THIRD EDITION

ETHICS
for Accountants and Auditors

Louise Kretzschmar • Frans Prinsloo • Martin Prozesky
Deon Rossouw • Korien Sander • Jacques Siebrits • Minka Woermann

OXFORD
UNIVERSITY PRESS
SOUTHERN AFRICA

OXFORD
UNIVERSITY PRESS
SOUTHERN AFRICA

Oxford University Press Southern Africa (Pty) Ltd

Vasco Boulevard, Goodwood, Cape Town, Republic of South Africa
P O Box 12119, N1 City, 7463, Cape Town, Republic of South Africa

Oxford University Press Southern Africa (Pty) Ltd is a subsidiary of
Oxford University Press, Great Clarendon Street, Oxford OX2 6DP.

The Press, a department of the University of Oxford, furthers the University's objective of
excellence in research, scholarship, and education by publishing worldwide in

Oxford New York

Auckland Cape Town Dar es Salaam Hong Kong Karachi
Kuala Lumpur Madrid Melbourne Mexico City Nairobi
New Delhi Shanghai Taipei Toronto

With offices in

Argentina Austria Brazil Chile Czech Republic France Greece
Guatemala Hungary Italy Japan Poland Portugal Singapore South Korea
Switzerland Turkey Ukraine Vietnam

Oxford is a registered trade mark of Oxford University Press
in the UK and in certain other countries

Published in South Africa
by Oxford University Press Southern Africa (Pty) Ltd, Cape Town

Ethics for Accountants and Auditors – Third edition
ISBN 978 0 19 904245 6

© Oxford University Press Southern Africa (Pty) Ltd 2012

The moral rights of the author have been asserted
Database right Oxford University Press Southern Africa (Pty) Ltd (maker)

First published 2006
Second edition published 2009
Third edition published 2012
Fourth impression 2015

All rights reserved. No part of this publication may be reproduced,
stored in a retrieval system, or transmitted, in any form or by any means,
without the prior permission in writing of Oxford University Press Southern Africa (Pty) Ltd,
or as expressly permitted by law, or under terms agreed with the appropriate
designated reprographics rights organization. Enquiries concerning reproduction
outside the scope of the above should be sent to the Rights Department,
Oxford University Press Southern Africa (Pty) Ltd, at the address above.

You must not circulate this book in any other binding or cover
and you must impose this same condition on any acquirer.

Publishing Manager: Alida Terblanche
Copy Editor: Marguerite Lithgow
Designer: Brigitte Rouillard
Cover Designer: Louise Topping
Indexer: Adrienne Pretorius

Set in Kepler Std Light 10.5 pt on 13 pt by Barbara Hirsch
Cover image: Getty Images
Printed and bound by ABC Press, Cape Town
122787

Acknowledgements
The authors and publisher gratefully acknowledge permission to reproduce copyright material
in this book. Every effort has been made to trace copyright holders, but if any copyright
infringements have been made, the publisher would be grateful for information that would
enable any omissions or errors to be corrected in subsequent impressions.
   The text on page 247 relating to the International Federation of Accountants (IFAC)
is an extract from the International Federation of Accountants, published by the
International Federation of Accountants (IFAC) in 2010, and is used with permission of IFAC.
(www.ifac.org/about-ifac/organization-overview).

Contents

Special acknowledgements xii

Contributors xiii

Preface xiv

Part 1: Principles of ethics
Introductory case study: A dilemma in professional and business ethics

Outcomes	2
Overview	2
Case study: A dilemma in professional and business ethics	3
Questions for discussion	15

1 Key concepts in business and professional ethics   DEON ROSSOUW

Outcomes	16
Overview	16
Introduction	17
Ethics or morality	17
Ethics and values	18
Moral dilemmas	19
Business ethics	20
Personal and organisational ethics	22
Ethics and the law	23
Professional ethics	24
Professional virtues	24
Conclusion	25
Questions for discussion	25
Bibliography	26

2 Religious and secular moral value systems for Professionals in South Africa   LOUISE KRETZSCHMAR

Outcomes	27
Introduction	27
The purpose of this chapter	28
Approaches used in this chapter	29
A few key terms	30
Case study: Thandi and government tenders	31
Where are we? Moral challenges facing our country	32
Social, environmental and economic challenges	32
Ethical issues facing accountants and auditors	33
Ethics and the family	33

Traditional African Ethics	34
What is an African ethic?	34
What is *ubuntu*?	35
Who are the ancestors in African tradition?	35
The ancestors as guardians of morality	36
African ethics in a twenty-first century context	36
Summary	36
Ethics in Judaism	37
Christian ethics	39
Commonalities between Jewish and Christian ethics	39
Jesus of Nazareth	39
Key elements of a Christian world view	40
Moral virtue and character	42
Ethics, the economy and business	42
Critical comments and questions	45
Summary	46
Islamic ethics	47
Introduction	47
The general character of Islamic ethics	47
The three sources of Islamic ethics	47
An ethic of action	49
A modern debate within Islam	49
Summary	50
Conclusion	50
Hindu ethics	50
Introduction	50
Hinduism as a way of life	51
Karma and *dharma*	52
Sources of Hindu ethics	53
Controversial practices	54
Revitalising Hinduism	54
Conclusion	55
Modern value systems	55
Introduction	55
Secular humanism	56
Communist ethics	57
Human rights and responsibilities	58
Feminist ethics	60
What is required to address the moral problems we face?	61
Why should anything be valued? What is a credible view of reality?	61
What is a good life? Re-establish the link between business and morality	64
Why should I be moral? How can moral individuals be formed?	65
What is the role of moral communities?	67
Questions for consideration	68
Bibliography	69

3 Philosophical foundations of ethics   *Deon Rossouw*

Outcomes	71
Overview	71
Introduction	71
Case study: Chris	72
Virtue theory	73
Virtues	73

Mean	74
Deontological ethics	76
The categorical imperative	77
Respect for persons	78
Utilitarian ethics	79
The Greatest Happiness principle	79
Criticism one: The theory is degrading to humans	80
Criticism two: Happiness cannot be the rational purpose of life	81
Criticism three: Utilitarianism is unattainable	81
Criticism four: Utilitarianism is self-serving	82
Criticism five: The theory is too time-consuming	82
Conclusion	83
Questions for consideration	83
Bibliography	84

4 Ethical decision-making   *Deon Rossouw*

Outcomes	85
Overview	85
Introduction	86
Case study: Jane Peterson's downsizing assignment	87
Making ethical decisions in business or the profession	88
Is it legal?	89
Application to Jane Peterson's assignment	90
Does it meet company standards?	90
Application to Jane Peterson's assignment	92
Is it fair to all stakeholders?	92
Application to Jane Peterson's assignment	93
Can it be disclosed?	95
Application to Jane Peterson's assignment	96
Conclusion	97
Questions for discussion	98
Bibliography	98

5 Resolving ethical dilemmas   *Deon Rossouw*

Outcomes	99
Overview	99
Introduction	100
Assumptions behind the RIMS strategy	101
Assumption one: Dissensus does not equal defeat	101
Assumption two: Dialogue can produce solutions	101
Assumption three: Focusing on motives is futile	101
Assumption four: Only moral arguments are allowed	102
The RIMS strategy	102
Step one: Generate and evaluate all points of view	103
Step two: Identify the implications	103
Step three: Find solutions	103
Case study: The email dilemma	103
Resolving the email dilemma: RIMS at work	105
Step one: Generate the moral points of view	105
Step two: Identify the implications	106
Step three: Find solutions	107

Conclusion 110
Questions for discussion 111
Bibliography 111

6   Case study using ethical skills and insights   *Martin Prozesky*

Outcomes 112
Overview 112
Introduction 113
Case study: Using ethical skills and insights 113
Questions for discussion 125

Part 2 Business ethics

7   Macro-ethics   *Minka Woermann*

Outcomes 128
Overview 128
Introduction 129
The rise of capitalism 131
    Capitalism versus Statism 131
    The dynamic nature of capitalism 133
Key features of capitalism 134
    Corporations 134
    Private property 135
    The profit motive 136
    Competition 136
Theories of justice 138
    Defining justice 138
    The utilitarian theory of justice 139
    The egalitarian theory of justice 140
    The libertarian theory of justice 143
Conclusion 147
Questions for discussion 147
Bibliography 147

8   The modern corporation and its moral obligations   *Deon Rossouw*

Outcomes 150
Overview 150
Introduction 151
Corporate social responsibility 152
    Milton Friedman 152
    Christopher Stone 154
Corporate moral agency 155
    Peter French 156
Stakeholder theory 157
    Edward Freeman 158
    Kenneth Goodpaster 161
Conclusion 162
Questions for discussion 162
Bibliography 162

9 Corporate governance *Frans Prinsloo and Jacques Siebrits*

Outcomes	163
Overview	163
Introduction	164
Why corporate governance is important	166
The importance of sound corporate governance to shareholders and other stakeholder groups	166
The importance of corporate governance to the company itself	167
The importance of corporate governance to a country	167
A brief history of corporate governance	167
Why the increased focus on corporate governance since 1980?	169
Superficial corporate governance and substantive corporate governance	170
Whom should the company's management serve?	170
The King Committee	172
Shareholder activism and the role of the institutional investor	175
Integrated reporting	177
Governance role of the auditing profession	179
Role of the audit committee	179
Role of external auditors	180
Role of internal auditors	181
Conclusion	181
Questions for discussion	182
Bibliography	182

10 Managing ethics *Deon Rossouw*

Outcomes	184
Overview	184
Introduction	185
Determining ethical risk	186
Ethical risk assessment	187
Codifying ethical standards	188
Directional codes	188
Aspirational codes	189
Institutionalising ethics	189
Strategic level	189
Systems level	192
Reporting and disclosing ethical performance	194
Conclusion	195
Questions for discussion	196
Bibliography	196

11 Case studies in business ethics *Deon Rossouw*

Outcomes	197
Overview	197
Introduction	197
Cheating	198
Case study one: Cheating and eating	198
Qualification fraud	200
Case study two: Credible credentials?	200
HIV in the workplace	201
Case study three: Aids anxiety	202

Black economic empowerment	207
Case study four: Black front, white back	207
Gifts and gratuities	208
Case study five: Tempting tickets	209
Employment equity	211
Case study six: Promotion problems	211
Company expenses	212
Case study seven: Three nights out of town	213
Whistle blowing	215
Case study eight: Suspicious invoices	215
Bibliography	216

Part 3 Professional ethics

12 Accountants and auditors as professionals *Frans Prinsloo*

Outcomes	218
Overview	218
Introduction	219
What is a profession?	220
One: Entrance into the profession requires an extensive period of education and training	222
Two: Professional knowledge and skill are essential to the wellbeing of the larger society	223
Three: Professions usually have a monopoly on the provision of professional services	226
Four: Professionals often have an unusual degree of autonomy when rendering their services	227
Five: Professionals claim to be regulated by ethical standards	227
Types of professionals in society	228
Professional bodies guarding the profession and its ethics	231
South African Institute of Chartered Accountants (SAICA)	232
South African Institute of Professional Accountants (SAIPA)	233
Chartered Institute of Management Accountants (CIMA)	233
Association of Chartered Certified Accountants (ACCA)	233
Institute of Internal Auditors (IIA)	233
Independent Regulatory Board for Auditors (IRBA)	234
The collapse of Enron and Andersen	235
Conclusion	237
Questions for discussion	238
Bibliography	238

13 Codes of professional ethics *Frans Prinsloo*

Outcomes	240
Overview	240
Introduction	241
What is a 'Code of Professional Ethics'?	241
One: Guidance on proper conduct for professionals	242
Two: Adherence to the Code assists in protecting the public interest	243
Three: Rationale for adherence even when pressured to violate code of ethics or moral conduct	243

Case study: Vanilla Investments (Pty) Ltd	244
Four: Providing a mechanism by which action can be taken against unethical conduct of professionals	244
Five: Achieving the objectives of the profession	245
Six: The Code provides a basis for debate about future changes and improvements to ethical standards	246
Dissemination and enforcement of professional codes of ethics	246
Codes of professional ethics in the accounting profession	247
International Federation of Accountants (IFAC)	247
Case study: Kool Trading (Pty) Ltd	249
SAICA's *Code of Professional Conduct*	252
Further analysis of selected fundamental principles of relevance to external auditors	254
Integrity	255
Independence	255
Professional competence and due care	259
The future of self-regulation	261
Conclusion	262
Questions for discussion	263
Bibliography	264

14 Case studies in accounting ethics Korien Sander

Outcomes	265
Overview	265
Introduction	265
Case study one: Recruiting and employing trainees	266
Case study two: Reporting time spent on timesheets	267
Case study 3: Networking and new clients	269
Case study 4: Parental leave and a BBBEE offer	271
Case study 5: Environmental and social impacts	272
Case study 6: Fraud red flags	274
Bibliography	276

Special acknowledgements

We would like to thank the following contributors to Chapter 2 'Religious and secular moral value systems for professionals in South Africa':

The late **Jocelyn Hellig** for the section on Jewish ethics. She was Associate Professor in the Department of Religious Studies at the University of the Witwatersrand, lecturing in world religions and specialising in Judaism. Thereafter, she was an independent scholar and writer based in Johannesburg.

Lucinda Manda for assistance with the section on Feminist ethics. Now on the staff of the University of Malawi, she was formerly a researcher in the field of African ethics at the University of KwaZulu-Natal's Unilever Ethics Centre, with special emphasis on issues affecting women and women's health in Africa.

Patrick Maxwell for the section on Hindu ethics. He is well known for his work on Hinduism in South Africa and the wider world. Formerly a Senior Lecturer in Religious Studies at the then University of Natal, his work thereafter focused on Information Studies at the University of KwaZulu-Natal, Pietermaritzburg.

Tahir Sitoto for the sections on African and Islamic ethics. He is a lecturer in the School of Religion and Theology at the University of KwaZulu-Natal, Pietermaritzburg, specialising in both African and Islamic religion and ethics.

We would like to thank the following contributors to Chapter 11 'Case studies in business ethics':

Lea Dippenaar for case study three, 'Aids anxiety'. She is Manager of Integrity Strengthening of the Independent Complaints Directorate (Pretoria) and teaches Business Ethics at UNISA on a part-time basis. She completed a BA degree and Higher Diploma in Education at Stellenbosch University before obtaining an MPhil in Workplace Ethics from the University of Pretoria.

Dr JM Elegido for case study seven, 'Three nights out of town'. He is Deputy Vice-Chancellor of the Pan-African University in Nigeria. He holds an LLM degree from Universidad Central de Madrid and an LLD from Universidad de Navarra in Pamplona, Spain.

Robin Stone for case study eight, 'Suspicious invoices'. He is a Chartered Accountant and the Chief Financial Officer of the University of Fort Hare. He holds a BCom Hons degree from the University of Cape Town, a Master of Business Leadership degree from UNISA, and an M Phil (Applied Ethics) degree from the University of Stellenbosch.

Contributors

Louise Kretzschmar is a Professor in Theological Ethics at the University of South Africa (Unisa). She is also involved in the teaching of Business Ethics at Unisa. Currently, her main areas of interest include Ethics, Leadership and Christian Spirituality. She lectures locally and overseas and has published widely in these and other areas.

Frans Prinsloo is Director of the School of Accounting at the Nelson Mandela Metropolitan University. He is a Chartered Accountant (SA) and obtained his BCom (Accounting), BCom Hons (Accounting), and MCom (Accounting) degrees with distinction from the University of Port Elizabeth. He serves as a member of the Committee for Auditing Standards of the Independent Regulatory Board for Auditors (IRBA), and contributes actively to the professional education functions of the South African Institute of Chartered Accountants and the IRBA. He serves as a member of a number of audit committees in the public sector.

Martin Prozesky is Founding Director of the Unilever Ethics Centre and Emeritus Professor and Senior Research Associate of the University of KwaZulu-Natal. He has a great deal of experience in running applied ethics workshops for various clients, including the accountancy profession. His most recent book is entitled *Conscience: Ethical Intelligence for Global Well-Being*, published by the University of KwaZulu-Natal Press.

Deon Rossouw is CEO of the Ethics Institute of South Africa and Extraordinary Professor in Philosophy at the University of Pretoria and at the University of Stellenbosch. He was the Founding President of the Business Ethics Network of Africa (BEN-Africa) and served as President of the International Society of Business, Economics and Ethics (ISBEE). He was a member of the Research Team of the Second King Report on Corporate Governance and is a member of the Sustainability Committee of the *Third King Report on Corporate Governance for South Africa*.

Korien Sander CA(SA) is a business ethicist and researcher.

Jacques Siebrits is Senior Lecturer at the Accounting department at the University of the Western Cape.

Minka Woermann is a Lecturer in the Philosophy Department and Head of the Unit for Business Ethics and Public Integrity in the Centre for Applied Ethics at the University of Stellenbosch.

Preface

Professionals play a hugely important part in society because of their expertise and skill in matters of great importance, from accountancy to engineering and medicine, to mention just a few examples. Expertise of this kind is a form of power, and power must always be governed by the highest ethical standards so that it does not lead to exploitation and abuse. It is to their great credit that the various professional bodies understand this need and have long taken measures to foster high ethical standards, typically by means of Codes of Conduct for their members and measures to enforce them.

The accounting profession in South Africa and indeed elsewhere therefore provides its members with a very detailed and comprehensive Code. This has long formed part of the education of aspirant members of the profession in their tertiary level studies. Now the profession in this country has taken a very important further step by requiring that students complete a course on applied ethics relevant to accountancy and auditing, as both a foundation for and an extension of their study of the Code itself, and as further ethical grounding for their work and personal lives. This is a welcome recognition of the fact that all of us will benefit from a deeper and wider-ranging understanding of the great practical ethical issues that face us as citizens and professionals.

Such is the background to this textbook. Written by a team of highly-qualified authors, it is designed in the first instance for students taking the new, required course, but is also directly relevant to their lecturers' needs and to practising members of the profession. The approach throughout is to ground ethical knowledge and wisdom in the real world of practical examples and cases relevant to the accounting profession in a region of great cultural diversity, and to write clearly and engagingly in ways that will foster debate and discussion rather than rote learning.

The book follows the design of the syllabus approved by the South African Institute of Chartered Accountants, which is shaped on the educational principle of handling issues in ways that link them relevantly to their wider contexts. There is therefore a first part which includes chapters on basic general ethics, so that readers will be well grounded in key ethical principles and more aware of the cultural diversity of their clients and colleagues in a society rebuilding itself after apartheid and its enforced separations. A second part follows, focusing on business ethics as the sector of society of particularly great importance to accountants, auditors, financial managers and others. The third part of the book then proceeds to deal in its various chapters with ethics in the accounting profession itself.

The ideals that have given rise to this textbook are well captured by a paragraph in an article about professional ethics by Professor Solly Benatar in the *Cape Times* on 14 February 2006. He wrote as follows:

> 'Professionals play an important role in society. Indeed, society could not function effectively without trustworthy professionals. This raises questions about the ethics of how institutions operate and exert influence on those who work within them. In the face of the powerful forces eroding professionalism, there is a great need to promote core professional values.'

Part 1
Principles of ethics

In the chapters that make up this first part of the book, we provide the foundations on which Parts 2 and 3 rest by giving you the various principles and introductory explanations that define and shape ethics. Each of these chapters draws on real examples from the worlds of accountancy and business.

The *Introductory case study* takes us directly into that world by providing readers with an extended case study involving, among others, a fictitious main character who is a South African chartered accountant contemplating a lucrative but ethically troubling job offer in a fictitious country called Nalanda.

In *Chapter 1*, we introduce ethics. We define key terms such as 'ethics', 'morality', 'values', and 'virtues', and explain the basic meaning of moral dilemmas. We then link ethics to the worlds of business and to the professions, also explaining the relationship between ethics and law and the connection between ethics and professionalism. A key point in this first chapter is the ethical importance of the structures in which we live and work.

This is one of the reasons for *Chapter 2*, where we introduce the most widely followed value systems in South African society. In a democratic South Africa, we can at last experience the reality and importance of our exceptionally rich cultural diversity in a spirit of respectful understanding, and thereby enhance our professional ability to relate ethically to colleagues, clients, and customers who come from different ethical traditions.

In *Chapter 3*, you will be introduced to philosophical insights into ethics. Three highly influential theories about the morally good life are presented:
- The view that the practice of virtue builds an ethically strong character, going back to the ancient Greek thinker Aristotle
- The theory that duty and universality are central to ethics as propounded by the eighteenth century German philosopher Immanuel Kant
- The approach taken by John Stuart Mill and other utilitarians, which emphasises the consequences of our actions and the principle of maximising happiness.

The heart of ethics is not, however, theory-based but practice-based, focusing on making wise choices. *Chapter 4* deals with the vital question of ethical decision-making. It provides a clear, practical process for making such decisions. It is followed in *Chapter 5* by a practical method of resolving ethical dilemmas.

Part 1 concludes with *Chapter 6*. This chapter takes readers back to the extended case study in the Introduction and especially to the important ethical dilemma with which it ends, and shows them how the ethical concepts, insights and skills of the preceding chapters can be used to resolve that dilemma.

Introductory case study: A dilemma in professional and business ethics

Outcomes

After working through this case study, you should be able to do the following:
- Understand ethical issues in the context of a real-life situation involving both business and the accountancy profession
- Appreciate the complexity of such situations, ethically and professionally
- Understand the different interests at work on the part of those who feature in the case study
- Appreciate the powerful ethical factors, both personal and professional, that are at work in the case study

Overview

Nothing reveals the nature and relevance of ethics in the worlds of the accountancy profession and business more effectively than real-life examples. Accordingly, this book opens with just such an example. It takes the form of an extended case study involving an ethical dilemma on the part of the principal character in the story, who is a fictitious South African chartered accountant called Rob Abrahams. He is asked to consider driving a new national lottery project in an imaginary Black Sea country called Larnia, which he visits in order to gain first-hand insights into the lucrative job offer that has been made to him to drive the new venture. His experiences there and his deliberations on returning home, shared with his wife Miriam, reveal just how challenging it can be to wish to act ethically in conditions where powerful but unethical forces are at work, and how vital ethical commitment is in such situations.

Case study: A dilemma in professional and business ethics

Introduction

Rob Abrahams had just finished a first read-through of the new Code of Professional Practice of the South African Institute of Chartered Accountants that he as a CA(SA) was required to follow when the phone rang. A long conversation followed during which he made notes and asked questions. 'That was a strange call', he said to himself after putting the phone down. He had not spoken to Mike van Tonder, an old classmate from his BCom days and fellow CA, for several years. In fact, their last face-to-face meeting was at Rob's wedding, just after he had danced with Mike's 'trophy wife', Samantha.

Six foot tall and an international model already at the age of 17, Samantha had come home from Paris quite disillusioned with the fashion scene that turned women, or rather girls, into mere objects. She buckled down at her studies and was now an assistant professor in philosophy at a local university. She had become very involved in gender politics, fighting for what she believed was still a very uneven playing field for women in the workplace. Still, as the story had been told to Rob a few years earlier, Mike had deserted his first wife the very week he laid eyes on Samantha, and they were married shortly afterwards.

Well, that was Mike, always busy chasing after the next big thing, even since varsity days, where he had left many a friend and girlfriend angry with him for his lack of lasting loyalties as he kept on re-inventing himself for every new conquest – whether girlfriends or business deals. Mike was ambitious and hard-driving, some of the very qualities that make for a good Chartered Accountant (SA), or at least so Rob thought.

The invitation to join

Rob sat down to stare at the notes he had taken during their telephone conversation. If he had understood correctly, Mike, who had qualified as a CA (SA) a few years before and completed his training contract with a well-known South African audit firm, was now working as financial consultant at a blue chip South African investment bank and travelled the globe assessing business deals.

One of Mike's clients was a consortium that had just secured in the country of Larnia the lucrative licence to operate what was sure to become a very large lottery. Mike's team had done their due diligence on the business opportunity and the required investment, had liked what they had seen in the project, and were considering investing in their client's venture. Yet they had one reservation. How had Mike put it again? 'It's the jockey that makes the project fly or fall, and without someone like you at the head of this venture's start-up, we would not consider getting involved. Can you make time to meet with our client?'

There was no harm in listening, so Rob agreed to meet with the father and son who were majority shareholders of the privately-owned South African company that was part of the successful licence consortium referred to above. As Rob had never heard of this company before, he spent the week beforehand digging deeply into Google and beyond to learn what he could about the international lottery business as well as about Larnia, which he had heard was arguably one of the most corrupt countries in the world.

His research quickly supported this notion. Transparency International, the most trusted source on the measurement of corruption, placed this country high on its corruption list year after year. Rob wondered how this South African consortium had managed to secure a licence to operate such a lucrative business in a different continent altogether.

Lotteries as industry

More encouragingly, Rob's research also revealed that lotteries internationally, or 'the gaming industry', as they preferred to call their industry these days, had been busy cleaning up their act. There were fantastic examples of the effect that the funds raised by the Georgia State Lottery had had on the education system in that region of the USA, and the UK Lottery prided itself on the immense social impact it had had through its distribution of charitable funding in the arts, sports and to welfare organisations.

Mike van Tonder had mentioned that the idea behind this new lottery was to raise funds for youth and sport development, with 30 per cent of lottery ticket revenue to be earmarked for this purpose. As for Larnia, Rob was likewise encouraged to learn that, after some years of corrupt dictators, the country finally had a democratically-elected government, and apparently this lottery project had the blessing of the highest office in that land as a way of starting to plough development assistance back to the local people.

The morality of gambling

Rob felt somewhat uncomfortable still with the idea of gambling. His was a suburban Christian upbringing, and he recalled how his parents used to stay mum about their occasional sojourns to Sun City in the days when it was still illegal to gamble in South Africa.

On the other hand, Rob felt that his religion also went to great pains to emphasise good deeds in service of the poor, and it sounded as if this project was aimed at achieving exactly that. Miriam, his non-observant

Jewish wife, shared some of his reservations about gambling, reminding him that they had come across a statement on the Internet that called it 'a tax on people who cannot count'.

However, her religious upbringing and the history of Jewish persecution had instilled in her a very strong sense of social justice, and she too felt that there might be merit in the social objectives of this project, even if it meant that they would both have to relocate to Larnia for at least a year.

Spin doctors and dealmakers

Before meeting with the father-and-son team from Mike's client who formed part of the consortium to operate this new lottery venture in Larnia, Rob and Mike, were joined by Arnold Booysen for a cup of coffee in Melville's trendy 7th Avenue. Mike explained that Arnold was the real mover behind this deal coming together for the consortium. A lawyer by training, Arnold had spent years as a government liaison and public relations officer for South Africa's largest cigarette company, and had then become involved as one of the lawyers who had drafted South Africa's new gaming legislation. Arnold never spoke of 'gambling' – he preferred to talk about 'gaming'.

Arnold told Rob how he had befriended Larnia's Ambassador to South Africa over the past few years, had picked up the tab every time this man's family visited Sandton and stayed in some fancy hotel, and had eventually managed to get him to open doors to the Minister of Sport in Larnia, under whose auspices this licence would be awarded, gaming being part of that Minister's portfolio.

Any fears about a potential religious backlash against the proposed lottery were quickly disposed of, as Arnold had been given the assurances by the Ambassador that his own brother, the highest-ranking religious leader in an important part of Larnia, had appointed a proxy to hold some shares for him in the company incorporated by the consortium. His own brother, a senior religious figure, would deal with anyone in his religious family who became too vocal in complaining about the new gaming venture.

The real powers that be

So it was with both a bit of healthy scepticism and some excitement about the potential good of this massive project in mind that Rob stepped into his first meeting with the South African family who now steered the consortium about which Mike had spoken. As Rob sat in the waiting area, he noticed the photographs on the wall of some of these family members meeting with some of the most powerful leaders in Larnia and its neighbouring countries. Handshakes and smiles – row after row.

From some of the literature spread around the waiting area, one could quickly surmise that this family had fingers in many pies, but most visibly, in the arms industry. They could supply any government or rebel leader with whatever fire power they desired – on land or from the sky.

The meeting was fairly uneventful. Present was the father who had built the family business, and one of his sons, who was most active in Larnia with a variety of ventures that included mining concessions, refitting the entire police force with small munitions, and some other deals of which Rob would rather not know.

Rob felt he was sitting in the pound seats, as he knew that their project was dead in the water if the investment bank did not come on board, and he had assurances from Mike that he could name his fee. For good measure, Rob negotiated a rate equivalent to about 150 per cent of what he was earning as an international management consultant, plus all expenses paid and free business class return flights for him and Miriam to South Africa once a month. This was accepted without anyone batting an eyelid. Rob wondered how his previous CA (SA) colleagues would react if they knew what he was earning now.

The rest of the meeting was spent on sorting through the details of a first exploratory trip to Larnia the following week by Rob and Arnold. The intention was to meet with the Minister of Sport, his local representatives, who would hold 51 per cent of the shareholding in the company formed by the consortium, and also the local office of their firm of external auditors, as well as several advertising agencies. The show had to get on the road, and it was agreed that Rob would make a final commitment only upon his return after this first visit.

First impressions

It was a bumpy ride flying north with the national carrier, yet Rob took it in his stride and enjoyed the creature comforts of the business class section. He was counting the extra frequent flier miles and wondering where he and Miriam could jet off to over December if the miles continued to grow at this rate. At his previous places of employment, all frequent flier miles had accrued to the corporate travel budget, and he had never received the benefit of what he considered to be the inconvenience of having to travel to fulfil his auditing or consulting assignments. Rob thought guiltily about the fact that he had almost decided by now that when someone else paid, he would fly business class, but when he had to pay for himself, he would suffer the cattle truck and save the money to spend on the other side. It appeared that clients expected one to relax and enjoy the luxurious extras. Why should he do it any differently? He resolved to discuss the ethics of his partly-made decision with Miriam when he was home again.

After checking in at the expensive hotel, Rob quickly unpacked. Having lived in hotels at client expense every so often, he grabbed a pricy can of cooldrink out of the mini-bar on his way out to the pool, not thinking twice about the expense. Things are just so much easier to buy with other people's money, he smiled to himself in the elevator. Again he felt a twinge of conscience at thinking this way.

A quick dip in the pool, and then he sat down with Arnold, who was well into his third gin and tonic, with little umbrellas and cherries, the works. Arnold laid out the plans for the next few days, and having said goodbye to Rob, dropped in at the casino at the entrance of the hotel after dinner, with a few beautiful local women accompanying him. This was not Rob's idea of fun, and he went instead for a long walk on the beach in the moonlight.

The intended beneficiaries

As he walked, he passed the ramshackle shelters that homeless locals had converted into their homes. The average life expectancy in Larnia was falling for both men and women. Infant mortality ranked among the highest in that part of the world. The sounds of crying babies and resonating boom-boxes shared the air with the smoke from charcoal fires – the national forests were being chipped away day after day to supply hungry people with fuel for their cooking.

There were no working ablution facilities on the beach, and Rob soon learnt that the high-water mark served the same purpose for these street-dwelling locals as did the Gents/Women signs in public spaces back home. Over the dunes he could make out the kneeling prayer party of Muslims from the country's substantial Islamic minority, faces turning towards Mecca for their fifth and final prayer session of the day.

This was a country with a substantial population, many of its people very poor and with the main source of national revenue, petrodollars, ending up either in corrupt politicians' pockets, or in foreign bank accounts. Arnold was telling him just the previous evening that very little was produced in this country any more. After years of political instability, anyone with cash would stash it away in a Swiss bank account as quickly as possible, and there was an elaborate scheme of over-invoicing with which to move funds. In fact, Arnold proposed that in their meeting with their auditors later that week, they should try to figure out how the new lottery company could do exactly the same.

Arnold had also dropped a few anecdotes into their conversation about how their mutual acquaintance, Mike van Tonder, had done many a trip with Arnold to former Soviet states to 'facilitate' the purchasing of weapons for rebel groups fighting across Africa. The South African consortium members had contacts with powerful people, and there was good reason why the newly-elected President of Larnia was happy to sanction South African participation in the lottery.

After a restless night with boom-boxes distorting the song blaring out directly underneath his beach-facing window, Rob had a quick cup of coffee in the room while getting into his jogging gear. He took his morning run past schoolchildren on their way to buildings in need of maintenance, and wove through the morning traffic stalled by potholes in the road and even bigger puddles of rank water from blocked drains.

He ducked away from generator fumes in the neighbourhood – the city was suffering another break in its power supply. Drains on the side of the road were clogged with slimy water that had him gasping for fresh air, and vendors were selling everything you could imagine by the roadside. He had seen much the same in some African countries, but had not expected such neglect in Larnia. Clearly, very few of this country's petrodollars did any work for its citizens.

The Chairman of the Board

On their way to their first meeting, Arnold briefed Rob on the Chairman of the Board of the new lottery company they were about to meet. He was to be called 'Chief I', his official title as former presidential candidate and owner of the largest football team in the country. Rob's research had offered up a little gem on this Chief. He had been Larnia's Olympic Chairman a few years ago during the Atlanta Games, and there was the matter of a few million dollars that had remained unaccounted for under his stewardship. Rob held back the information from Arnold, deciding to play along as the day unfolded.

The larger-than-life Chief welcomed them in his home, and barked orders at domestic staff scampering around in a very subservient manner. To Rob, this seemed like a snapshot from his childhood in apartheid South Africa, although he found out later when talking to Sasha, the Chief's driver, that all the staff hailed from the Chief's home area, where he was revered as a great man for 'putting bread on our tables'. Sasha had not seen his wife and three children back home for over two years, despite the Chief's flying down to this home city on his own airline every second week. It had never crossed the Chief's mind to take Sasha along, and more striking to Rob was that Sasha had never thought of querying this state of affairs. He was happy to be of service to the Chief and to send home the equivalent of about $20 per month to feed his family. Clearly, thought Rob, labour unions and workers' rights are not very active in this country.

The Chief explained his vision for the lottery to Rob and Arnold, and minced no words about the fact that it would be he, as Chairman, and not the lowly, in his opinion, Minister of Sport who would decide what charitable funds would remain for distribution and to which organisations. He also explained how the local shareholders would take out a four per cent management fee, to be paid offshore, despite the original agreement being that the South African shareholder would be responsible for managing the operations.

When Rob pointed out that there were only 100 percentage points available to share among prize-winners, management fees, operations, charitable distribution and shareholder profits, the Chief laughed at his accounting and said: 'Yes, we promised the Minister of Sport and the President that 30 per cent will go to charity, but there are many ways to calculate 30 per cent. I suggest we give them 30 per cent of what is left after lottery prize-winners, management and operations have been paid out. That will leave us shareholders with a decent profit.'

Rob's quick calculation in his mind estimated that with the Chief's sleight-of-hand accounting, the proposed beneficiaries were about to have their receipts from the lottery cut to about one-tenth of what the amount would have been had they received 30 per cent of gross receipts. The Chief furthermore insisted that his daily newspaper receive the lion's share of advertising spend for marketing the lottery, and that his airline would carry all cash from the lottery from across the nation at a fee of two per cent of gross revenue.

Potential business partners

After being stuck in traffic back to the hotel for two-and-a-half hours, Arnold postponed the meeting with the partners of the lottery company's auditors for the following day. The hotel front desk had 17 messages from complete strangers, all claiming to be friends of the Chief, who insisted on a meeting to come and introduce themselves as potential business partners. Arnold shrugged it off, saying that they would come to the hotel anyway, and that trying to return telephone calls on this country's derelict telephone system was a waste of time. Besides, it was time for Arnold's regulation gin and tonic down at the bar.

Rob ducked off to find an Internet café, as he desperately wanted to share some of his thoughts and impressions with Miriam, who he believed might be able to help him separate the wood from the trees. He was starting to doubt whether his optimistic hope that the best place to change any system was from within could ever materialise, having met the Chairman Chief, a man so evidently set in his ways and beliefs, and even more evidently not interested in hearing anyone else's thoughts on any matter. And it was only day one!

The next few days, Rob and Arnold hardly left the hotel, being tracked down and kept busy by a myriad potential business partners in the lottery. Rob felt as if he could not face one more cold soft drink on the hotel patio, where other heavy-weights like the Chief, judging by their expensive suits, were gathering round the clock, with big black duffle bags under their tables and large quantities of hard currency disappearing into these bags during virtually every meeting that Rob could witness from where they were sitting. He was starting to wonder if anyone in this place ever did any honest business, and even if there was any room for someone to survive on a day-to-day basis if choosing to be honest.

Local morality

In these meetings with the friend of the Chief, Rob listened to stories about how the system really worked locally; how school fees and exam fees were in fact bribes in order to get promoted; and how local politicians received petrodollars from the central government and then essentially paid off their own local civil servants in order to maintain political support. Advertising and public relations types pitched their business for the proposed lottery, all claiming some association with big international names in New York, Paris or London. Fancy degree certificates were produced as people tried to hustle for a spot on the lottery management team, and the brand managers of several major consumer goods companies tried to secure the exclusive distribution rights to the lottery. The word was out that there was a new lucrative project in town, backed by foreign money, and everyone wanted to get in on the action.

To the capital

On the fifth day of the visit, Rob and Arnold flew to the nation's capital city, where they were to have a meeting with the Minister of Sport. A death-defying taxi ride to the airport, with people using their hooters rather than their brakes, got them to the check-in counter on time. There were no pre-assigned seats on what looked like a fifty-year-old plane operated by Bulgarian pilots, who would have been a better fit outside a New York night club as bouncers than behind the controls of this flying death trap.

During the two-hour flight they encountered some storms, and lightning struck close to the wing where Rob was staring out in dismay and gripping the seat handles with white knuckles. He kept on reminding himself that these pilots must have someone who loved them, and that he could trust them to land the plane safely. Rob was drenched with sweat and then rain, and felt totally drained by the time he checked into their hotel, with hardly enough time before their pick-up to go off and meet the Minister.

INTRODUCTORY CASE STUDY: A DILEMMA IN PROFESSIONAL AND BUSINESS ETHICS

Hurry up and wait

Two hours passed after their supposed meeting time with the Minister before someone finally asked them to come through to have their audience. The Minister made no reference to their three-hour wait – it was just the way things were done in this place. You sit outside an office hoping that 'the man is on seat', as the locals would say. And more often than not, Rob was beginning to learn, the man is never there!

The Minister was charming, welcoming them and sharing with them his latest pride and joy. It was the signature of soccer great, Maradona, who had visited the previous week and signed the Minister's visitors' register. Rob could not care less at this stage about being just a few lines below the great man in this book. He was fuming with all the ceremony and the lack of direct discussion of the task they had at hand. In his own mind, he had made the decision that should he undertake to manage this start-up, he would run the company according to global best practices, and teach these locals a thing or two about running a proper business, including showing some respect for other people's time.

The Minister disclosed to Rob and Arnold who all the local shareholders in the lottery company would be, but the names meant nothing to them. They suspected by now that these were all proxies for bigger fish who could not be seen to hold a direct share in a national project of this nature. Then the Minister landed his bombshell, namely that his idea of youth and sport development was to use all the funds raised by the lottery to build a national football stadium that could host the Black Sea Confederation Cup of Nations in a few years, and that the stadium was destined to be named after him. Likely also to be built by some of his cronies? Rob listened to Arnold trying desperately to express what he understood the President of Larnia's wishes were for the project, as well as those of the South African shareholder, yet he was sure it was water off a duck's back. Arnold was plainly wasting his time.

That night they had a sumptuous Middle-Eastern dinner with one of the Lebanese construction tycoons who would be one of the shareholders, before they retired to the hotel bar. Here, Arnold finally gave Rob his thoughts on the day, and his summation wasn't good. He did not like the plans of the Minister at all, and the two of them put in a late-night conference call to the South African shareholders to talk tactics. Arnold was told to leave it until the morning and for them to stay in the capital for a possible meeting with the President of Larnia the following day. Rob could only wonder how these people would manage to get them an audience with the President on such short notice, with their being this far away. Rob went to bed with too much on his mind and no chance to share any of it with Miriam.

The plot thickens

The next morning over breakfast, Arnold confirmed that he had a very early call from the Presidential villa around the corner, and that they were expected to be there just before lunch. Before then, they would also have to deal with one other matter that their South African principals thought would be well timed, namely to try to squeeze a crude oil allotment out of the Presidential office while they were there. After breakfast, they were to meet with a representative of a Swiss oil-brokerage company that had ties with the South African group, and together with the head of the country's oil shipping agency, they would craft a strategy to put to the President.

Arnold laid it all out for Rob as the sun started beating down on them on the hotel patio. The South African group, Rob learnt, was actually not all that interested in the lottery business. Their main interests in the region were mining and oil concessions, and arms supply. They had long-standing relations with senior politicians in the region, and had several old apartheid luminaries on their payroll as consultants. If Rob read between the lines correctly, this South African group had built a considerable part of their fortune during the apartheid years when they had helped the South African political establishment in their 'grey marketing' endeavours.

'Grey marketing' was the euphemism for sanction busting, where South Africa supplied some of the regional states with their essentials, despite these states being vocal critics of the South African government in the public spotlight. Friendships with politicians in these states were forged, and today's meeting regarding oil-shipping consignments was really based on calling in a favour. After 1994, these relationships could come out in the open, and business was booming for this group.

The favour being called today, Arnold explained, had its origin in an older favour, when the current President had at some stage been incarcerated by the dictator then in charge of Larnia, and would have been executed had it not been for the intervention of a senior South African politician, now serving as consultant to the South African group that Arnold and Rob represented. In fact, there was a strong chance that this well-known politician would be present for this meeting by midday, with the South Africans having laid on one of their private jets overnight to get him here to help resolve both the oil-shipment issue and the looming problems with the Minister of Sport regarding the lottery.

Rob's head spun. This was a lot to swallow at one go, and decidedly not the kind of stuff he wanted to be involved in. On the other hand, he was thrilled to meet with the President, a man he understood truly to have taken a stand for democracy and who seemed almost as though he could be the Mandela of his own damaged nation.

Fiddling with his tie back in his room, he finally managed to speak to Miriam on the phone and shared some of what was taking place. She was speechless, and wished him a safe return by the weekend.

The President

It was no surprise that they had to wait a while before seeing the President. Joined by the somewhat exhausted South African ex-politician who had flown in overnight, still smelling slightly of his dinner drinks, for which he had developed a reputation over the years, Rob and Arnold were really just flies on the wall. There was a lot of insincere flattery, plenty of talking, yet in Rob's view, once again no commitment to anything concrete. It was fascinating to witness the diplomatic skills of the two senior gentlemen in the room, who both clearly had their own agendas and constituencies at the back of their minds while mixing it up in a friendly fashion. At some stage, when the lottery came up for discussion, Rob and Arnold were requested to excuse themselves, with a promise to meet up with the South African ex-politician at the hotel.

A new agreement

That afternoon, it was explained to them that the agreement reached with the President that morning was that the South African shareholder would now own the majority share in the lottery company, and that the President wanted the previously-designated chairman of the company replaced with his own confidante. He did not trust any of the Minister of Sport's nominees, some of whom had political agendas. The Minister was also about to be sacked. The President's chairman nominee owned a bank and would finance the Larnia shareholders' working capital. The cheque would be deposited the following day, and the show with the lottery could get under way upon the South African team's return a few weeks down the line.

For the first time it dawned on Rob that everyone here just assumed that he had taken the job, despite his reserving his commitment until after his return from this week in Larnia. He did feel somewhat relieved at the news of the President's intervention. Perhaps the idea that this lottery could deliver some true benefit to the local population was in safe hands once again, and perhaps there was a chance to turn the proposed lottery into a model corporate citizen in this troubled country.

Decision time

It took more than one swim in the ocean and a few glasses of chilled white wine at their favourite Camps Bay restaurant, a quick stroll down from their apartment on the beach, for Rob to feel that he had washed the dirt of Larnia and the unsavoury people he had met the previous week off him. Sitting with a notepad on the starched linen of the restaurant table, Miriam started drawing up the pros and cons of Rob's accepting the assignment in Larnia.

On the pro side, Rob quickly listed the great financial progress the two of them would make from taking care of this start-up phase during year 1 of the lottery. They would likely be able to put aside in excess of R1 million, and place it offshore for that matter, as the newly-proposed residency tax system being discussed for South Africa was not yet in effect. Secondly, there was the real possibility that this kind of project would be part of the major reconstruction of a new democratic society in Larnia, and Rob trusted his instincts that the newly-elected President was quite serious about the social impact this lottery could have. By their team's estimate, they would end up directly and indirectly creating about 3 500 jobs in year 1.

Finally on the plus side, Rob had to admit that intellectually, as a former management consultant, he was getting really excited about trying to build the lottery company against seemingly-impossible odds. As a postscript, Miriam added the thrill of living in a new country and the chance to travel in the region. Rob had no other immediate consulting assignments lined up, so the price of taking this assignment was only the one-year postponement of a four-month overland trip through Botswana and Namibia that they had tentatively planned.

On the negative side, the list grew quickly. Neither of them was convinced that 'gaming' was an acceptable industry to join. The South African lottery experience had shown that it was often the poorest of the poor who poured critical household income into the hope of winning untold millions. Then there was the matter of the South African shareholders' other business ventures, and especially their arms supply to rebel groups in several war-torn parts of the world.

Rob had devised a section in his draft employment contract that he called a 'morality clause', which stipulated that he had the right to resign within 24 hours if any of the shareholders' other activities which in his opinion would negatively impact on his own reputation came to light. Yet he was not sure that one could properly ring-fence the lottery from all their other activities, as the recent experience with the oil-shipment business had shown at the meeting with the President of Larnia.

Lower on the list were issues related to living conditions in that country – health, safety, and the way in which people treated their fellow citizens. Would Rob be allowed the budget to compensate staff according to rights that they were entitled to under international labour law standards? If he refused the assignment, Rob was certain that they would find someone else, perhaps quite unscrupulous, to manage this

INTRODUCTORY CASE STUDY: A DILEMMA IN PROFESSIONAL AND BUSINESS ETHICS

> start-up, and that would mean the end of the opportunity to create something that could help turn the tide of corruption in this society.
>
> As the waiters started clearing the tables from the patio, turned off the music and switched on the bright lights to call an end to the evening's dining, Rob and Miriam just stared at each other across the table – not one step closer to making a final decision about something that was sure to affect their lives dramatically one way or another. Normally an impulsive decision-maker, Rob could just not decide what would be the right thing to do.

Questions for discussion

1. What is understood under the statement 'uneven playing field for women in the workplace'? Do women have equal opportunity in the auditing and accounting professions, and what arrangements have major auditing firms made internationally and in South Africa to accommodate working mothers?
2. Look at South Africa's standing in the corruption ranks on the Transparency International website at <www.transparency.org>. How was this determined, and do you believe it is a justifiable ranking?
3. Does the Government have the right to enforce morality upon its citizens, or should they allow any business venture in a free market to operate and leave to individual choice the decision to gamble, for example?
4. Do you believe it is acceptable to use a euphemism such as 'gaming' for gambling, and why do you think it is wrong or right?
5. Do you think Rob, Mike and Arnold have good personal morals? Find examples in the case that support your opinion on each of the men.
6. Can a person with dubious personal morals live by the professional code of ethics that professions such as lawyers (Arnold) or accountants (Mike and Rob) prescribe? Discuss in a short paragraph.
7. Should Rob accept the local customs in Larnia, such as the manner in which the Chairman treats his employees, or the local perceptions about bribery and corruption, even when these are in contrast to the standards he is used to at home? What do you think he should do in these circumstances?
8. Make a list of pros and cons to add to the list of decision-making criteria Rob and Miriam were considering.
9. Should this venture go ahead? Motivate your answer.
10. Should Rob accept this assignment, and why do you think he should, or should not?

1

Key concepts in business and professional ethics

Deon Rossouw

Outcomes

After working through this chapter, you should be able to do the following:
- Define the concepts 'ethics', 'business ethics' and 'professional ethics'
- Identify the relationship between ethics and values
- Distinguish between personal and social moral dilemmas
- Discern the three levels at which ethics in economic activity is being studied and identify the core issues that are studied on each of these levels
- Indicate why ethics needs to be addressed on both the personal and organisational levels
- Make a clear distinction between morality and legality
- Demonstrate why professionals need both professional ethics and professional virtues.

Overview

'Ethics', as the term is generally used, will first be defined around three core concepts: the 'self', the 'good' and the 'other'. Ethical behaviour is characterised by the fact that it is unselfish and balances what is good for oneself with what is good for others. The relation between ethics and values will also be explored.

This definition will then be extended to the field of business. A number of concepts that are closely related to business ethics will also be introduced. These include concepts such as **'law'** and **'moral dilemmas'**. The difference between personal and **organisational ethics** will also be demonstrated by introducing the metaphor of good and bad apples and good and bad barrels.

Finally, the relation between ethics and professions in general will be explored. By referring to the typical features of professions, it will be shown that ethical standards and virtues count among the distinguishing features of the accounting and auditing profession.

Introduction

In the case study in the previous chapter, several incidents were referred to that can be labelled as unethical, illegal, or at least dubious. These incidents included the exploitation of employees, arms trafficking, corruption, fraud, deception and a host of other unsavoury practices that eventually left Rob in serious doubt about whether he should take up the very lucrative position that was offered to him. In order to make sense of the ethical dimension of a situation like the one that Rob was facing, one needs to have a proper understanding of key concepts in ethics. Understanding such key concepts provides one with a vocabulary to make a meaningful analysis and assessment of the ethical dimension of situations. In this chapter, we will explore what ethics entails. In doing so, we will draw a number of important distinctions and clarify the relation between ethics and some closely related concepts like values, virtues, moral dilemmas and the law.

Ethics or morality

The term 'ethics' originates from the Greek word *ethikos*. When the Greek term was later translated into Latin, it was translated as *moralis*. The common origin of the terms 'ethics' and 'morality' explains why it has become fashionable to use the two terms interchangeably. When we refer in ordinary language to unacceptable or irresponsible behaviour, we call such behaviour 'unethical' or 'immoral'. The words are therefore used as synonyms – what is unethical is immoral and what is immoral is unethical. Some people try to forge a distinction between ethics and morality, but based on the lack of distinction between ethics and morality in ordinary language, that distinction will not be maintained in this book.

> The common origin of the terms 'ethics' and 'morality' explains why it has become fashionable to use the two terms interchangeably.

In both its Greek and Latin versions, ethics (or morality) refers to the *character* or *manner* of a person. The focus is therefore on the kind of person that someone is (that person's character) and on how the person interacts with others (that person's manner). This shows that ethics is about the 'self' and its interactions with 'others'. There is, however, still a missing element: the quality of the interaction between the 'self' and 'others'. This introduces a third essential concept for defining ethics, namely the concept of the 'good'.

Around these three concepts of the 'self', the 'good' and the 'other', we can develop an adequate definition of **ethics**. Behaviour can be classified as 'ethical' when it is not only good for the self, but also good for others. An action is unethical or immoral if the actor (the person doing the action) is concerned only about what is good for her or him without any regard for how others will be affected by it. We usually classify such behaviour as selfish, because the actor is interested only in what is good for the self without caring about what is good for others.

Figure 1.1 The three concepts inherent in a definition of ethics

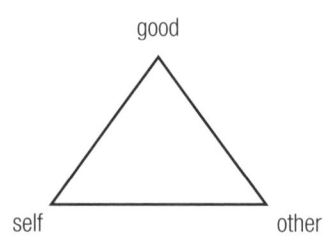

```
           good
            /\
           /  \
          /    \
         /_____\
       self    other
```

While selfish behaviour constitutes the opposite of ethical behaviour, it does not imply that ethical behaviour requires one to act selflessly – that is, totally disregarding one's own interests for the sake of others. It is likely that such a standard of behaviour would be unattainable for most human beings. We are constituted in a manner that makes it almost impossible for us not to consider our own interests and well-being. This reality is captured in the golden rule of ethics: that we should do to others as we would like them to do to us. Being moral, therefore, does not require that we should totally disregard our own interests. It does, however, require that we should not merely consider what is good for us, but also consider what is good for others.

Applying this understanding of ethics to the case study in the Introduction, we can see how at the end of the case study Rob and Miriam are battling with the question about whether a deal that will be financially good for them will also be good for those who will be affected by the new lottery company that Rob will head up. There are also numerous examples of unethical behaviour where persons are so selfishly focused on their own self-interest that they could not care less about the interests of others. A glaringly obvious example of such selfish behaviour is the behaviour of the Chairman of the Board of the new lottery company, Chief I.

Ethics and values

There is a close relationship between ethics and **values**. 'Values' can be described as convictions about what is good or desirable. In that sense, our values provide content to the concept of the 'good' in the above definition of ethics. For example, because we are convinced that freedom, human dignity, equality, or honesty are good, we use these standards to determine whether an action is not only good for us, but also good for others. Should an action only promote my freedom, but compromise the freedom of others, for example, it cannot be considered good.

People do not share the same values. We often find that both between and within groups, there are disagreements about what is good. Or we find that although two persons both agree that freedom and equality are important, the one may regard freedom as being more important than equality, while the other person may regard equality as being more important than freedom.

> 'Values' can be described as convictions about what is good or desirable.

Differences in people's values are due to a variety of factors. Culture, religion, climate, social and economic status, personal experiences, age, gender and a host of other factors can all have an impact on our values. It is therefore quite natural to expect that people's values would also be different. These differences between the values that people hold lead to the differences in ethical judgements that we typically find among people.

Although values determine our ethical judgements, it does not mean that all values are ethical values. A person's values indicate what he or she considers important. Such convictions about what is important influence the way in which persons decide and act. What persons consider to be important inevitably has an effect on how ethical their decisions and actions would be. In the case study in the introductory chapter it became clear that some persons were so concerned with their own reputation and income that they could hardly be bothered with the interests of others. Rob's personal values, to the contrary, had a marked impact on his ethical assessment of his own situation, as well as on his ethical assessment of the situation of other persons, such as Eddie, the driver of the Chairman of the Board. It clearly also had an impact on his ethical evaluation of the striking contrast between the desperately poor people and the wealthy elite that he encountered in Larnia. It is thus clear that despite the close link between values and ethics, values cannot be equated with ethics.

Moral dilemmas

A moral dilemma occurs when an ethical evaluation of a situation produces two or more conflicting judgements. Such moral dilemmas can be of either a personal or a social nature. When conflicting judgements occur within a person, we refer to it as a **personal moral dilemma**. A **social dilemma** occurs when conflicting ethical judgements arise not within one person, but between people or groups. An issue such as affirmative action can easily turn into a social dilemma, as some people regard it as good, while others regard it is wrong and unfair. It is therefore typical of moral dilemmas that they divide opinion on whether something is right or wrong.

> A moral dilemma occurs when an ethical evaluation of a situation produces two or more conflicting judgements.

At the end of the introductory case study, it was clear that Rob and Miriam were facing a moral dilemma. On the one hand, they felt that taking up the assignment in Larnia might be a good thing, because it might create jobs and raise funds in support of social reconstruction in Larnia; but on the other hand, they were concerned that by being involved in the lottery, they might be party to luring poor people into losing the little money they had.

In ethics, it is important to realise that there are not only moral dilemmas. There are many matters that we regard as right, and there are many things that we regard as wrong. Only some situations turn into moral dilemmas. We widely agree that respecting the dignity of all human beings, keeping promises and telling the truth, for example, are right or good, and we also share the conviction that humiliating others, breaking promises and telling blatant lies are wrong. Moral dilemmas arise only in some instances such as in the case of affirmative action, which gives rise to conflicting ethical judgements.

The fact that people differ from one another in their ethical judgements of situations or actions does not mean that ethical dilemmas cannot be resolved. In most dilemmas, the conflicting parties are able to reach compromises that accommodate the ethical concerns of both parties in a dilemma. Such solutions are sometimes referred to as **'creative middle way solutions'** (Harris, Pritchard and Rabins, 2005:69). Such solutions can be achieved only if the parties are willing to discuss the dilemma with one another and arrive at solutions that can accommodate the *moral concerns* of both parties. Moral dilemmas are therefore not irresolvable in principle, but they do require us to be willing to discuss our moral differences in order to resolve them.

Business ethics

Economic activity always has an ethical dimension. Even if we look at business (or economic exchange) in its most rudimentary form, the ethical dimension of business is evident. A business transaction consists of exchanging a product or service for money. The buyer receives the product or service and the seller receives the money. If the exchange is fair, both parties benefit and therefore both parties' interests are served or enhanced. It clearly is a case of interaction between the two parties that is good for not only one party, but also the other. This satisfies the basic test of ethics: interaction between a 'self' and an 'other' that is 'good' for both 'self' and 'other'. Of course, these transactions can go horribly wrong: products or services may be of inferior quality and not live up to the buyer's expectations; the seller may charge an unfair price; buyers may renege on their promise to pay the seller. These are only a few of the malpractices that may haunt business transactions.

Business ethics focuses on what is good and right in economic activity. It engages in a moral analysis and assessment of economic practices and activities. This moral evaluation can occur on three levels, namely:

1. the economic system level (macro-economic level)
2. the organisational level (meso-economic level), and
3. the intra-organisational level (micro-economic level).

> Business ethics focuses on what is good and right in economic activity.

- The *economic system (macro-economic)* level refers to the policy framework within which economic exchange occurs. This framework is determined at national level by the political power of the state. On the international level, the policy framework is determined through multilateral or international trade agreements.

    Economic systems or macro-economic policies have an impact on people. They can be designed to enhance the freedom of people or to meet a specific social or political objective such as protecting the poorest people in society. Whatever their objective may be, such economic systems or policies have consequences for people. These consequences can be either positive or negative or have positive outcomes for some people, but negative outcomes for others.

    Advocates of economic systems and policies often justify a specific system or policy in terms of how they impact upon the wellbeing of people or society. Adam Smith, the founding father of capitalism, justified capitalism by arguing that capitalism is the system that would best serve the wellbeing of society. Karl Marx, who opposed capitalism and proposed socialism instead, rejected capitalism on moral grounds and defended socialism, because he believed that socialism would be the best system for all people in society.

    On the macro-economic level, business ethics evaluates economic systems and macro-economic policies and trade-agreements to determine whether they are fair and just.

- The *organisational (or meso-economic) level* refers to business organisations, such as corporations, and their relations with the rest of society. Business enterprises have an impact on *society*. They have an impact on people, such as on their customers and suppliers. They also have an impact on *local communities*, local culture and on the *natural environment*. This impact can once more be either beneficial or detrimental to those affected by the operations of a business company. This raises many questions, for example:

    - Should the business sector take responsibility for its impact on society?
    - Should the state regulate businesses to ensure that business practices do not harm society or natural ecology?
    - Should businesses be regarded as corporate citizens with responsibilities to protect and contribute towards the societies in which they operate?

At the organisational (or meso-economic) level of business ethics, what is being studied is precisely this ethical impact that business has on society.

- The *intra-organisational (or micro-economic) level* of business ethics focuses on economic activity within business organisations. It concentrates on the moral dimension of business practices, policies, behaviour and decisions that occurs within a business.

Business enterprises also have an impact on the people who work for these enterprises. Very often, employees and managers are faced with moral problems in different situations which arise at work. They may be expected to perform duties or participate in practices that clash with their personal values. It can also happen that people are discriminated against, humiliated or harassed in the workplace. Employees' physical or mental health may be at risk because of their working conditions. The culture, policies or systems of an organisation may also be such that it breaks down trust between people in the organisation.

Within organisations, relations at work are therefore ethically charged. These situations have an effect on people and often determine the quality of people's lives. Because of these and other ethical implications of work situations, ethics also needs to be studied on the intra-organisational (or micro-economic) level.

> Business ethics, as an academic field, is the study of the ethical dimension of economic activity on the systemic, organisational and intra-organisational levels.

Business ethics, as an academic field, is the study of the ethical dimension of economic activity on the systemic, organisational and intra-organisational levels. As such, it is a multidisciplinary academic endeavour as scholars from various disciplines such as philosophy, economics, business management, human resource management, theology, psychology, sociology and accounting all contribute to this field of study.

Personal and organisational ethics

From the above discussion on the ethics of the three levels of economic analysis, it is clear that business ethics is not merely about personal moral decisions and actions in business. Business ethics is also about the ethics of economic systems and organisations. It is a big mistake to focus only on personal ethics and to ignore the ethics of organisations and systems. This distinction between personal and organisational (or system) ethics is well captured in the metaphor of apples and barrels.

Unethical behaviour in organisations is often attributed to unethical individuals. Such individuals are termed 'bad apples'. They are seen as morally corrupt and it is often suggested that the solution to unethical behaviour in business lies in removing the bad apples.

This is a gross oversimplification. Individuals can influence organisations, but organisations can also influence individuals. Individuals are affected by their social setting in the same way that apples are affected by the barrels in which they are kept. If an apple is placed in a dirty and unhygienic barrel it will not last as long as an apple in a clean, hygienic barrel.

The same principle applies to organisations. The social settings or organisations (barrels) within which individuals work can also have either a good or a bad (corrupting) influence on their moral character. People with dubious or even good moral characters can turn to unethical behaviour if they find themselves in organisations where unethical conduct is the norm. In this way, bad barrels can corrupt dubious or even good apples. The opposite is equally true. Dubious or even bad apples can be restrained from unethical behaviour should they find themselves in organisations that do not tolerate unethical behaviour, but reward ethical behaviour.

Table 1.1 The relationship between personal and organisational ethics

	Good barrels	Bad barrels
Good apples		
Bad apples		

The distinction between apples and barrels draws attention to the fact that ethical behaviour should be addressed not only on the individual level, but also on the systemic and organisational levels.

> Ethical behaviour should be addressed not only on the individual level, but also on the systemic and organisational levels.

Ethics and the law

Is there is a difference between ethics and the law? Is something that is ethical also necessarily legal? Or is anything that is legal also at the same time ethical. Could it be possible that something is ethical but illegal, or unethical but legal?

There are obvious similarities between ethics and the law, but there are also significant differences. Both ethics and the law intend to determine what is right. The law does so through a public and political process and employs the power of the state to ensure that all people abide by the law. Ethics emanates from personal values; as such, the sense of obligation to do what is right is internal as opposed to external, the latter being the case with the law, since the law is enforced through external pressures such as state authority.

> Is something that is ethical also necessarily legal? Could it be possible that something is ethical but illegal, or unethical but legal?

Although ethical and legal behaviour often coincide, they also sometimes differ. Actions can be both ethical and legal. An example of behaviour that is both ethical and legal would be when a company publishes accurate statements of its income in accordance with accepted accounting standards. An example of ethical but illegal conduct is when an individual exceeds the speed limit in an effort to get a seriously injured person to a hospital in an effort to save the injured person's life. An example of action that was unethical but legal was the legal discrimination that occurred under apartheid in South Africa. Actions can also be both unethical and illegal as in the case of fraud. Table 1.2 illustrates the four possible relationships that can occur between morality and legality.

Table 1.2 The different relationships that can occur between morality and legality

	Legal	Illegal
Ethical		
Unethical		

Professional ethics

It is not only persons and business organisations that adhere to ethics. Specific groups in society also adhere to **ethical standards**. A profession is a typical example of a group of people who adhere to a set of ethical standards. Professions are distinguished from other occupations by a number of distinct features that will be discussed in Chapter 12. One of these features is that professions adhere to a self-imposed set of ethical standards (*cf* Cotell and Perlin, 1990:180). The purpose of these ethical standards is to ensure that members of a profession act in accordance with the spirit and purpose of the profession as well as to the benefit of the clients and community whom they serve. The accounting profession is a clear example of a group of professionals who adhere to such a set of ethical standards.

Accountants therefore have at least three different sets of ethical standards by which they have to abide. They have their personal ethics and professional ethics as well as the organisational ethics of the firms or companies that they work in. In an ideal situation, these three sets of ethical standards will coincide, but sometimes they do not. This poses difficult moral dilemmas to professionals when they have to make choices among these three sets of values.

Professional virtues

A **virtue** can be described as a character trait that predisposes one to doing the right thing. These character traits can be developed over time. A man with a short temper whose anger flares up at the most insignificant incident can deliberately try to change this kind of behaviour that leads to personal embarrassment for himself and harm being inflicted upon others.

Over time, he can restrain himself until he has gained control over his temper. Through his deliberate attempts, he can succeed in overcoming his fierce temper and develop the virtue of being even-tempered. Virtues are therefore learned forms of behaviour that become second nature to us. The opposite of a virtue is a **vice**. Whereas virtues predispose one to doing the right thing, vices do the exact opposite.

> A virtue can be described as a character trait that predisposes one to doing the right thing.

Part of one's training in becoming a professional involves having the virtues of the profession to which one aspires inculcated in oneself. In the case of the accounting profession, there are a number of important virtues that accountants should acquire. The most important virtues are *integrity*, *competence* and *objectivity* (Maurice, 1996:18; Mintz, 1992:5). There is a general belief within the profession that when accountants and auditors have cultivated these virtues, they will each be well disposed to act with integrity and enhance their own reputation and that of their profession, while also serving the wellbeing of their clients and society.

Conclusion

This chapter introduced some of the key concepts that will be encountered in the rest of this book. Being familiar with these concepts provides one with the vocabulary that is required to converse about ethics in organisations and professions. In the rest of the book ideas, theories and issues that are relevant to ethics in business and in the accounting and auditing professions will be introduced.

Questions for discussion

1. Define the concept 'ethics'.
2. What do business ethics and professional ethics respectively entail, and how can they be differentiated from each other?
3. Distinguish the three levels on which ethics in business is studied and give an example of an ethical issue that is typical of each of these levels.
4. What is the difference between personal and social dilemmas?
5. How can moral dilemmas be resolved?
6. Give one example of an action or practice within the accounting or auditing profession for each of the following categories:
   - ethically right
   - ethically wrong, and
   - ethical dilemma.
7. Can an action be both legal and unethical? Explain your answer by providing an example.

8. What are professional virtues and why are they deemed important? Provide examples of professional virtues in the accounting and auditing profession.

Bibliography

Cotell, PG & Perlin, TM. 1990. *Accounting ethics: a practical guide for professionals*. New York: Quorum Books.

Harris, CE, Pritchard, MS & Rabins, MJ. 2005. *Engineering ethics: concepts and cases*, 3rd ed. Belmont (CA): Wadsworth.

Maurice, J. 1996. *Accounting ethics*. London: Pitman Publishing.

Mintz, SM. 1992. *Cases in accounting ethics and professionalism*, 2nd ed. New York: McGraw-Hill.

2

Religious and secular moral value systems for professionals in South Africa

Louise Kretzschmar

Outcomes

After working through this chapter, you should be able to do the following:
- Understand the more widely followed and influential value systems that will be encountered among colleagues and clients in professional life in South Africa and be able to function in a context of moral pluralism;
- Understand the way in which people's histories and cultures shape their ethical values, behaviour and working lives;
- Become more aware of the relevance of religious and other moral world views for the accounting and auditing professions;
- Develop an increased moral consciousness – an awareness of your own ethical convictions and those of others;
- Recognise the importance of ethics for the accounting and auditing professions and the importance of acting in a morally responsible manner.

Introduction

What do you value? It is useful to commence with this question since a proper evaluation of the views of others should be preceded by a reflection on our own approach to life. Rank the following statements from 1 to 14, with 1 being the most important to you. Be as honest as possible in this process. Do not consider what others may think, or how you feel you ought to rank these statements.
- Gain significant financial prosperity.
- Protect and nurture my family.

- Live a life of integrity.
- Follow the company's Code of Ethics.
- Obey significant leaders in my context.
- Attain a sense of achievement from doing my work well.
- Work towards a better life for all.
- Do what is right in God's eyes.
- Live a life of personal freedom and independence.
- Gain a high position and the admiration of others.
- Use my position to assist my own family and social group.
- Do what is right.
- Accumulate wealth and retire early to enjoy my life.
- Be respected by others as a moral leader.

If you engaged in this exercise honestly, the results will reveal what you regard as important in life. What you value will determine how you will behave. Your actions will, in turn, have consequences for your family, workplace and society as a whole.

Sometimes we deceive ourselves about our real values. We may claim to be guided by values such as integrity and accountability, but in practice we do not walk the talk. Individual interests (what will benefit me) or group interests (what will benefit my group) may dominate our lives. Often, when personal or group interests are at stake, all our principles fly out of the window. Actions – which reveal our true values – often speak louder than words.

The purpose of this chapter

The purpose of this chapter is to:
- Identify what ethical norms and values (or principles) are;
- Ask from where (or Whom) they are derived, and
- Establish the role they can play in an accounting and auditing environment.

This chapter forms the basis of subsequent chapters. Codes of conduct within business and the accounting profession stress the importance of values such as integrity and accountability. But what do these terms mean, and on what are they based? The following key questions will be answered in the course of this chapter:
- Why should anything be valued?
- What is a good life?
- Why should I be moral?
- What is the role of moral communities?

We begin with the question: Why is a chapter on religious and secular ethics important in a book on ethics for accountants and auditors? It is important for two reasons. First, millions of people in our country have identified themselves as religious adherents. For them a particular religion is important for their lives and the way they ought to conduct themselves in the workplace. Second, many of those who do not associate themselves with a particular religion still stress the importance of morality. As noted below, many of the moral values they uphold have their roots in an earlier religious ethic.

According to the 2001 South African census, 79.8% of the population are Christian, 0.2% Jewish, 1.5% Muslim and 1.2% Hindu. Those who stated that they follow no religion accounted for 15% of the population.[1] This last figure is controversial, since the census did not list traditional African religion. Approximately 5-10% of the population are adherents of traditional African religion. These figures reveal that the majority of South Africans identify with a religious faith. Their religious adherence ranges from 'strongly committed' to 'mere lip service'. Nevertheless, to some extent their faith remains a source of moral norms and values.

In Africa, as elsewhere in the world, religion has shaped morality, society and the economy for centuries. Any discussion of ethics, society and business that fails to take note of the religious ethics of this large group of people is splitting faith from life for such people, impoverishing both. More recently, other approaches such as secular humanism, communism, human rights and feminist ethics have become influential. They are also discussed below.

Approaches used in this chapter

A dialogical approach is used in this chapter. The first dialogue takes place between the concrete situations we face and the moral value systems to which people adhere. We first note some of the social, environmental and economic challenges we face, as these form the broad context within which professional ethics operates. Thereafter we describe some of the main moral approaches upon which accountants and auditors can draw, especially in a South African context.

A second dialogue is between religious and secular ethics. These approaches to morality are described and some critical questions are asked. We also ask in what ways a religious ethic differs from a secular ethic. An attempt is made to evaluate the importance for professional ethics of the various approaches to morality outlined in this chapter.

A third dialogue is between the religions. There is a significant measure of similarity between the moral teachings of a number of religions. For example, they agree that business should *not* be pursued in a grasping and unjust manner, and that stealing, lying and selfishness are wrong. They

---

1 The data from the most recent (2011) census is not yet available.

also agree that honesty, responsibility and trust are right and valuable. However, it is not true that all religions are the same. To say this would do a disservice to their distinctive world views, traditions and belief systems. Hinduism and Islam, for example, arise within different social contexts, look to different leaders and provide different systems of thinking about reality and the purpose of life. People who do business in India and/or the Middle East need to understand something about these faiths and the differences between them as they influence the way in which people live and make ethical decisions in these contexts.

Contemporary South Africans live in a multicultural society. People of different faiths, cultures, ethnic groups, social contexts and educational backgrounds rub shoulders in the business environment. In a pluralistic context, we need to learn to deal with both moral consensus and the conflict of values. It is essential to understand both our own heritage and that of others. This does not mean that we will agree with everyone. Nor does it mean that our critical or moral faculties should be suspended. It means that knowledge and insight should precede moral judgement.

A few key terms

What is religion?

The term 'religion' can be defined both specifically and more generally. A specific definition would be that religion is a system of beliefs and practices about God and/or the nature of reality, which includes moral teachings, traditions, rituals and customs. We could therefore refer to the Christian or Muslim religion or faith tradition. Some religions, such as Hinduism, include a vast range of beliefs and practices and others, like Buddhism, do not include belief in God.

A broader definition of religion or faith would be that which is of 'ultimate concern' to a person or group. Our ultimate or primary concerns are what we most value. As we saw at the beginning of this chapter, each of us values something. What is of 'ultimate concern' to a person or group could include belief in God; the pursuit of self-gain, pleasure or power; a life dedicated to the care of others; the adoption of an ideology, such as communism, capitalism, secularism or black consciousness. Whatever is of 'ultimate concern' to us will motivate our actions.

What are ethics and morality?

What is ethical or moral is not simply what is legal or culturally acceptable. It is what is inherently right and good, not only for ourselves, but also for others, society and the natural environment.

A norm is behaviour that is normative or obligatory. The prescriptions of the Ten Commandments, as contained in the Bible, are examples of norms. The eighth commandment simply instructs: 'Do not steal' (Exodus 20:15). Other norms include: 'be compassionate', 'treat others fairly' and 'assist the poor'.

Narrowly understood, moral norms are rules that prescribe certain actions, such as those contained in codes of conduct. But norms are also broad principles, such as: 'Do not oppress the alien, the orphan, and the widow' (Jeremiah 7:6). In a modern context, this principle can be understood to mean: Act with justice and compassion towards the stranger, the vulnerable and the marginalised. Norms are important because they restrain selfishness and stress obligations towards others.

Values derive from norms and define what we regard as important and 'valuable'. Examples include integrity, justice and compassion. (Not all values are moral values – someone may value only their personal material advancement – no matter how it is achieved.) Virtues, in turn, are human attitudes and actions that express moral norms and values. We speak of a moral person as being honest, fair and caring in his/her dealings with others. Norms, values and virtues are essential to life, society and business operations, as they facilitate constructive social interaction.

Case study: Thandi and government tenders

Thandi is a young woman who completed a BCom degree in auditing. She looks for work for several months, in the context of an economic downturn. Eventually, she is employed by a large government department near her home in the Eastern Cape. She comes from a close-knit extended family with strong religious commitments. She attends church regularly and is involved in its ministry to prisoners. Her African parents are dedicated Christians and educated professionals. From an early age, both at home and in her religious environment, Thandi has been taught the importance of doing what is right and caring for others. Her love for God is strong and she wishes to honour and serve God in her relationships, workplace and social context.

In the government office where she works, Thandi is eager to learn, hard-working and capable, although she lacks knowledge and experience due to her age. She begins to gain experience and pursues her studies.

After several years, she completes her articles and passes the Board examination, gaining her Chartered Accountant certification. She is told that she is in line for a new post that carries additional responsibility and a significant increase in salary. Her new post will involve acting as an advisor for the procurement section of the department, and making professional judgements concerning irregularities in tender applications and the awarding of government contracts.

> Her politically well-connected uncle, Sipho, invites her to lunch. He requests insider information concerning tenders on a regular basis. He comes from a distant branch of her extended family. Sipho lost both his parents to HIV/Aids at an early age, and was brought up by his father's brother, who is rumoured to be involved in shady business practices. Her help will enable him to advise firms in their bids for contracts to supply goods or services to this department. In return, he promises her a percentage of this potentially lucrative arrangement. When Thandi says that she is not prepared to supply him with this information, he threatens to use his connections to spread rumours about her in her workplace, block the promised promotion and even to cause her to lose her job. Lunch ends with him saying that he will contact her in a week's time. What is Thandi to do? What resources does she have at her disposal?

Where are we? Moral challenges facing our country

Social, environmental and economic challenges

As we examine briefly the state of our world and our country in the early twenty-first century, we are confronted with a series of challenges. In social terms, our country needs to deal with broken families, racial tension and many forms of violence. Many old people are neither valued nor cared for, and children are often neglected or abused. Local politicians engage in seemingly endless power struggles, while solvable problems, such as the maintenance and development of infrastructure and service delivery, are neglected. Young people are bombarded with the conflicting voices of consumerism, care for others, group loyalty and moral relativism.

Environmental groups warn us of present and impending disasters such as a shortage of clean water, global warming, burgeoning populations, toxic waste, threatened habitats and the extinction of increasing numbers of plant and animal species.

Economic recession, poverty, unemployment, crime, incapacity, unequal distribution and corruption are prominent features in the economic context. The Gini coefficient shows no sign of narrowing: the rich are getting richer, and the poor are getting poorer. Because of the global recession, businesses and banks have shown massive losses locally and/or globally, and many people have lost their jobs, houses, savings or investments. Officially, unemployment stands at about 25%, but many believe the real figure to be much higher. Politicians, economists, business leaders, labour unions and many others fiercely debate which economic systems and strategies can best address these problems.

But what, you may ask, does all of this have to do with the accounting and auditing professions? This is, in itself, a revealing question as it requires us to ask what the very term 'accounting' means. Is it simply to ensure that the books balance and reflect fairly the health or otherwise of a business?

Ethical issues facing accountants and auditors

Scandals resulting from unethical actions such as fraud, embezzlement, tax evasion and the underreporting of profits in the auditing and accounting fields have resulted in the credibility of accountants and auditors being questioned. Individuals have been declared bankrupt or imprisoned, and firms have gone under. Even though only a few people were implicated in the Enron debacle, the Arthur Andersen accounting firm collapsed and an estimated 85,000 people lost their jobs. The increase of lucrative consulting fees for management advisory services has resulted in increased conflicts of interest when both consulting and auditing services are offered.

We now hear of triple bottom line accounting, corporate governance, fiduciary responsibility, business ethics, codes of conduct, integrity and accountability. These terms reveal a growing concern with moral issues in the workplace and society generally.

What moral value systems can we draw on to address these ethical challenges? We begin with a brief description of the role the family plays in the development of our moral convictions. Then we outline the ethics of several religious faiths. We begin with African ethics, followed by the ethics of Judaism and Christianity. As the latter is the major religious tradition in South Africa, we examine it in more detail. We then describe key elements of the ethics of Islam and Hinduism. Even though there are very few Muslims in South Africa, about 40% of the population of Africa are adherents of this faith. Islam is also a significant player on the global stage. Hinduism is discussed because it has a significant presence in KwaZulu-Natal, is an important Eastern religious tradition, and India is playing an increasingly significant role in the global economy. In addition to these religious faiths, we also discuss the moral approaches of secular humanism, communism, human rights and feminist ethics.

Ethics and the family

Even though it is not discussed in detail here, it would be a mistake to omit the role of the family, as it is extremely important in the early formation of moral values and actions. Parents and other members of the family are very influential in forming the world views and behaviour of children and young people – for good or ill.

As we illustrated in the case study, both Thandi and Sipho were influenced by their family background. Most people continue to live according to what they were taught when they were young unless they make a deliberate decision later to adopt a different moral approach. As we note below, the role of the family is stressed by religious faiths, not only in terms of teaching, but also in terms of attitudes and actions. Religious rituals (for example, baptism, funerals and communal prayer) and festivals (for example, Easter, Diwali and Ramadan), illustrate and reinforce the moral teaching of these religions.

Traditional African Ethics

What is an African ethic?

Can we speak of an African ethic on our vast continent? In terms of specific details, we would need to identify particular traditions from different parts of the continent. But scholars tend to agree that there are sufficient common elements in African traditional religion to enable us to speak of an African ethic.

An African ethic draws on the moral taboos, rules and customs of African people developed over centuries. Often these are transmitted through pithy proverbs, stories, and the rituals of African traditional life. From these, certain values have emerged, including: solidarity with the group, sharing, moral obligations to your family and clan, harmony, respect for life and human dignity. According to Gbadegesin (2005:419-421), traditional African values include: truthfulness, industry, moderation, generosity, patience, respect for elders and respect for the community. An African ethic emphasises not the moral autonomy of the individual, but the wellbeing of the group and moral obligations (duties) within the community.

Also important is *seriti*, a Sotho-Tswana word that refers to the energising or dynamic force which is at the core of every human being. Often linked with the life force, personality or blood of a person, *seriti* can also be understood as vitality or energy (from the Latin, *vita*, meaning life). *Seriti* is the 'energy or power that makes us ourselves and unites us in personal interaction with others' (Shutte, quoted in Boon 1998:35).

An African ethic has further been described as holistic because it is applicable to the whole of life, including nature. For instance, some Africans believe that they have a special relationship with animals, plants and sacred sites. These animals, plants and sites become respected symbols, totems or family emblems. It may therefore be taboo to pick certain plants except for medicinal purposes. This demonstrates very clearly the interconnectedness of life in the traditional African world view.

The central concern of African ethics is managing life and maintaining wellbeing *within society*. Individual ethical choices are made within the context of the community. In such a context, individual actions are evaluated and judged based on the effect that they have on the life of the community. Within the South African context, this view finds expression in the concept of *ubuntu*.

What is *ubuntu*?

In Africa, many speak about the ethics of *ubuntu*. This term is derived from the Xhosa or Zulu phrase: *Umuntu ngumuntu ngabantu*, meaning that a person is a person through (or because of) other people. Or: 'I belong, therefore, I am.' In African society, a person is perceived as 'being-in-relation' because 'the individual does not exist alone except corporately' (Mbiti 1969:108-109). A person who has *ubuntu* is a real, fully human person, because he/she cares about the needs of others and fulfils his/her social obligations. Personhood and personal morality develop through relationships in the context of community. Equally, social relationships can increase or impede social justice through the network of family and clan relationships.

The emphasis on *ubuntu* ethics in the South African context is extremely important because of its contribution to the values of holism, hospitality, sharing, justice and compassion within the context of community and social relationships. However, it is one thing to speak about *ubuntu* and African values, but quite another to live according to these values. Self-enrichment, violence, theft, nepotism and xenophobia reveal that, without ethical practice, talk is cheap. Similarly, some are replacing the traditional conviction that: 'I belong, therefore I am,' with a consumerist value system, which claims: 'I have possessions, therefore I am.'

Who are the ancestors in African tradition?

In African tradition, ancestors are humans who have passed to the world of the deceased. They are those who have lived a good, honourable life and who were regarded as custodians of knowledge and wisdom in their families and communities. To qualify for 'ancestorhood', the departed must have descendants who can look after them when they pass into the world of the nonliving.

In African tradition, the community consists of both the living (visible) and the invisible worlds. In ethical terms, this implies that maintaining sound societal relationships is based on the need to safeguard this crucial link between the visible and invisible worlds. The ancestors are the vital link between the two. But what exactly are the moral and ethical implications of such a view?

The ancestors as guardians of morality

The ancestors are perceived as the guardians of the ethical traditions in African societies. Arguably, such a view stems from the understanding that, since the ancestors are those who have lived exemplary lives in the world of the living, they continue to be preoccupied with regulating the affairs of their communities from the spirit world. They are therefore still concerned about the moral integrity of their communities. Disregard for moral virtues renders the community vulnerable to harmful spirits, misfortune, and subsequent destruction.

The notion of what is right and wrong, desirable and undesirable, acceptable or unacceptable is evaluated on the basis of whether it has the approval or nonapproval of the ancestors. Those who practised cruelty, murder, cheating or stealing could be ostracised through appropriate public censure.

African ethics in a twenty-first century context

As African ethics are linked to African traditional religion and culture, we can ask whether its moral teachings, community-based guidance and deterrents still apply. The fragmentation of families, urbanisation, secularism, the incidence of child-headed households and the adoption of other faiths such as Christianity lead us to ask to what extent the ancestors and elders still exercise this moral guardianship (Nürnberger 2007:206).

In post-colonial Africa, respect for elders has sometimes meant that leaders are not questioned. Distorted loyalty to a person or group can mean that leaders are not held accountable. Even though the wellbeing of the entire community is central to an African ethic, powerful individuals and groups have arisen who proclaim *ubuntu,* but promote their own material interests. We saw in the case study that, although, as an African Christian, Thandi respects her elders, she regards her faith and the wellbeing of the community as more important than obedience to her uncle, Sipho. Indeed, Sipho appears to be acting contrary to the requirements of an African *ubuntu* ethic.

Summary

1. The history of the community and the community members' collective life experiences are the sources of African ethics. These include social customs, religious beliefs, regulations, social taboos, proverbs and certain symbols.

2. In ethical terms, the collective wisdom of the ancestors and elders become the basis of moral decisions that the individual or community makes, with respect being an important moral principle in African ethics.
3. Morality is the creation of the community and emerges from its social institutions. It is a living concept within the community. What an individual does, affects the whole of society, either directly or indirectly. Tradition therefore demands that those who have committed shameful or immoral acts must be cleansed before they can be accepted back into the community.

Ethics in Judaism

Jewish ethics are grounded in the *Torah*, the five Books of Moses at the beginning of the Hebrew Bible. They are given clear and unambiguous force in the prophetic books of that Bible, and have been elaborated on by rabbis centuries later, in a way that has made the *Torah* an inextricable part of the fabric of Jewish life. In rabbinic Judaism, which was normative until the emergence of newer forms of religious expression with the eighteenth-century European Enlightenment, ethics may not be separated from the ritual commandments. All God's commandments must be observed, including the ritual ones, which are not a replacement for (as is often thought), but a reminder of the ethical commandments or *mitzvoth*.

> Jewish ethics are grounded in the *Torah*, given clear and unambiguous force in the prophetic books of that Bible, and elaborated on by rabbis in a way that has made it an inextricable part of the entire fabric of Jewish life.

Jews base their ethics on their collective memory as slaves. They believe that God chose them, a small and undeserving people, as His instruments to perfect the world. He delivered them from bondage, and took them to their promised land. Their obligation was to live their lives in obedience to the covenant He had entered into with them and to observe all His commandments (Hebrew: *mitzvoth*). Fundamental to Jewish ethics is the commandment for Jews to love and care for the stranger, because they themselves were strangers in the land of Egypt. The good life in Judaism therefore extends from duties to the self to duties towards the whole of humankind. Since all human beings are children of God, all are equally entitled to justice and mercy.

Judaism teaches that humans were created in God's image, and should therefore imitate God in their behaviour, exhibiting the godly traits that are inherent in them. Since God is just and merciful, to live in God's image is to emulate his mercy and justice. Jews can fulfil this only by observing the *mitzvoth*. Jews claim no inherent superiority over other people. They merely assert that they have been given a special advantage in receiving the *Torah*. It is in the very terms of the *Torah* that their duties towards all of humankind are commanded.

Except by virtue of character and conduct, no one human being is better than any other. Judaism demands that you care for the stranger, the orphan and the widow, and that you love your neighbour as yourself. So central is the Jew's duty to his fellow human beings that Rabbi Hillel (first century BCE), when asked to encapsulate the whole essence of Judaism while his hearer (a potential convert to Judaism) stood on one foot, formulated the golden rule of Judaism: 'That which is hateful unto you, do not do unto others. Thou shalt love thy neighbour as thyself. This is the whole *Torah*, all the rest is commentary. Now go and study.'

The prophets, in whose words the ethical content of the *Torah* is brought into sharp and unambiguous focus, decried ritual practice that was not accompanied by social justice. They castigated the Jews' failure to show concern for those whom temporal power habitually shunts to the sidelines. They did not condemn possessions or wealth, but called for its more equal distribution. Jewish ethics teach that all people have the right to possess things by which to live. The *Talmud*, a very influential Jewish text commenting on and explaining the biblical faith of Israel, therefore forbids the Jew from encroaching in any manner whatsoever on the capacity of any other person to make a living. It demands scrupulous honesty in business transactions and obligations towards employees. In fact, the highest form of charity is not the mere giving of money to the indigent, but giving in a way that empowers them to make a living with dignity.

Prophecy laid the foundation for social protest which, in turn, aims to create a better and more equitable world. It has been pointed out that underlying prophecy is the twin conviction that the future of any people depends largely on the justice of their social order, and that individuals are responsible for both the condition of society and the tidiness of their personal lives. Prophecy is grounded in the assumption that the prerequisite for political stability is social justice. Injustice breeds its own demise and, since God demands the highest of standards, He will not forever tolerate exploitation, corruption and mediocrity. Countries that have been influenced by the prophetic vision have the greatest potential for the achievement of social justice.

Christian ethics

Commonalities between Jewish and Christian ethics

Jesus and most of the very early Christians were Jews. The first commonality for Christians and Jews is that morality is an inextricable part of religious life. Morality and faith cannot be separated; a moral life is a result of a genuine spirituality.

Secondly, moral goodness is believed to have its source in the perfect goodness of God. God's nature and dealings with humanity, as revealed in the Scriptures, are an external point of reference, or authority, for morality. Humanity is ultimately accountable to God for the way they live their lives. For Jews, God's moral guidance takes the form of the Hebrew Bible (which Christians call the Old Testament). Christians regard both the Old and the New Testaments as their authoritative Scriptures. Also important as sources are tradition (customs, rituals and theology), reason and experience.

> For Jews and Christians morality and faith cannot be separated; a moral life is a result of a genuine spirituality.

A third feature common to the Jewish and Christian traditions is their emphasis on both a high standard of personal moral behaviour and social justice. (See the stress on doing what is right in the case study of Thandi as discussed earlier). Personal morality, justice and compassion are cardinal moral values for both Jews and Christians. Social justice takes the form of special concern for vulnerable groups such as the poor, the oppressed, the sick and the outcast.

The value systems of the Judaeo-Christian and African ethical traditions probably constitute the most influential source of ethical values in South African society.

Jesus of Nazareth

Jesus of Nazareth entered human history in approximately 4 BCE and lived in what was then Palestine, a part of the Roman Empire. According to the New Testament, his birth (which is still celebrated in the festival of Christmas) was accompanied by wonders and signs. According to Christian belief this was no ordinary birth, but the incarnation ('enfleshment') of God in human form. (Based on the revelation of the Scriptures and their experience of God, the doctrine of the Trinity later developed; the understanding of God as 'three coequal Persons', the Father, the Son, and the Holy Spirit.)

After growing up in Nazareth and pursuing the trade of a carpenter, Jesus began to preach about the kingdom (rule) of God and called twelve disciples who became his closest followers. His central teaching was that, in him, the kingdom (rule) of God had been inaugurated. The signs of this kingdom were there for all to see: multiple healings, authoritative preaching, the raising of Lazarus from the dead, his power over the sea and storms. Jesus exemplified the biblical values of justice and mercy: the hungry were fed, false religion was condemned and arrogant exploiters exposed. People were amazed at his wisdom, drawn by his compassion, and huge crowds began to pursue him everywhere.

In the so-called golden rule (echoing Leviticus 19:18 and Rabbi Hillel), Jesus taught: 'Love the Lord your God with all your heart and with all your soul and with all your mind and with all your strength ... Love your neighbour as yourself' (Mark 12:30-31).

After a three-year ministry, Jesus was arrested by the Jewish authorities and handed over to the Romans, who crucified him. Most of his disciples ran away. Only John and some of the women who had followed him were present at his death. He was buried in the tomb of a Jewish leader, which was sealed. A Roman guard was set to prevent his body from being stolen by his followers. On the third day, some women went to the tomb to find it empty. The risen Christ appeared to them, and later to many of his disciples, including 'doubting' Thomas. His frightened followers were transformed into bold witnesses of the resurrection and they proclaimed Jesus as the Christ (Messiah). Saul, who had previously persecuted the followers of Christ, became a believer after his dramatic encounter with Christ on the road to Damascus. Many Jews, and later even more Gentiles, were converted to the Christian faith. The church began to spread across the Roman Empire and beyond.

Today the Christian faith is a global one, with churches spread across all five continents, representing all the major traditions, including the Orthodox, Roman Catholic, Protestant, Pentecostal and Charismatic. Approximately two billion people worldwide, or 33%, identify themselves as Christians, making it the most widely followed religion.

Key elements of a Christian world view

The Christian faith is God-centred. All of life is to be lived in the presence and through the power of God. Human beings find their true selves by living to the glory of God.

The story is told of a master woodcarver working on a cathedral in the 1400s. A visitor, who had come to see how work was progressing, saw the craftsman carving a beautiful pattern on a section of the back of the bench of the choir stalls. These choir stalls, which provided seating for the monks or nuns during religious services, were to be placed against the wall of the choir area. The visitor asked the craftsman, 'But why are you carving designs on the back of the stalls? No-one will see them.' The craftsman replied, 'God sees them.'

This man worked for the glory of God. Every aspect of his life and work was focused on loving and serving God. For Christians, to be known and loved by God is to be set free to participate joyfully and gratefully as a co-creator with God in the world, and to be accountable to God for our use of creation and the gifts that God has given us. To be truly human is to live alongside God, imitating the character of the One in whose image we were created. God is not seen as a distant, judgemental figure, but an ever-present God of love and justice, who invites human beings into an intimate relationship. Human beings are seen as God-breathed creatures who find their true identity in relation to God.

> Human beings are seen as God-breathed creatures who find their true identity in relation to God.

Christians believe that the universe was created by God (Genesis 1 & 2) and proclaimed to be 'very good'. Human beings are God's special creation, made in God's image, which includes their intelligence, self-consciousness, moral responsibility and creativity. They have also given authority as the trustees or stewards of creation. However, as represented in the narrative of the Garden of Eden (Genesis 3), human beings chose to disobey God. The result was what theologians have called 'the Fall', which brought alienation between God and humanity, between people, and between humanity and the rest of creation. But evil has no existence of its own, Augustine taught, it is the absence of goodness.

The next major element of a Christian world view is salvation or redemption. Out of love, God took the initiative to restore this relationship by calling Israel to be a special people and a light to the Gentiles. For Christians, the culmination of this initiative is reached in the New Testament. Through the death of Christ on the cross, all of humanity can be saved and their relationships with God, each other and all of creation can be restored. This insistence on the need for salvation is born out of the very realistic view that Christians have of human nature. The Bible and experience show us that human beings are capable both of loving, self-sacrificial actions and brutal, selfish actions. Human moral incapacity is clearly evidenced in our newspapers that report endlessly on fraud, violence, greed, corruption, theft, indifference towards others, rape and murder. Christians believe that human beings are unable to restore their relationship with God through effort, discipline or reason alone. As Jesus explained: 'For out of the heart come evil intentions, murder, adultery, fornication, theft, false witness, and slander' (Matthew 15:19). In short, without God's forgiveness, and the empowerment of the Holy Spirit, we cannot become who we were created to be. The drama of the death and resurrection of Christ, now celebrated in the festival of Easter, stresses the triumph of goodness over evil.

What, then, is the good life according to Christians? It is to live a life of intimacy with God so that relationships with others and creation can be restored. Faith in God comes first, followed by hope. This hope is based on the conviction that the world is created and sustained by God. The kingdom of God, which began in the coming of Jesus to this world, will one day be fully realised and fulfilled. Finally, a life of love for God, others and the world is a truly human life. Thandi can draw on this world view in her decision-making process. Rather than being driven by the threats of her uncle, she can do what is right in God's eyes.

Moral virtue and character

The religious roots of many current business values are often forgotten. The notion of fiduciary responsibility is based on *fides*, which means faith and faithfulness. Integrity means both honesty and wholeness and is derived from biblical texts which stress speaking the truth (e.g. Psalm 15; Zechariah 8:16-17; Ephesians 4:15, 25-32). Similarly, many would argue that the philosophical value of beneficence (doing good, assisting others) is rooted in the Jewish and Christian teaching of loving our neighbour as we love ourselves. Donald Hay (1995) has argued that markets need persons who have virtues in order to operate well. For example, the market is dependent on trust, people speaking the truth and acting on their promises.

A Christian ethic prizes the following virtues: love; goodness; prudence, insight or wise judgement; moral courage; being just in our social dealings and not supporting unjust policies or structures; temperance (or wholeness); self-control, honesty and trustworthiness; endurance; respect for other people; compassion (caring action) and respect for creation. These moral virtues do not take root overnight. They develop as a result of intimacy with God, a personal commitment to obey God, the regular practice of spiritual disciplines such as prayer and service, and the ongoing critique and nurture of the Christian community.

Ethics, the economy and business

The Bible and Christian theology, which were written over several centuries, do not support a particular economic system. Rather, their moral teaching on economic matters stresses certain important moral norms in the area of money and the economic wellbeing of society.

As we have noted, Christian ethics draw on Jewish ethics. Several of the Ten Commandments provide basic prescriptions that are relevant to business. For example, 'do not steal', 'do not bear false witness', and 'do not covet' (Exodus 20:15-17; Deuteronomy 5:19-21). Instead of greed or economic exploitation, the Bible stresses the fundamental principles of compassion, justice, respect, generosity, truth and love. A Christian ethic does not simply promote fairness or refusing to harm others, but actively pursues what is right and good for others. The family is the basic social and economic unit, so it must be assisted to function well. Christians also stress the importance of the relief and elimination of poverty and the necessity to resist economic injustice.

Even though the Bible was written long ago, many of the issues which it addresses, such as theft, corruption, bribery, lying, greed and exploitation remain all too common. Ethical prescriptions such as 'tell the truth', 'love your neighbour as you love yourself', 'practise righteousness', and 'care for creation' remain relevant and form the basis of many current business and accounting codes of conduct. Where specific biblical teaching relating to twenty-first century issues is absent, existing Christian norms and values need to be reinterpreted for new contexts. Perhaps the best way to explain Christian teaching concerning morality in business is to note a few historical examples.

Benedict of Nursia (480-550) founded what became the Benedictine Order of monks. Their motto was prayer and work (*ora et labora*). All monks, whether from a high social class or not, worked in the monastery. Especially during the Dark Ages (fifth to tenth century) in Europe, they preserved agriculture, craftsmanship and learning, and provided health care, education, hospitality and a welfare system for the poor. Their churches and other buildings, plumbing systems, fish farms, brew houses, bakeries, crops, animal husbandry and financial accounting systems provided not only for their own needs, but for those of many others.

> The Benedictine motto was prayer and work (*ora et labora*).

Several centuries later, Luca Pacioli, a member of the Franciscan Order, published the book *Summa de arithmetica, geometria, proportioni, et proportionalita* (1494). He is sometimes called 'the father of accounting' (although he acknowledged the earlier work of Benedetto Cotrugli). He discusses double-entry bookkeeping in this book. By using a trial balance, he says, if the two balances are not equal, 'that would indicate a mistake in your Ledger, which mistake you will have to look for diligently with the industry and intelligence God gave you'.[2]

The early church fathers, Catholic teaching in the medieval period and much of its teaching today stresses that all land and resources are owned first by God, the Creator of the world. This teaching is a reminder that all property, even when apportioned to particular individuals, must nevertheless serve the interests of the common good. The owner of the property has the right to reap the fruits of his/her labour, but the notion of property as something that we can do with as we like, without considering the needs of others, was entirely foreign.

---

2   http://www.canhamrogers.com/HDEB.htm [Accessed 16 Aug 2011].

> A key emphasis of Catholic social ethics was their stress on the common good. The State and those with possessions, property and resources needed to assist others to become participating and responsible members of society. Fair access to and the just distribution of economic resources were central to their teaching.

For several centuries the church was opposed to interest being charged on loans as this would conflict with Christian charity and cause the poor to be further indebted. A key emphasis of Catholic social ethics was their stress on the common good. The State and those with possessions, property and resources needed to assist others to become participating and responsible members of society. Fair access to and the just distribution of economic resources were central to their teaching.

The teaching of the sixteenth-century Reformer, John Calvin, on usury (lending money on interest for investment purposes) enabled the early Protestants in the city of Geneva to pursue trade and banking. In common with earlier teaching, he believed that lending to the poor or a neighbour should not be subject to interest. Other restrictions included just loan conditions, fair rates and the common good. He believed that all of life, including the economy, should to be governed by faith in God. Business should therefore be practised within the same moral code that governed good personal relationships, family life and community needs.

Calvin believed that Christians should make God's will and kingdom visible through their actions in the world. Each Christian is called (*vocatio*) by God to be active in different spheres, including the home, civil government, the law or business. This meant that all of life, not just attending a religious service on a Sunday, was part of the Christian's worship of and service to God.

This motivation to do one's best and to serve God in the world became the basis of what Max Weber later called the Protestant work ethic. Ironically, it was the moral values of honesty, loyalty, thrift and dedicated work, as well as the limitations on consumption and luxury, that enabled the new Protestant communities to accumulate capital for business purposes. A secular version of this ethic removes the moral framework and motivation of the Christian faith, leaving only work as effort. Similarly, when a 24/7 life replaces the norm of a weekly Sabbath rest, we should not be surprised when mental breakdown and physical illness are the result.

During the early years of the industrial revolution in England, John Wesley (the founder of Methodism) was deeply concerned about matters such as poverty, illiteracy, unemployment, drunkenness and slavery. In his sermon *On the Use of Money*, he warns believers of the dangers of the love of money. He urges them to 'gain all you can', taking into account their health, their minds and souls, and the wellbeing of their neighbour. They are to 'save all they can' rather wasting money on luxuries. They are to 'give all you can' to assist their family, those in the Church and the many others who are in need. This basic teaching is very different to those contemporary approaches that stress profit maximisation at the cost of others and spending what you do not have. For Wesley, economic activity in itself is not wrong, but the way in which it is pursued and what is done with the wealth that is accumulated need to be governed by a moral framework.

Several nineteenth-century entrepreneurs were active Christians who combined faith and business. For example, the Quaker family, the Cadburys, and their colleague, Joseph Rowntree, not only built up businesses which still exist today, but also provided their employees with well built houses, libraries and schools for their children. They were encouraged to cultivate gardens, attend church, be better educated and improve the lot of their families (Bradley 1987).

More recently, many Christian theologians have been very critical of the injustice, selfishness and brutality of the type of capitalism that is all too often practised today. When business is separated from a moral and religious framework, moral relativism and self-centred materialism often emerge in their place.

> Each Christian is called (*vocatio*) by God to be active in different spheres, including the home, civil government, the law or business. This meant that all of life, not just attending a religious service on a Sunday, was part of the Christian's worship of and service to God.

Critical comments and questions

It is always difficult to assess a religious tradition as old and diverse as Christianity – which examples of its witness does one select and emphasise? Do the extensive positive examples already discussed outweigh the distortions and abuses also perpetrated in the name of the Christian faith? Three types of social interaction can be identified. First, as we have already seen, Christianity provided the cement that held society together. It provided educated people to administer the political machinery of government, and it supplied education, health services, hospitality and social welfare. Second, Christians have also supported and legitimated the status quo. For example, from the 4th to the 15th centuries, Christianity was the 'official' religion of Europe, and the Church became rich and powerful. It supported feudalism, military conquest, the Crusades, and the 'divine right' of kings. After the 16th century, brutal religious conflicts encouraged the growth of rationalism and secularism. More recently, the exposures of the sexual abuse of children by some priests has caused some people to turn their backs on the Church. A third form of social interaction was that of providing a vital source or religious renewal and of socio-political and economic critique, e.g. the Franciscan movement, the Reformation, the Evangelical revival in England and North America, anti-slavery movements, and many movements of political and economic resistance and change.

Bearing in mind the many millions of those who claim to be Christians on the African continent, some critical questions need to be asked. Are these millions actually followers of Christ or are they only nominal (in name only) Christians? Also, if they are genuine believers, why is their faith not having a much greater critical and constructive moral impact in terms of combating corruption, poverty, crime and violence? Christians need to more actively promote integrity, healthy family life, safe local communities, a more equitable distribution of wealth and social responsibility within the continent as a whole.

Summary

1. Christians ought to combine a God-centred and inspired life with a deep and practical concern for all members of society.
2. Christians believe that God created the universe, therefore they ought to appreciate, respect, protect and wisely use the natural environment.
3. Moral integrity of character and conduct are expected of those who call themselves Christians.
4. A sense of social responsibility and the values of love, justice and compassion ought to govern social, political and economic relationships, movements and structures.
5. Historically, and today, some Christians have legitimated unjust political systems such as colonialism and apartheid. At other times some Christians have gone to the other extreme and withdrawn from any social involvement. Both blind obedience and escapism need to be abandoned and replaced with a model of constructive and critical engagement.
6. Contemporary Christians can draw on the many positive examples of their heritage and be moral examples and leaders in contemporary society and the business world. Genuine Christian faith or spirituality can have a constructive impact on society and the engagement of humanity with the natural world.
7. Christians believe that all human beings are accountable to God for their conduct.

Islamic ethics

Introduction

To appreciate Islamic ethics, it is vital first to understand something about Islam, a religion that has its origins in the Arabia of the seventh century CE. Since then, the religion has become a faith with approximately a thousand million followers, spread across the world, although it has a minority status in South Africa.

The word 'Islam' means peace. In its religious sense, it implies engaged surrender or submission to God or Allah's will. The central belief in Islam involves the acceptance of God's oneness and the prophethood of Muhammad. Accordingly, Muhammad as God's final prophet and messenger is seen by Muslims as the recipient of the sacred scripture of Islam called the Holy *Qur'an*. The *Qur'an* and, in second place, the Prophet Muhammad are the major sources for the Islamic tradition. Sharia, commonly referred to as Islamic law, is derived from these two sources. Sharia gives most Muslims their legal and ethical framework.

> The word 'Islam', in its religious sense, implies engaged surrender or submission to God or Allah's will.

The general character of Islamic ethics

Muhammad drew on both Judaism and Christianity and, like them, Islam does not separate religious from worldly pursuits, its ethics are part and parcel of the religion. Given the centrality of the doctrine of the unity of God, ethics in this tradition tend to be God-centred. In other words, God's will becomes the basis for evaluating ethical behaviour. Human actions become purposeful in such a God-centred world view, driven by the goal to serve, submit to, and surrender to Allah's will.

The three sources of Islamic ethics

The *Qur'an*

The *Qur'an*, through its supreme status in the Islamic tradition, not only gives general guidelines about the beliefs and religious practices of Muslims, but also becomes the central source for deducing Islam's ethical and moral guidelines. These moral guidelines emanate mostly from Qur'anic passages that describe the attributes of the Muslim God. God is called, for example, 'the most merciful', 'the compassionate', 'the forgiving' and 'ultimate peace'. Flowing from these attributes, good Muslims are those who are perceived to have assimilated and internalised these attributes in their interaction with others.

Prophet Muhammad's example

In the Muslim tradition, Prophet Muhammad is inseparable from Islam. His conduct, teachings and example constitute – next to the *Qur'an* – a major source of Islamic ethics. Seen by Muslims as the embodiment of human perfection, Muhammad is the norm and standard by which the ethical ideals of the Muslim community are often judged. Islamic ethical attitudes towards the environment derive mostly from Muhammad's teachings and personal conduct. The destruction of the environment by Muslim armies in times of war is forbidden. Muhammad's statements such as '[i]n avenging the injuries caused to you, do not destroy their means of subsistence, neither their fruit trees, nor their date palms' (Bowker 1998:81) often serve as moral guidelines for Muslims in such contexts.

> Seen by Muslims as the embodiment of human perfection, Muhammad is the norm and standard by which the ethical ideals of the Muslim community are often judged.

Sharia (Islamic law)

If ethics can be defined as the way we make decisions about right and wrong, and the values that underlie such decision making, then sharia, in addition to the *Qur'an* and Prophet Muhammad's example, represents a vital source of reference for the ethical regulation of Muslim life and activity. All rules concerning prohibitions and what is permissible, from rules governing ritual observances to social transactions such as commercial and family laws, are supposed to be sanctioned by sharia. For most Muslims, sharia represents the very will of Allah that must be carried out.

To facilitate this acting out of God's will, sharia classifies human actions into five basic categories. These are as follows:

1. *Obligatory acts*, such as the prescribed five daily prayers, fasting in the Muslim month of Ramadan, giving alms to the needy, pilgrimage to Mecca and defending the faith.
2. *Recommended acts*, such as visiting the sick, kindness to animals and respect for the environment.
3. *Reprehensible but not essentially forbidden acts*, such as silence against injustice and smoking.
4. *Forbidden or reprehensible acts*, such as stealing, bribery, cheating and dishonesty.
5. *Being indifferent or morally neutral*. These are human actions on which the *Qur'an*, Muhammad's example and Islamic law are either vague or silent regarding their permissibility or impermissibility.

Two points arise from this classification of human actions. First, it is clear that there are grey areas in which the Islamic ethical code becomes ambiguous. Second, the classification seems to suggest that there is a close relationship between ethics and law in Islam.

An ethic of action

Islam is often described as an action-based religion. In other words, beliefs must be accompanied by necessary actions. The ethical implication is that the human intention to do good is not sufficient. To support this view, Muslims often cite this statement from Muhammad: 'Whoever amongst you sees an evil or wrong, change it by your hand, and if unable to do so, talk against it, and if still unable to talk against it, then at least reject it with the heart, and rejection by heart is the weakest form of faith.'

> Whoever amongst you sees an evil or wrong, change it by your hand, and if unable to do so, talk against it, and if still unable to talk against it, then at least reject it with the heart, and rejection by heart is the weakest form of faith.'

A modern debate within Islam

Like most traditions, Islam is not free from diverse points of view. From the discussion above of sharia, it would seem that Islamic morality is very much an enforced morality. The question is then: To what extent does the imperative to do what Muslims see as God's will through application of sharia involve an enforced morality? A cursory glance at some Muslim countries seems to support this view. Countries such as Saudi Arabia and northern Sudan have made sharia the law of the land. Even in countries where Muslims live within secular democracies, such as parts of Europe and Nigeria, they have not shied away from demanding that sharia should govern them. (Some groups have even committed acts of violence.) Can it be assumed from these cases that Muslim ethical conduct is achieved only through the enforcement of God's law? Is this a true reflection of morality within Islam? Does the Islamic tradition have other perspectives, or is this the only perspective?

> Can it be assumed from these cases that Muslim ethical conduct is achieved only through the enforcement of God's law? Is this a true reflection of morality within Islam?

Based on the centrality of Muhammad within Islam, a less legalistic ethic has emerged that stresses the compassionate side rather than the punitive dimension of God, running parallel to legal or sharia-based ethics. This view holds that the compassionate side of God is very much reflected in Muhammad's personality.

This approach to Islamic ethics is located mostly within Sufism, the spiritual dimension of Islam. While Sufis accept the significance of Islamic law, they assert that a body of ethics that draws reference mainly from sharia tends to emphasise the punitive side of God. From their perspective, such a morality fosters an enforced notion of morality. Such an enforced morality cannot serve as the basis of true morality. True morality, according to Sufis, is achieved when humans act out of love rather than fear of God's retribution, anger and punishment. Such love is achieved when individuals are detached from the material and physical world and have moved towards a closer union with God. Sufis place most emphasis on the voluntary surrender of the individual (or community) to God's will.

Summary

To sum up, it can be noted that morality in Islam is based on the following basic beliefs and principles:

- Allah is the source and creator of all goodness, truth and beauty.
- Humans are representatives or agents of God on Earth.
- All things are created for the service of humans.
- Allah, as a just God, does not place unnecessary burdens on humans.
- All things must be done in moderation.
- Except for the explicitly forbidden, all things are permissible.
- The ultimate goal is to attain the pleasure of Allah.

Conclusion

Islam has laid down regulations that have moral and ethical implications for organising human life, in the form of religious and social duties. These are intended to assist Muslims in their quest towards moral progress and the improvement of relations between human beings.

Hindu ethics

Introduction

A number of ethical traditions originated in India, namely Hinduism, Jainism, Buddhism, and Sikhism. We will discuss only Hinduism, as the Hindu community in South Africa is bigger than these other religious traditions.

'Hinduism' is a recent Western name for the oldest of the Indian religious traditions. The preferred Hindu name for their own spiritual and ethical heritage is 'the eternal way'. Hinduism had no specific historical founder. It is a rich and complex cultural and historical tradition. A variety of beliefs, practices, customs and trends can be found within the wider Hindu universe, past and present, which is embraced by 850 million of the earth's inhabitants. Three illustrations of this variety follow below.

1. There are a number of ways or paths in Hinduism that enable the seeker to achieve final spiritual liberation from the problems of suffering, bondage and ignorance. The three main paths are: the path of works done in a spirit of unselfishness; the path of inner spiritual realisation, and the path of loving devotion to a personal God (for example, Shiva, Vishnu) or to the great Goddess.
2. There are many Hindu scriptures. A Hindu may choose to focus on one (or more) of these as a preferred holy book: the popular Bhagavad-Gita, the Four Vedas or the Ramayana, with its colourful stories and characters.
3. It is sometimes said that ahimsa (practising nonharmfulness toward all living creatures, a theme stressed by Mahatma Gandhi) is universal in Hinduism. This is not the whole truth. Once again, we encounter a number of different viewpoints. While many Hindus (especially Gandhi) have followed a consistently nonviolent lifestyle, others have supported what the West calls the 'just war' teaching, that certain types of wars are acceptable, provided that they are carried out in a spirit of restraint and in self-defence. Some Hindus interpret the Bhagavad-Gita as teaching nonharmfulness, while others see it as supporting the just war teaching.

Hinduism as a way of life

Hinduism is often thought to be a tolerant and flexible tradition. While there is some truth in this, the flexibility and freedom of choice lie in the realm of Hindu beliefs and ideas rather than in the areas of religious practice and social organisation. Religious and social practice is crucial. Hinduism (like Judaism) is a tradition in which doing and acting are more fundamental than believing, although beliefs are not unimportant. This doing can take many forms, including: popular worship, various ritual performances, yoga, prayer, chanting, good deeds, participation in festivals and pilgrimages. An important context in which Hinduism has been learned and lived out over the centuries is the family.

Some suggest that Hinduism is the most otherworldly or spiritual of the world religions. The otherworldly model does not do justice to the full range of Hindu values, as can be witnessed by the four goals of life and the Bhagavad-Gita.

> The substance of the four goals of life, some of which are clearly worldly in character, is:
> 1. Moral and ritual action;
> 2. Economic and political activity;
> 3. Desire and pleasure (including sensual and sexual desire);
> 4. Ultimate spiritual liberation.

One of the most significant teachings of the Bhagavad-Gita is that you do not need to leave the world and society behind in order to find God. You continue to live fully in the world in all sorts of ways, but you do so in a spirit of 'action without attachment' – action without desire, ambition, selfishness or vested interest.

Karma and *dharma*

If we want to understand the basic workings of Hindu morality, we need to understand the two important themes of *karma* and *dharma* that have been accepted by all branches of Hinduism. Simply put, *karma* means *actions* (any actions, whether right or wrong) as well as the various consequences of these actions; *dharma* means *right or appropriate actions*, including moral actions and appropriate ritual actions.

Karma

Karma, in Hindu history, has always been linked to the idea of reincarnation: when your body dies at the end of this life, the real, eternal 'you' or eternal self lives on in body after body, life after life. The general circumstances of each of your reincarnated lives are governed by the law of *karma*. (We can understand *karma* as a sort of automatic moral and spiritual law of cause and effect.) Act morally, and this will affect your future lives for the good; act selfishly and negatively, and you will experience negative and miserable circumstances in your future lives. Moral considerations therefore lie at the heart of important Hindu teachings.

Karma often results from a Hindu's intentional acts, though it is possible for Hindus to gather *karma* without realising it, for example, by breaking a ritual purity rule and becoming polluted. For a Hindu, *karma* can have ritual ramifications as well as moral implications.

Karma in Hinduism does not involve a fatalistic belief that there is no human freedom, that everything is always predetermined. Although what a Hindu is right now is a result of past (and unchangeable) forces and influences, from this moment on, the Hindu is relatively free to shape his/her future destiny.

When the West first encountered Hinduism, the question was soon raised: How easily does belief in *karma* lead to a lack of concern for human suffering? We might be tempted to say: 'Why interfere and help this poor, suffering person? Leave him to work out the consequences of his own past actions!' Modern Hindus would lean in the other direction, stressing that it is our clear moral duty to help people in need. By doing so sincerely, we will improve our own *karma*.

Dharma

Dharma is a very important theme in Hinduism, and its claims affect all Hindus. Even those Hindu saints who have withdrawn from the world are achieving their spirituality on a foundation of *dharma* practised over many years. *Dharma* finds meaning in two main contexts:

1. Applied to the universe, *dharma* implies order (orderliness, coherence) in a comprehensive sense; the overall order of the universe or nature.
2. Applied to the human and social realms, *dharma* implies proper action, right action, moral action. It is sometimes translated simply as 'duty'.

The link between these two meanings is simply this: dharmic action is right action *that conforms to the order* that lives in all things.

Some dharmic virtues are universal and obligatory for everyone, such as: truth telling, self-control, patience, hospitality, kindness, and honouring parents. Other applications of *dharma* are contextual. These depend, firstly, on the *class* or *caste* to which you belong. The four classes, from high to low, are: Brahmans (for example, priests); rulers and warriors; farmers and traders, and servant workers. Secondly, they depend on the *stage of life* you are passing through. The four stages of life are: the spiritual student, the married householder, the contemplative forest dweller, and the sannyasi – a devout holy wanderer.

Dharma is often contextual: the dharmic obligations of a married warrior will be different to those of an elderly (and celibate) Brahman wanderer.

Sources of Hindu ethics

What are the sources of Hindu moral awareness? The situation is not as clear-cut as in some other traditions, where there is one infallible sacred scripture that enshrines the will and commands of God. The most useful sources of Hindu values would include certain Hindu scriptures, as well as the living examples of Hindu teachers and holy people. In scriptures like the Great Epic, the popular Ramayana, and the Bhagavad-Gita, we can find many useful models of practical *dharma*: people whose lives are characterised by virtues such as: courage, unselfishness, faithfulness, honesty, and so on. The heroic Rama and his wife Sita in the Ramayana are two of the best known of these morally admirable characters.

Controversial practices

There are a number of traditional social practices in Hinduism that have proved to be significantly controversial. We briefly cite two examples: caste, and the situation of Hindu women.

The caste system means that Hindus are born into a particular caste (social slot, social niche), each characterised by specific features and restrictions. We have seen that four great classes underlie the caste system, as well as thousands of specific castes. A specific caste will have rules about various things: whom you may marry, whom you may eat with, and what occupation you may practise. Below the caste hierarchy was an underclass called the outcastes or untouchables. (Mahatma Gandhi supported them and called them 'children of God'.)

Caste discrimination is outlawed in India today, yet caste is still observed more than we might expect. Not surprisingly, many modern Hindus regard the practice of caste as morally unacceptable. In a contemporary climate of moral equality and human rights, caste is seen as immoral by its critics.

> The place and treatment of women in traditional Hinduism is also often seen as regrettable from a modern perspective. Although women were not always treated as subordinate, many women in Hindu history would have experienced the truth of the famous saying from an ancient Hindu law manual: 'A woman is protected by her father when she is young, by her husband during her marriage, and by her sons when she is old.' In addition, women were traditionally accorded a relatively low caste status. The controversial practices of child marriage and widow burning that occurred in India from medieval times were believed to emphasise, respectively, the Hindu woman's purity and her devotion.

Revitalising Hinduism

During the last century or so, many Hindus have attempted to revitalise their tradition. This includes at least two elements. The first involves calling people back to certain fundamental teachings of Hinduism: there is one ultimate Divine Reality; the need for Hindus to combine their religious practices with genuine spiritual development; the key Hindu virtues of unselfishness and compassion, and spiritual liberation as the result of increasing closeness to God. This emphasis on religion as a force for good is echoed in the most popular of the modern Hindu festivals, Diwali, which symbolises the triumph of light and goodness over darkness and evil.

The second revitalising element is criticising what is seen as regrettable developments and innovations that emerged during Hindu history: child marriage, widow burning, the plight of outcastes, the relative lack of humanitarian concern in previous centuries, and the crudeness of some traditional image worship.

> Mahatma Gandhi is of particular interest: he taught that the *moral* dimensions of Hinduism should take precedence over all other dimensions. He acted out the practice of satyagrahi (putting truth into practice in an actively concerned yet nonviolent manner).

Conclusion

While South Africa's Hindu community is relatively small and more evident in KwaZulu-Natal and Gauteng than elsewhere in the country, its values have helped to reshape the modern world through the influence of Gandhi and his followers. Gandhi's years in this country were crucial for his development. As India with its large Hindu majority undergoes rapid economic growth, the Hindu ethic is set to become an increasingly significant factor in globalisation.

> As India with its large Hindu majority undergoes rapid economic growth, the Hindu ethic is set to become an increasingly significant factor in globalisation.

Modern value systems

Introduction

We proceed now to a brief account of four important secular approaches to morality that have emerged since the French and American revolutions of the late eighteenth century. They differ radically from each of the religious traditions we have covered, approaching ethics in secular terms. Some of these secular moralities regard all beliefs about the existence of a supernatural Being or spiritual world as mistaken and even harmful, holding that the physical universe is the only reality. We look briefly at secular humanism, the communist value system, the human rights movement and feminist ethics.

Secular humanism

The original meaning of the term 'secular' (from the Latin word *saeculum*, meaning 'this present age, world or generation'), is 'neutral about the truth or otherwise of religion'. In the term 'secular humanism', however, the word has come to mean that the present, natural world or cosmos is the only reality. Secularists deny the validity of any belief in God and many are determinedly antireligious. As we have seen, secular humanists place great emphasis on ethics, understood as humanity's achievement in discovering and practising that which is right and good.

> The key to secular humanist ethics is the conviction that moral values come from nature, human nature, and the lessons of our experience as human beings.

As an organised movement, secular humanism is very small. This is especially true of South Africa. But secular humanism has an influence that reaches far beyond the numerical size of the organised humanist movement of countries like Britain and the USA. This influence is also felt in South Africa, and is particularly evident among some of the more highly educated members of society. In addition, secular humanist ethics seek to build a global ethic that would embrace the central, time-honoured moral values of the older, religious approaches to ethics, while separating these values from their religious foundation.

The key to secular humanist ethics is the conviction that moral values come from nature, human nature, and the lessons of our experience as human beings. We see quite clearly the secular humanist belief that the whole point and purpose of moral goodness is to make life on this planet more enjoyable and meaningful. The American philosopher Paul Kurtz (1988), a leading secular humanist writer, has stated that the 'ethics of personal excellence' must include joyful living – in this present life, of course, not as something that might await us beyond death.

> Kurtz's four-point statement of the 'common moral decencies' offers a more detailed statement of core humanist values:
> 1. *Integrity*, which involves truthfulness, promise-keeping, sincerity and honesty;
> 2. *Trustworthiness*, which involves fidelity or faithfulness, and dependability;
> 3. *Benevolence*, which includes goodwill, nonmalfeasance (malfeasance = harm) to persons and property, sexual consent and beneficence (acting in a way that benefits others);
> 4. *Fairness*, which involves gratitude, accountability, justice, tolerance and cooperation.

Clearly these moral values correspond quite closely to those endorsed by most religions. Many believers regard moral principles as universal truths because they have their source in the perfect goodness of God. But secular humanists do not believe in God. Instead they draw on the sources that are available to them: nature, including human nature. Humanists believe that we can study these sources by means of open, critical enquiry and that we can overcome personal and cultural bias. Secular humanists regard ethics as something that has always evolved according to changing realities and will continue to do so in the future. They believe that humanity learns from experience: which values foster the greatest wellbeing, and which values reduce harm as much as possible.

Communist ethics

Communism, as an economic and political movement advocating collective ownership of the means of production, has declined as an international force since the fall of the Berlin Wall in 1989. In South Africa, however, it is still an influential partner in the country's ruling political alliance at the time of writing. This makes it important to have a basic grasp of its values. Since these are based on the work of Karl Marx (1818-1883), understanding communist values requires a basic grasp of the essentials of Marxist philosophy.

Marxism holds that the physical universe is the only basic reality. Human existence is governed by the need to meet material needs, so economic forces drive our actions. As history unfolds, economic classes emerge with conflicting interests, giving rise to class struggle. In our present capitalist stage of history, the opposed classes are the wealthy and powerful, who control the means of production, and the great mass of workers, who are exploited by the capitalist pursuit of profit. It is therefore in the interests of the workers to overthrow capitalism and replace it with a new socialist economic and political order, where exploitation will be a thing of the past.

> Marxism holds that the physical universe is the only basic reality. Human existence is governed by the need to meet material needs, so economic forces drive our actions.

If matter is the only basic reality, ideas of all kinds, such as laws, religious teachings and morality itself, must be outgrowths of the material and economic conditions in which they appear. In the words of the 1990 essay, *Has Socialism Failed?*, by the late Joe Slovo, a leading South African communist: '[A]ll morality is class related,'[3] and reflects the interests of the dominant class. Marx himself rejected the belief that moral principles can be universal and timeless. The well-known Marxist rejection of religion follows logically from such a philosophy.

---

3   South African Communist Party website, www.sacp/org.za [Accessed 20 February 2009].

> Marxist ethical doctrine has as its governing value the goal of overthrowing all exploitation of persons by persons, and with it the capitalist system. What communism values most is action that furthers this goal, such as: active commitment to the common good, as communism understands it; loyalty to the party; self-discipline, and human equality. Science is greatly valued as our most reliable way to discover truth. It rejects as evil: all exploitation; all that deludes people, which includes religion according to this value system, and all that undermines the communist project of overthrowing capitalism.

Leading South African communists like Joe Slovo and Jeremy Cronin insisted that the movement can thrive only if it is democratic and supports human rights. They argued that the repressive acts of the Soviet Union and its allies were "a grave bureaucratic distortion of socialism" brought about by Joseph Stalin's dictatorship, and that this distortion led to the failure of communism in Europe. Marxist socialism, they argued, remains essentially valid.[4]

Human rights and responsibilities

The current human rights debate is often pursued by secular thinkers and is entrenched in a variety of Bills and Constitutions. We need to remember, though, that the notion of human rights is implicit in a Judaeo-Christian ethic. The biblical view of humanity as created in the image of God, with moral obligations towards others, and the moral norms of justice and mercy provide a foundation for the idea that any form of neglect or abuse of human beings is morally wrong.

> The human rights movement has become a global force for change in safeguarding individuals from the power of the State and other individuals.

The human rights movement seeks to entrench basic human rights in laws, national Constitutions and internationally accepted documents like the Universal Declaration of Human Rights. Starting with the American and French Revolutions in the late 1700s, this movement has become a global force for change in safeguarding individuals against the power of the State and other individuals.

The usual way of doing this is to assert in a Bill of Rights that all people are by nature entitled to certain freedoms, such as freedom of speech, movement and association, and certain rights, such as the right to a healthy environment and to a belief system of their choice, if they are to achieve their human potential. By the same token, the human

---

4 Ibid.

rights movement also guarantees that all people will be free of unfair discrimination, such as discrimination on grounds of race or gender. The desire to entrench and protect human rights is a development of great ethical importance. Its purpose is to foster conditions that promote our wellbeing against forces that might lead to tyranny, exploitation, domination, violence, and other evils.

The Constitution of the democratic Republic of South African of 1996 is a much-admired document, especially the Bill of Rights contained in Chapter 2. Of great interest is the set of core values on which it is built. Contained in its opening clause, the set 'affirms the democratic values of human dignity, equality and freedom'.[5] As a key part of the basic law of the land, these three values enjoy legal supremacy in South Africa.

Ethics is, however, about much more than just these three values. South Africa's Moral Regeneration Movement has produced a more comprehensive set in its Charter of Positive Moral Values, launched in 1998.[6] The Charter calls on people to pledge to do the following:

- Respect human dignity and equality;
- Promote freedom, the rule of law and democracy;
- Improve material wellbeing and economic justice;
- Enhance sound family and community values;
- Uphold honesty, integrity and loyalty;
- Ensure harmony in culture, belief and conscience;
- Show respect and concern for all;
- Strive for justice, fairness and peaceful coexistence;
- Protect the environment.[7]

One important weakness of this movement is that too much emphasis is placed on individual human rights, which can foster self-concern, and neglect responsibility towards others and community life. This has given rise to continuing attempts in South Africa to produce a Bill of Moral Responsibilities that will counter such one-sidedness. A second weakness, which we return to below, is whether a concern for the rights of others can be supported by a purely humanistic ethic. Some argue that it opens to door to moral relativism which, in turn, can offer little or no moral critique of any human beliefs, actions or movements.

---

5   'Human dignity, the achievement of equality and the advancement of human rights and freedoms', Constitutional Law No. 108 of 1996, South African Government website, www.info.gov.za/documents/constitution/1996/a108-96.pdf [Accessed 10 September 2011].
6   www.mrm.org.za [Accessed 20 February 2009].
7   *Ibid.*

Feminist ethics

Feminist ethics can be described as rethinking those aspects of traditional ethics that fail to do justice to women's collective moral experience, including ethical qualities often linked with women, such as care and compassion. There are many contributors to this significant new development. We will review the work of Carol Gilligan and Nel Noddings and feminists from the Christian tradition.

> Feminist ethics can be described as rethinking those aspects of traditional ethics that fail to do justice to women's collective moral experience.

Carol Gilligan's seminal and frequently cited book, *In a Different Voice: Psychological Theory and Women's Development*, sparked much debate and discussion around women's moral thinking. Her motive was to counter fellow psychologist Lawrence Kohlberg's theory of moral development. In her study, Gilligan collected data through interviews with women who were making important decisions in their lives. Her analysis reveals women's moral thinking when confronted with various ethical dilemmas such as abortion. Gilligan discovered that women's handling of moral problems prioritises care and responsibility rather than rights and rules.

What emerged indicates that women's moral judgements can differ from those of men as they are often tied to feelings of empathy and compassion, and are concerned with real problems, rather than hypothetical dilemmas. According to Gilligan's analysis: 'Care becomes the self-chosen principle of judgment' (Gilligan 1982:74). Such an ethic logically also emphasises the interconnectedness of life: an activity that is perceived as potentially destructive to self and others is bad, while an activity that promotes happiness and wellbeing for self and others is good.

Equally influential in feminist ethics is Nel Noddings. Her book, *Caring: A Feminine Approach to Ethics and Moral Education*, echoes Gilligan, but also expands on the ethic of care. The caring of women is 'rooted in receptivity, relatedness, and responsiveness' (Noddings 2003:2). This does not mean that men do not have the capacity to care. Through experience and practical wisdom, they, too, can engage successfully in the ethic of care, especially if it is acknowledged that caring is a source of survival for humanity.

> The feminist ethic of care places enormous importance on the development of morally sensitive and caring beings, who are aware of their relatedness and connectedness to others.

The feminist ethic of care places enormous importance on the development of morally sensitive and caring beings, who are aware of their relatedness and connectedness to others. In this moral paradigm, which is similar to the African ethic of *ubuntu*, there is a definite departure from individualistic ethics to a more communalistic ethic in which values of compassion, care and friendship are integral to morality.

Feminist and African women theologians have engaged in the task of both ethical deconstruction and reconstruction.

For example, they critique abusive patriarchy in both Western and African cultures, and those theological interpretations and religious practices that fail to recognise the image of God in women. In addition, they have written theologies and liturgies that take into account the insights and contribution of women, empower individual women and women's groups, and assist women who are financially dependent on men that abuse them. They also insist that the bodies of women and children need to be valued and protected and they promote both ordained and lay female leadership. Finally they assist churches to enable both women and men to be more active in promoting what is right and good in terms of the family, culture, social structures, politics and the economy (Phiri et al. 2002). Women like Thandi in our case study, are faced with complex and important moral challenges; they have the opportunity to work alongside those who wish to create better societies in which to live.

What is required to address the moral problems we face?

We have outlined some of the ethical challenges we face and the various religious and secular moral value systems on which we can draw to find solutions to these challenges. In this final section, we ask what we need to be able to address the ethical problems we face. Which of these approaches to ethics can provide a basis for a professional ethic for auditors and accountants in South Africa today? Below it is argued that financial systems cannot be reconstructed nor trust in accounting and auditing practices ensured without a credible view of reality, a moral understanding of life and work, the reawakening of moral conscience and conduct, and the formative role of moral communities.

> ... financial systems cannot be reconstructed nor trust in accounting and auditing practices ensured without a credible view of reality, a moral understanding of life and work, the reawakening of moral conscience and conduct, and the formative role of moral communities.

In the remainder of this chapter, we address the key questions posed at the outset of the chapter:
- Why should anything be valued?
- What is a good life?
- Why should I be moral?
- What is the role of moral communities?

Why should anything be valued? What is a credible view of reality?

This chapter has stressed the importance of moral integrity, responsibility and action – but on what are these to be based? It could be argued that a credible view of reality needs to provide an explanation of the origin of the universe and answer the question of whether there is any purpose and meaning in life. It needs to account for the existence of both good and evil and explain why human beings believe that life itself, people, society and the natural world ought to be valued. It further needs to provide a sense of belonging and hope for the future.

Strengths and weaknesses of religious world views

The strengths of the many religious world views have already been outlined in some detail. They provide explanations of the origins of life and the world, the future and reasons why people ought to be moral. They further explain why faith and life, particularly socio-economic life, ought to be linked rather than separated. In the Judaeo-Christian view of reality, for example, faith and morality are inextricably linked. The prophet Amos (5:12, 15, 24) could record God's condemnation of social injustice:

> For I know how many are your sins – you who afflict the righteous, who take a bribe, and turn aside the needy from the gate ... Seek good and not evil, that you may live; and so the Lord, the God of hosts, will be with you ... Hate evil, and love the good, and establish justice in the gate ... But let justice roll down like waters, and righteousness like an ever flowing stream.

Thus, the ethicist Hans Küng (1997:142-43) has argued that in contrast to secularism, religious faith provides a comprehensive framework and motivation for ethics. It supplies: an unconditional, transcendent basis for morality; an explanation for the existence of both evil and goodness; ultimate meaning and belonging, and a reason to protest against injustice, even when a situation appears hopeless.

What then are the weaknesses of a religious ethic? To begin with, people adhere to different religions and these do not all have the same view of reality. Hindu, African and Muslim views of the world and God/the gods are different. Further, the religious elements of social conflicts such as those between Catholics and Protestants for many years in Ireland, between Hindus and Muslims in India and Pakistan or between Muslims and Jews in Israel/Palestine need to be acknowledged. Finally, instances of distorted teachings (e.g. defending slavery or colonialism) and brutal practices (such as the Spanish Inquisition or placing bombs that kill innocent people, e.g. in Iraq, India or Nigeria) form the core of secular critiques of religion.

How do religious adherents respond to these critiques? As we saw earlier, certain beliefs and practises perpetrated by religious adherents in the past are now being questioned or rejected by their successors. Religious ethicists also argue that because of the influence of religion, both historically and in many contemporary societies, those in power often seek to either eliminate religion (e.g. in the former USSR), or to use religion to legitimise their actions (as in the case of apartheid). Thus, a particular religion cannot be rendered illegitimate on the basis of an action that is not defensible in terms of that religion's moral teaching. Not all who claim to be acting on the basis of religious convictions are indeed doing so. Similarly, in the aftermath of the Enron and other scandals, the accounting profession was not discarded, although the credibility of some of its practitioners was questioned and steps put into place to avoid ongoing malpractice.

Strengths and weaknesses of secular world views

Contemporary secular humanists hold that reason and experience are sufficient to explain our physical and moral realities. Their views are not new, as some earlier thinkers have also been critical of religious world views and the worst examples of religious practice. Members of human rights movements and both feminist thinkers and activists, for example, have fought long and hard to combat exploitation and inequalities in society and many find secular world views to be convincing.

Secular humanists, communists and some within the human rights and feminist movements discard belief in God and a religious world view, while seeking to retain a stress on the importance of morality. To a large extent, this is the legacy of the philosopher, Immanuel Kant (see Chapter 3). He believed that what is right could be determined by autonomous human reason, independently of religion. On the basis of reason alone, people could identify the moral duties and obligations that govern life and apply them to practical living. Kant was raised by Christian parents, but he was not a practising Christian. As MacIntyre (1966:197) argues: '... the Kantian doctrine is parasitic upon some already existing morality.' His philosophical system drew on the norms and values of the Christian faith. But his stress on the moral autonomy (freedom) of the human agent meant that this Christian moral basis was later abandoned by those who sought to separate religion and morality.

What, then, are the weaknesses of a secular view of reality? One criticism of secularism is whether it can provide an explanation as to why anything ought to be valued at all. Many secularists believe that this material world is all there is; there is no God or transcendent reality. But on what basis, a religious ethicist may ask, can a secularist insist that morality or reason is important (Haught 2008:15-27)? If the world and human beings are the chance result of chaos and/or natural selection, why should anyone be morally obligated towards others or care for them? Why should anything be right or good in a purposeless, conditional and material universe? Furthermore, human experience differs and is influenced by culture. How can reason alone determine what is right if what my reason tells me differs from what your reason tells you?

Consequently, Alastair MacIntyre (1985:11-12) argues that, in a postmodern context, many people no longer believe in ethical obligations or absolutes. Many have little clarity about what is right or wrong and have little or no sense of purpose, meaning or direction. As a result, decisions are made on the basis of personal preference (emotivism) rather than reason, faith or moral obligation. This results in ethical relativism, although some would argue that moral absolutes can be sustained independent of religion (Prozesky 2007; cf Kretzschmar 2008).

Ethical relativists argue that there are no moral principles that are applicable to all. The adage: 'When in Rome, do as the Romans do', encapsulates relativism. Moral relativism is difficult to defend because it undermines itself. The statement: 'Everything is relative' is making a universal claim, while relativism says that no universal claims can be made. Further, relativism is incapable of solving practical social problems because a relativist cannot logically or fully commit him or herself to a moral belief or course of moral action.

Where does ethical relativism leave us as a society? One result is selfish individualism. In our case study, Sipho admits to no moral obligations to society. Such persons feel no moral obligation towards others. This is evidenced in the actions of those who defraud shareholders, lie to clients and enrich themselves at the expense of tax payers and the poor. Another practical result of ethical relativism is immoral collectivism. Certain powerful groups enrich themselves and each other at the cost of others. While it is true that individuals wish to care for their families and those close to them, a fraudulent enrichment of your family members (nepotism) or friends (cronyism) causes deep damage to our society.

Finally, the abuse of power and immoral actions are not limited to religious practitioners. For instance, in the name of the communist ideology, Stalin (Russia) and Mao Tse Tung (China), together with all those who supported them, caused the death of millions of their own people. Also, some secular business people have polluted the rivers and oceans, destroyed huge forests and other natural habitats, and poisoned the very air that we breathe.

What is a good life? Re-establish the link between business and morality

As a result of the increased specialisation of knowledge, one can complete a degree in economics, management accountancy, auditing, financial accounting or internal auditing without any study of history, religion, politics, sociology or moral philosophy. This has resulted in an increasingly fragmented rather than a holistic understanding of reality. This was not true for the seminal thinker, Adam Smith (1723-90). For him ethics and economics could never be separated. His book, *Theory of Moral Sentiments* (1759), preceded the publication of his *The Wealth of Nations* (1776). His emphasis on self-interest must not be misunderstood to be selfishness, but rather a natural drive to preserve and improve your economic position in life. But, greed and ruthlessness are incompatible with religious faith, secular morality or stable communities. Economic aims and actions ought to be pursued within the framework of the law and moral convictions and further the interests of all the members of society, not just the powerful few.

We have a very different situation today. For many, the market, competition, profits and material benefits are all that is important. Coupled with individualism and consumerism, a very materialistic and increasingly selfish view of what life is about has emerged in many parts of the world, including South Africa. When businesses and audit firms strive to be lean and mean, not just profit, but profit maximisation becomes the main criterion for decision making. If profit maximisation becomes the main object, indeed the dominant 'value' of a society, we should not be surprised when business people deliberately make claims to deceive shareholders and enrich themselves. Immorality in business was well illustrated in the film *Wall Street* starring Michael Douglas in the role of Gordon Gekko. His creed was: 'Greed, for lack of a better word, is good.'[8] But what is the personal, family and social cost when thousands, if not millions of people, lose their jobs, or have never had a job? Can an emphasis on production and consumption alone lead to a good life? Human beings obviously have material needs, but we also need meaning and good relationships – a sense of where we fit into the vastness of the universe.

> Economic aims and actions ought to be pursued within the framework of the law and moral convictions and further the interests of all the members of society, not just the powerful few.

Some would argue that the value of a religious world view is that it is concerned with the whole of life. For instance, in a Jewish ethic, a God-centred life seeks to resemble God's character and follow God's moral guidance. In Hinduism, *dharma* is associated with the overall order of the universe and right action in the human and social realms. Individual moral action is obligatory on the basis of this overall understanding of the universe. As we saw earlier, those that question or oppose a religious ethic may argue that a secular ethic can provide the necessary link between business and morality on the basis of human reason and experience – what has proven to be good for humanity and the world can be identified and practised.

Why should I be moral? How can moral individuals be formed?

Virtue ethics is a long-standing approach in both religious ethics and moral philosophy. You will read more about the ethics of Aristotle in the next chapter of this book.

---

8   en.wikipedia.org/wiki/Gordon_Gekko [Accessed 10 September 2011].

It is clear that greed and selfishness are at the root of many of the problems we face. But how can the immoral actions of unscrupulous individuals be eliminated or significantly reduced? What or who will cause them to become moral? Furthermore, how can those entering the fields of accountancy and auditing be convinced of the importance of morality, not just in theoretical terms, but as a way of life? In his book entitled *Ethics in Business: Faith at Work*, Childs says:

> ... some are saying that our preoccupation with ethical problem solving has resulted in a neglect of concern for 'character', the sorts of people we are. These newer voices are suggesting that our moral development, our ethical formation and a shaping of our conscience are even more important than formulating the rules of right and wrong and applying them. Persons of integrity and communities with strong, clear ethical traditions possess the 'character' needed to do the right thing. An overemphasis on decision making puts the cart before the horse. (Childs 1995:72)

No-one can doubt the importance of moral virtue and character in the workplace. It would be foolish to trust a financial manager who is obsessed with the need to accumulate huge sums of money so that he can retire at before the age of 40. Lust, the uncontrolled desire to possess and control another person sexually, is likely to exhibit itself as sexual harassment in an office environment. It is difficult to work well with a person you do not trust because he/she has a proven record of lying and attempting to manipulate facts and people.

Religious adherents and those from other belief systems, such as secularist approaches to human rights, need to practise what they preach. Honesty, trust and fairness are welcome in any context. Actions always speak louder than words; the best testimony to the validity and relevance of any moral system is to live a life of integrity. This does not mean that Muslims can insist that sharia law can be imposed in a country or corporation that is not Muslim. Any more than a Christian can insist that everyone attends readings of the New Testament every morning before work.

An important difference between Christians and Muslims is their understanding of the relation between faith and the State. As we have seen, many Muslims seek to have sharia law imposed on all citizens, whether Muslim or not. Most modern Christians uphold the separation of Church and State. This does not mean that your religious faith cannot be taught or practised in public spaces. It does mean that the State cannot use its power to impose a certain faith, or lack thereof, on the citizens of a country.

It is necessary for individuals, business, society and the accounting profession to be able to answer the question: Why should I be moral? Above

> Religious adherents and those from other belief systems, such as secularist approaches to human rights, need to practise what they preach.

various answers to this question have been outlined. For instance, we have seen that a Christian ethic is spiritually motivated: love for God requires moral character and conduct from God's followers. This is why a Christian ethic is prescriptive rather than merely descriptive. Or, a Hindu may say: Act morally in this life and these actions will have an impact on your eternal destiny. In short, a genuine spirituality results in ethical character and conduct. Secular humanists and/or materialists hold that moral values can be derived from human nature, reason and experience, and that human beings can discover and practise what is right and good. Thus, the secular thinker Kurtz argues that the humanist 'four common decencies' of integrity, trustworthiness, benevolence and fairness need to be practiced.

But human nature is not simply good and well meaning. How can the ruthless and damaging evil actions we see perpetrated by many individuals be accounted for and combated?

Therefore, in addition to knowing what is right and good, and why we ought to be good, it is important to ask: How can I become a good person? How can integrity, fairness and responsibility be formed in individuals? This necessitates a process of moral formation. No-one becomes a moral person or a moral leader overnight. We need to admit and learn from our mistakes, learn to distinguish right from wrong, discern falsehood, and develop moral courage. A secularist may argue that human beings can become good people who do what is right as a result of their own efforts. A Christian may say that without the grace and empowerment of God, we will not succeed. Who is right?

What is the role of moral communities?

Because an individual can only do so much, moral communities of different kinds are required to transmit values, form moral character, deter immorality and encourage moral conduct. It is interesting that Bolman and Deal (2003:347) argue: 'Organisational ethics must ultimately be rooted in the soul – an organisation's understanding of its deeply held identity, beliefs, and values ... The most important responsibility of managers is ... [to be] models and catalysts of such values as excellence, caring, justice, and faith.' For example, if the members of a professional body such as the South African Institute of Chartered Accountants (SAICA) provide moral leadership, stress moral norms and values and insist on accountability from their members, they can function as a moral community.

Moral example and leadership in the workplace is extremely important. Work communities can either promote or impede the moral formation of individuals. An accounting clerk doing his/her articles in a practice in which morality is taken seriously by the partners and senior staff is far more likely to practise in a moral, professional manner than a clerk working in a practice where profit alone is regarded as important.

Other communities, such as the family and faith communities, also play a vital role. As was noted in the case study, Thandi's family and church have already formed her character. Her desire to preserve these family and communal relationships acts as both an encouragement to do what is right and a deterrent to avoid doing what will bring disrepute and shame on all. An ethic of integrity and responsibility can grow when individuals are nurtured and critiqued by a moral community. This raises the question: Which of the moral systems discussed in this chapter can best create and sustain such communities of moral accountability?

Finally, within the nation as a whole, in addition to a moral example being provided by influential leaders, a proper legal framework needs to be maintained and implemented. Such a legal framework can protect individuals such as Thandi against baseless rumours and slander, penalize wrong actions and uphold what is morally right.

If the entire auditing profession were made up of people of high moral fibre, unscrupulous members of business, government or other groups would not be able to hide their nefarious practices. Instead of millions being wasted, stolen or misused, they could be disbursed to pay for schools, houses, job creation, welfare, hospitals, rural renewal, environmental protection, roads and much more. In this way the actions of a few honest individuals can ensure a more just society and a better life for all.

> Moral example and leadership in the workplace is extremely important. Work communities can either promote or impede the moral formation of individuals. ... Other communities, such as the family and faith communities, can also play a vital role.

Questions for consideration

1. What are norms, values and virtues? What have you learnt about what you value in life?
2. What are the key ethical challenges facing us as a country?
3. With which of the value systems discussed in this chapter do you agree? Why?
4. Have you learned anything new as you read this chapter?
5. What contribution can a religious ethic make to a business environment?
6. What contribution can a secular ethic make to a business environment?
7. Why is morality in business, accounting and auditing circles important?
8. Do you have a sense of vocation that influences the way you approach accountancy or auditing? If so, what is that vocation?
9. Do you consider yourself to be morally motivated in your work? If so, what is the source of this motivation?
10. Are you sustained and critiqued by a moral community?

Bibliography

Bolman, LG & Deal, TE. 2003. Reframing ethics and spirit. *Business Leadership: a Jossey-Bass reader.* San Francisco, California: Jossey-Bass, 330-348.

Boon, M. 1998. *The African way.* Sandton: Zebra Press.

Bowker, J. 1998. *What Muslims believe.* Oxford: Oneworld Publications.

Bradley, IC. 1987. *Enlightened entrepreneurs.* London: Weidenfeld & Nicolson.

Carew Hunt, RN. 1978. *The theory and practice of communism.* Harmondsworth: Penguin Books.

Childs Jr, JM. 1995. *Ethics in business: faith at work.* Minneapolis, Minnesota: Fortress.

De Gruchy, J & Prozesky, M (eds). 1991. *A southern African guide to world religions.* Cape Town: David Philip.

Elkington, J. 1999. *Cannibals with forks: the triple bottom line of 21st century business.* Oxford: Capstone.

Gbadegesin, S. 2005. Origins of African ethics. *The Blackwell companion to religious ethics*, edited by W Schweither. Oxford: Blackwell, 419-421.

Geering, L. 1991. *Creating the new ethic.* Wellington: St Andrew's Trust.

Gilligan, C. 1982. *In a different voice*: psychological theory and women's development. Cambridge, Massachusetts: Harvard University Press.

Haught, JF. 2008. *God and the new atheism: a critical response to Dawkins, Harris and Hitchens.* London: Westminster John Knox Press.

Hay, D. 1995. Do markets need a moral framework? *Journal of the Association of Christian Economists,* No. 19, 22-35.

Holm, J & Bowker, J (eds). 1994. *Making moral decisions.* London: Pinter.

Kretzschmar, L. 2002. Integrity and consensus: a Christian perspective on ethical management and education in South Africa. *Koers* 67:4, 365-386.

Kretzschmar, L. 2008. Christian spirituality in dialogue with secular and African spiritualities with reference to moral formation and agency. *Theologia Viatorum* 32/1, 63-96.

Kretzschmar, L. 2010. Cultural pathways and pitfalls in South Africa: a reflection on moral agency and leadership from a Christian perspective. *Koers* 75:3, 567-588.

Küng, H. 1997. *A global ethic for global politics and economics.* London: SCM.

Kurtz, P. 1988. *Forbidden fruit: the ethics of humanism.* Buffalo, New York: Prometheus Books.

Kwenda, C, Mndende, N & Stonier, J. 1997. *African religion and culture alive!* Hatfield, Pretoria: Collegium.

MacIntyre, A. 1966. *A short history of ethics.* London: Routledge & Kegan Paul.

MacIntyre, A. 1985. *After virtue: a study in moral theory.* Notre Dame, Indiana: University of Notre Dame.

Mbiti, J. 1969. *African religions and philosophy.* London: Heinemann.

Moosa, E. 2003. Ethics and social issues. *Encyclopedia of Islam and the Muslim world.* New York: Macmillan Press.

Moral Regeneration Movement. 1998. *Charter of Positive Moral Values.* [Online]. Available: www.mrm.org.za [accessed 20 February 2009].

Morgan, P & Lawton, C (eds). 1996. *Ethical issues in six religious traditions.* Edinburgh: Edinburgh University Press.

Noddings, N. 2003. *Caring: a feminine approach to ethics and moral education*. Berkeley, California: University of California Press.

Nürnberger, K. *The Living Dead and the Living God*. Pietermaritzburg: Cluster, 2007.

Phiri, IA, Govinden, DB & Nadar, S. 2002. *Her-stories: hidden histories of women of faith in Africa*. Pietermaritzburg: Cluster Publications.

Prozesky, M & De Gruchy, J (eds). 1995. *Living faiths in South Africa*. Cape Town: David Philip.

Prozesky, M. 2007. *Conscience: Ethical Intelligence for Global Well-Being*. Pietermaritzburg: University of KwaZulu-Natal Press.

Richardson, N. 1996. Can Christian ethics find its way, and itself, in Africa? *Journal of Theology for Southern Africa* 95:37-54.

Shutte, A. 2001. *Ubuntu: an ethic for a new South Africa*. Pietermaritzburg: Cluster Publications.

South Africa. 1996. Constitution of the Republic of South Africa, 1996. Pretoria: Government Printer [Laws].

South African Communist Party website. [Online]. Available: www.sacp/org.za [accessed 20 February 2009].

Stackhouse, M, McCann, DP & Roels, SJ (eds). 1995. *Business: classical and contemporary resources for ethics in economic life*. Grand Rapids, Michigan: Eerdmans.

3

Philosophical foundations of ethics

Deon Rossouw

Outcomes

After working through this chapter, you should be able to do the following:
- Understand what virtue ethics entails
- Gain insight into deontological ethics
- Discern the distinguishing features of utilitarian ethics
- Apply the above theories to specific cases in accounting and auditing.

Overview

In the history of philosophy, a number of ethical theories have emerged that can provide guidance in judging whether actions or decisions are ethical or not. Three such theories have gained particular prominence. They are the virtue theory, the deontological theory, and the utilitarian theory. We will discuss each of these theories by referring to their most prominent representatives.

Introduction

Virtue theory will be introduced through Aristotle's version of this theory. This theory emphasises that what matters in ethical behaviour is the integrity of a person's character. We can expect consistent ethical behaviour only from persons with a well-formed ethical character. Deontological theory shifts the focus from a person's character to the qualities inherent in an ethical action. It claims that to qualify as an ethical action, there are specific qualities to which an action should comply. Immanuel Kant is an exemplar of a deontological approach to ethics, and his version of deontological ethics will be explored. Utilitarian ethics focuses on the consequences of actions in order to decide their ethical worth. John Stuart Mill's version of utilitarian ethics in which he asserts that actions can be judged as ethical if they bring happiness to most people will be discussed.

> **Case study: Chris**
>
> Chris could not believe his luck when a newly listed mining company contracted his company to provide them with external audit services. Chris is the senior partner in an auditing firm which he started with two of his former university classmates. After having struggled for more than a year to build the client base of their firm, they were nowhere near where they had envisaged they would be. At one point, they had seriously considered closing down their firm, but that was before they were contracted by this newly-listed mining company. This contract dramatically changed their entire situation, as this single client was generating more income for them than all their other clients combined. It rescued their company from demise and raised their hopes that they were about to break into the big league.
>
> After completing their first audit of this mining company, Chris found that there were irregularities in their financial accounts and realised that he had no option but to issue a qualified audit statement. As senior partner of the firm, he informed the client of his intention. The financial director of the mining company reacted angrily when he learned of Chris's intention. He warned Chris that a qualified audit statement would spell the end of their relationship. He asked Chris whether he realised what damage a qualified statement could do to the company's share price and financial viability. Later in their discussion he promised Chris that they would sort out the irregularities during the next financial year on condition that Chris provide them now with an unqualified audit statement.
>
> Chris was very perturbed by this development. Before his discussion with the financial director, he knew what the right thing to do was. But all of a sudden, it was no longer that clear. If he were to issue a qualified audit statement, it might result in financial hardship and even the demise of both their firm and their client's company. In the mining company alone, about 4 700 employees could potentially lose their jobs. Wouldn't it be best for all to issue an unqualified audit statement – especially since the financial director had promised to rectify the matter before the end of the next financial year?

Dealing with an ethical issue like the one Chris is facing is tough. Where can one turn to find advice on whether an action is right or wrong? One source of guidance is ethical theories. Through the centuries a number of ethical theories have become prominent. These theories provide guidance on when an action or decision can be regarded as moral or not. Three of the most prominent ethical theories will be discussed in this chapter. You will also see how these theories could possibly apply to Chris's dilemma.

These three theories are:
1. Aristotle's Virtue Theory
2. Kant's Deontological Theory
3. Mill's Utilitarian Theory.

Virtue theory

The Greek philosopher, Aristotle, is commonly associated with **virtue theory**. His ethical theory is mainly to be found in a collection of his writings known as *The Nicomachean Ethics*, which was compiled into one source in the fourth century BC by his son Nichomachus and is generally referred to as *Ethics*.

> Aristotle believes that everything in life has a specific goal. He uses the Greek word *telos* when referring to the goal of something. The goal (or *telos*) of a knife, for example, is to cut. The *telos* of a pencil is to write. In the same way, all people share a common telos. (Aristotle, though, referred to men sharing a common *telos* as he used only the masculine in his theory, as was previously the custom.) In striving to reach their *telos*, people will find fulfilment and happiness. The Greek word that he uses to describe the *telos* of humans is *eudaimonia*. This is commonly translated into English as 'happiness'. This is not the best translation of *eudaimonia*: the original word has a more profound meaning than happiness. It suggests a life well lived. It describes the state of a person who has realised his full human potential.

To reach the *telos* of *eudaimonia* is no simple matter. It does not happen automatically. You need to develop and cultivate your human potential in order to reach the goal of happiness. He insists that the journey towards *eudaimonia* starts with self-love. Unless you love yourself and are willing to invest in your own development, you will never reach your goal in life. He does not consider self-love to be pejorative or bad. On the contrary, self-love is a pre-condition for reaching your full human potential.

Virtues

The way to develop your character is through the cultivation of virtues. A virtue, according to Aristotle, is a character trait that enables you to reach your *telos* or goal. The example of the knife can demonstrate this. If the *telos* of a knife is to cut, then the virtues of a knife are those characteristics that enable it to cut well. These may be the strength of the metal, the sharpness of the blade, and the

> A virtue, according to Aristotle, is a character trait that enables you to reach your *telos* or goal.

firmness of grip that the handle of the knife provides. If the *telos* of humans is *eudaimonia*, then the virtues required by humans are those character traits that enable them to reach their *telos*.

But what are these character traits (or virtues) that are required to reach one's *telos*? And how does one develop them? In answering these questions, Aristotle starts with our natural inclinations. We are born with certain natural inclinations. These are characteristics that predispose us to acting in a specific way. For example, some of us are naturally inclined to run away when confronted with danger, while others have the opposite inclination: they tend to face and fight any threat that come their direction. Aristotle refers to these inclinations as our **natural dispositions**. These dispositions should be controlled by rational thought and not be left to our natural instincts. Once these inclinations come under the control of our rational thinking, and we succeed in controlling them, they become established patterns of behaviour. That is, they become part of our nature, or what we often call our 'second nature'. Characteristics developed in this way are called moral virtues. Moral virtues are nothing other than rationally-controlled dispositions that become permanent character traits. Aristotle emphasises that virtues cannot be developed instantaneously, but that they should be developed and maintained throughout a lifetime.

> Aristotle describes the *mean* as the midpoint between excessive and deficient dispositions.

Aristotle introduces the concept of the 'mean' to assist us in developing rationally controlled dispositions. Our natural dispositions tend to cause us to err in one of two ways. Either we are too much inclined to do something or we are too little inclined to do it. That implies that we either have excessive dispositions or deficient dispositions. The mean is intended to correct these 'defective' dispositions. Aristotle describes the **mean** as the midpoint between excessive and deficient dispositions. This mean disposition can be achieved by taking rational control of one's dispositions.

Mean

When Aristotle refers to a mean (or the midpoint between excessive and deficient dispositions), he does not assume that there is a universal standard that applies to all people. On the contrary, he indicates that a mean is always relative to a specific person. Let us take the example of courage. Someone can tend to have either too much or too little courage. If you have too much courage, your disposition with regard to courage will be excessive. If you tend to have too little courage, your disposition is deficient. If person A is naturally inclined to behave too courageously by rushing in where angels would fear to tread, then he or she needs to take rational control of his or her behaviour in order to become less courageous. Person A's mean would therefore be in the direction of less courage.

Should person B be inclined to act with too little courage, his or her mean would be in the direction of displaying more courage.

What applies to courage in these examples also applies to our other dispositions. With regard to all of our dispositions, Aristotle envisages a spectrum that runs from excessive at one end through a mean position to being deficient at the other end. The table below gives an indication of his vision of the mean position with regard to a number of typical human dispositions:

Table 3.1 Aristotle's mean position with regard to some typical human dispositions

Sphere of action or feeling	Excess	Mean	Deficiency
Fear and confidence	Rashness	Courage	Cowardice
Pleasure and pain	Licentiousness	Temperance	Insensibility
Getting and spending	Prodigality	Liberalness	Illiberalness
Anger	Irascibility	Patience	Lack of spirit
Self-expression	Boastfulness	Truthfulness	Understatement
Shame	Shyness	Modesty	Shamelessness

Source: Adapted from Tredennick (translated from Aristotle), 1976:104.

Aristotle insists that the correct attitude towards pleasure is a precondition for achieving our personal means. Pleasure can be both detrimental and beneficial to establishing our personal mean. Aristotle maintains that we tend to indulge in those things that give us immediate pleasure. This results in excessive dispositions. Similarly we tend to avoid those things that give us the opposite of pleasure, that is, those things that cause us pain. This results in deficient dispositions. Our natural experience of pleasure and pain is the main cause of our wrong dispositions. So, we should avoid being guided by our natural instincts of pleasure. We should take rational control of our natural feelings of pleasure and pain and teach ourselves to find pleasure in achieving our personal means. Once our sense of pleasure has been altered so that we derive pleasure from achieving our means, pleasure becomes conducive to our moral development. We then find pleasure in doing the right thing. This, in turn, reinforces our virtues.

> Always acting in a virtuous way will provide you with a sense of wellbeing and joy.

For Aristotle, it is obvious that reaching your *telos* by always acting in a virtuous way will provide you with a sense of well-being and joy. The virtuous life is a life that will bring pleasure to the virtuous person. This does not mean that every little action will be guided by immediate pleasure. Sometimes one will have to postpone immediate pleasure in order to act with virtue. But the result of always acting in accordance with virtue is a life characterised by the pleasure of knowing that one is doing good and therefore living the good life.

Virtue is therefore developed by taking rational control of one's dispositions. Practising virtuous conduct over and over again slowly but surely becomes part of one's character. Virtuous conduct becomes a habit or our second nature. Persons who have cultivated virtues will be disposed to doing the right thing when they are confronted with difficult ethical situations. Let us now apply the virtue theory to the case of Chris, discussed at the beginning of this chapter.

If Chris simply follows his natural inclinations, he may be tempted to give in to his client's demand to issue an unqualified audit statement. As a professional, however, he hopefully has developed certain virtues as part of his professional training and formation. Virtues or character traits that are closely associated with the accounting profession are independence, objectivity, and integrity. As a professional person for whom it has become almost second nature to act according to these virtues, he will be disinclined to grant his client's wish. His integrity, independence, and objectivity will compel him to decline his client's request and to issue a qualified audit statement as he had initially intended to do.

Deontological ethics

Where the proponents of virtue ethics claim that morality depends on the moral quality of one's character, the proponents of **deontological ethics** insist that there are objective ethical standards of behaviour that everyone should respect. Deontological ethics therefore shifts the focus from the quality of agents (those carrying out ethical or non-ethical behaviour) to the quality of actions. The classical representative of this theory is the German philosopher, Immanuel Kant. His influential work on ethics is entitled *Fundamental Principles of the Metaphysic of Ethics*, first published in 1785.

Kant was convinced that our moral actions cannot be guided by our practical experience. People may be involved in severely corrupt practices which cannot possibly offer moral guidance. Similarly, he believed that we cannot find moral guidance in our natural instincts and needs. Instead, Kant believed that the only reliable source of moral guidance resides in our own independent thinking (our rationality). Consequently, we should turn our focus away from our natural needs and inclinations as well as from our present and past experiences and determine what the standard for good behaviour is through pure rational reflection. In addition, we need the discipline to follow this standard of behaviour that we have discovered through our own thinking, irrespective of whether we personally benefit from it. Kant referred to this internal discipline to

> The classical representative of deontological ethics is the German philosopher, Immanuel Kant.

act in accordance with the standard of good behaviour as the 'good will'. In fact, in the opening sentence of *Fundamental Principles of the Metaphysic of Ethics*, Kant says: 'Nothing can possibly be conceived in the world which can be good without qualification, except a Good Will.'

As human beings, we find ourselves in a constant tension between the demands of our natural inclinations and the demands issued by our rational thinking. It is for this reason that Kant referred not merely to the human will, but explicitly to the 'good will', which is the will that consistently follows the instructions of reason and not our natural inclinations. The human will can be corrupted if it gives in to the demands of our natural inclinations. Such a corrupted will can never ensure consistent moral action. It may be able to do so at times, but it can never sustain moral behaviour over time. Such consistent moral behaviour can be achieved only by the good will. Deontological ethics is therefore an ethic of *duty*: the duty always to abide by those objective standards of ethical behaviour that we have discerned through our rational thinking. For Kant, obeying objective standards of behaviour from a sense of duty is the hallmark of moral behaviour.

The categorical imperative

Kant's search for an objective standard for ethical behaviour through rational reflection led him to the discovery of an objective moral law against which all actions could be judged. He called this law the **'categorical imperative'**, thereby indicating that all persons should abide by it. The categorical imperative stated that an action can be considered ethical only if one is willing to allow all other people to perform the same action. In Kant's own words, it is stated as: 'Act only on that maxim whereby you can at the same time will that it should become a universal law'. This moral law is a purely formal law that does not apply to any specific situation. This is precisely because it has such a general and formal nature that it can be used as a criterion to judge any action that we might encounter on a daily basis. Kant offers an example of demonstrating how this seemingly abstract moral law can give moral guidance in making practical decisions. He wrote:

> Kant's search for an objective standard for ethical behaviour through rational reflection led him to the discovery of an objective moral law against which all actions could be judged. He called this law the 'categorical imperative'.

'Let the question be, for example: May I when in distress make a promise with the intention not to keep it? The shortest way, however, and an unerring one, to discover the answer to this question whether a lying promise is consistent with duty, is to ask myself, should I be content that my maxim (to extricate myself from difficulty by a false promise) should hold good as a universal law, for myself as well as for others? And should I be able to say to myself, "Everyone may make a deceitful promise when he finds himself in a difficulty from which he cannot otherwise extricate himself?" Then I presently become aware that while I can will the lie, I can by no means will that lying should be a universal law. For with such a law there would be no promises at all, since it would be in vain to allege my intention in regard to my future actions to those who would not believe this allegation, or if they over-hastily did so, would pay me back in my own coin. Hence my maxim, as soon as it should be made a universal law, would necessarily destroy itself.' (Kant, 1929: 21-23)

> From this example it is clear that in applying the categorical imperative, we should be guided by the principles of universalisability and reversibility. The **principle of universalisability** demands that we should be willing to make the principle of our proposed action into a universal law that will be followed by all other people. The **principle of reversibility** then demands that we should be willing to live in a world where everyone else behaves in accordance with this universal law. If we are not willing to live in a world where the principle of our action has become a universal moral law, then the proposed action is definitely wrong.

Respect for persons

Kant also provides us with an alternative formulation of the 'categorical' imperative. His second formulation of the categorical imperative is: 'So act as to treat humanity, whether in your own person or in that of another, in every case as an end in itself, and never as a means only.' It is this rendition of the categorical imperative that leads some authors to refer to Kant's theory as a 'respect for persons' theory (Harris *et al*, 2005). Through this alternative version of the categorical imperative, Kant once more set an objective standard against which all actions can be measured. If an action amounts to abusing other persons in order to reach our own objectives, then the action is wrong. We may never use other people as mere stepping stones to attain our own goals. Other persons may assist us in reaching our objectives, but they must do so willingly and with consent. This is clear from the following example provided by Kant (1929:57):

'As regards necessary duties, or those of strict obligation, towards others: he who is thinking of making a lying promise to others will see at once that he would be using another man merely as a mean, without the latter containing at the same time the end in himself. For he whom I propose by such a promise to use for my own purposes cannot possibly assent to my mode of acting towards him, and therefore cannot himself contain the end of this action.'

Kant's moral theory claims that there is indeed an objective moral rule that can guide all our moral decisions. We need to respect this moral rule and act on it out of a sense of duty. Let us apply this moral theory to the case of Chris, contemplating whether he should issue an unqualified audit statement.

Judging this situation from a deontological perspective requires determining whether one is willing to allow everyone else to perform the same action that one is contemplating. Chris therefore needs to universalise his action and ask himself what the world would be like if all auditors issue false unqualified audit statements whenever their clients request them to do so. Once he has universalised his action, he should then reverse the situation and ask himself whether a situation where auditors issue false unqualified audit statements on the request of their clients would be acceptable to him. Without any doubt, Chris would realise that such a situation is intolerable. It would make a mockery of the practice and profession of auditing and result in the destruction of the auditing profession. Consequently, Chris will have to reject his client's request, even though it may be detrimental to both himself and his client in the short run.

> Kant's moral theory claims that there is indeed an objective moral rule that can guide all our moral decisions.

Utilitarian ethics

The proponents of **utilitarian moral theory** focus on the quality of actions in the same way as the proponents of the deontological theory discussed above, but differ from the latter by claiming that we should look at the practical consequences of an action in order to determine whether an action is right or wrong. The classical representative of this theory is John Stuart Mill, whose influential book, *Utilitarianism*, was first published in 1863.

Mill was convinced that actions are good when they contribute towards fulfilling the ultimate goal of human beings. He defines this ultimate goal as happiness. He justifies his conviction that happiness is the ultimate end of all human beings by starting with the experience of the individual. According to Mill, each of us is motivated by one end only, and that is happiness. Whatever we do, we do merely in order to experience happiness. There are plenty of routes to be taken towards happiness, such as knowledge, love, power, or money. But ultimately, these are mere avenues to the final destination of happiness.

> According to Mill, each of us is motivated by one end only, and that is happiness.

The Greatest Happiness principle

Mill therefore concludes that an action should be considered good when it results in happiness for the majority of those affected by the specific action. He formulates this conviction succinctly in his Greatest Happiness principle (1965:281), which states that:

> 'Actions are right in proportion as they tend to promote happiness, wrong as they tend to produce the reverse of happiness. By happiness is intended pleasure, and the absence of pain; by unhappiness, pain or the privation of pleasure.'

> The practical implication of this **Greatest Happiness principle** is that whenever we are undecided on moral action, we should merely calculate which of our alternatives for action would result in the greatest amount of happiness for the greatest number of people. The option that promises to produce the most happiness and the least pain for the greatest number of people affected by our decision should be regarded as the morally right action.

Mill is convinced that there are firm grounds for believing that individuals have the capacity to strive not only for their own happiness, but also for the general happiness of society. He bases this conviction firstly on the social nature of humans. Individuals regard themselves almost invariably as belonging to a community. Further, Mill thinks that there is also external pressure on the individual to take cognisance of the interests of other people, as everyone needs the support of others throughout their lives. Without such support, we would face the threat of rejection and even expulsion from our communities. Finally, Mill argues that we have a natural inclination to sympathise with others. This manifests itself in our individual consciences which prevent us from doing harm to our fellow beings. The combination of these three factors, Mill believes, provides sufficient grounds for the conviction that individuals have the capacity to act for the sake not merely of their own happiness, but also in the interest of general happiness.

Mill sheds further light on the meaning and implications of his moral theory when he defends himself against the critique raised by critics of his theory. We will consider five of the most important points of criticism raised against Mill's theory and his response to each of them.

Criticism one: The theory is degrading to humans

The first objection to his theory is that it degrades human beings to the level of animals because his theory suggests that as human beings, our only goal in life is attaining pleasure.

In defence of his theory, Mill argues that this accusation is better levelled at his critics. It is they who equate the pleasures of animals with those of humans. The pleasures that excite humans differ vastly from those of animals. Mill introduces the distinction between bodily pleasures and mental pleasures to argue his point. Both humans and animals enjoy bodily pleasures such as eating, drinking, and sleeping. People also enjoy mental pleasures such as learning, aspiring, and caring. When mental pleasure is compared to bodily pleasure, humans assign a very definite priority to the former. When he propagates that humans should strive to increase the general happiness through their actions, he assumes that they will give preference to their mental or higher pleasures.

> The first objection to Mill's theory is that it degrades human beings to the level of animals because his theory suggests that as human beings, our only goal in life is attaining pleasure.

Criticism two: Happiness cannot be the rational purpose of life

A second objection to his theory is that the pursuit of happiness can never be regarded as the rational purpose of human life. Mill's critics list a number of noble people throughout history who sacrificed their own happiness in order to do good. They are regarded as noble exactly because they did not pursue happiness, but sacrificed their own happiness.

Mill's response to this is that they are probably regarded as noble simply because they sacrificed their own happiness for the sake of the happiness of the greater number of people. Far from contradicting the utilitarian standard, they were actually acting in accordance with it. Utilitarianism requires that one should act for the sake of the general good, even if it runs counter to one's own happiness.

> Mill argues that utilitarianism requires that one should act for the sake of the general good, even if it runs counter to one's own happiness.

Criticism three: Utilitarianism is unattainable

A third objection to Mill's theory is that the utilitarian standard is unrealistically high. Opponents claim that it is almost impossible to act always for the sake of the general happiness of society. Ordinary people will simply not be capable of constantly striving towards such a lofty ideal.

Mill's reply to this objection is that people would very rarely find themselves in situations where they have to act for the sake of the general happiness of society. We mostly find ourselves in situations where we need to consider only the interests of the few who are affected by our proposed actions. We merely need to consider the happiness of these few and not the happiness of humanity as a whole. Only a very few have the opportunity to act for the benefit of society as a whole, and then only on very rare occasions. Only people in such rare circumstances need to consider the happiness of society as a whole.

Criticism four: Utilitarianism is self-serving

A fourth charge against utilitarian theory is that it is an immoral doctrine because it will inevitably result in expediency. Critics insist that the utilitarian principle will be abused in order to serve the particular interests of the person making the decision.

> Critics insist that the utilitarian principle will be abused in order to serve the particular interests of the person making the decision.

Mill's response to this charge is that such expediency is incompatible with the utilitarian spirit. He uses the example of telling a lie to illustrate his point. According to Mill, it is unthinkable that someone would lie merely for the sake of the momentary benefit that it might hold. Each person has a conscience and a sense of veracity. Lying would violate these. This would cause so much unhappiness and pain to the liar that it would outweigh the immediate benefit that the lie might gain.

Criticism five: The theory is too time-consuming

A final objection to Mill's theory is that it would be too time-consuming to apply in practice. Critics allege that it would be impossible to sit down each time a situation requires a moral decision, calculate the amount of pleasure and pain implied by each alternative course of action, and then come to a conclusion based on the utilitarian calculus.

Mill also dismissed this objection against his theory by indicating that in most cases when we are confronted with an ethical issue, we know beforehand what is morally right or wrong. We know, for example, that it is wrong to lie, cheat, steal, or kill. This we have learned over years or have been taught by our elders. We need not sit down and first do calculations in utilitarian fashion every time we are confronted with a decision that may have moral significance. We can simply act on the basis of the moral knowledge that we have accumulated over years. Only in the rare case where we are confronted with a new moral dilemma, do we have to go through the entire utilitarian process of deciding which course of action would produce the greatest amount of happiness for the greatest number of people.

When we apply the utilitarian theory to Chris's dilemma of whether he should issue an unqualified audit statement as requested by his client, we should look at the consequences that such an action may potentially have on those affected by the action. Initially, it may seem as if most people would benefit should Chris issue a false unqualified audit statement. He would retain the mining company as a client and the adverse consequences that the company might suffer from being issued with a qualified audit statement would be avoided. The potential loss of 4 700 jobs that might follow in the wake of the bad news would also be avoided. On closer scrutiny, however, it becomes clear that other consequences should also be taken into consideration. Investors would be misled if a false unqualified audit statement were issued. Should this be uncovered at a later stage, it would cause huge damage to both Chris and the mining company's reputations. It might even lead to the demise of both Chris's firm and the mining company. The auditing profession as such would also be brought into disrepute. It is consequently clear that Chris would not be serving the greater good by issuing a false unqualified audit statement. This is not only clear when the potential consequences for all parties involved are considered, but would also run counter to Chris's conscience and to the accumulated knowledge of ethical behaviour that he had acquired through his professional training as an auditor.

Conclusion

Each of the virtue, deontological, and utilitarian theories discussed above provides its own criteria for assessing whether an action is right or wrong. Each of these theories represents an important ethical perspective that we should keep in mind when we evaluate actions, practices, or situations morally. Using these theories helps us to anticipate which moral concerns should be considered in making moral decisions, not only in our everyday lives, but also in the accounting and auditing profession.

Questions for consideration

1. Explain what the following concepts mean in Aristotle's virtue theory:
   - *telos*
   - *eudaimonia*
   - mean
   - virtue.
2. Explain how Aristotle uses the above concepts to formulate his virtue theory.
3. Explain what Immanuel Kant means by the following concepts:
   - a good will
   - the categorical imperative.
4. Use an example to illustrate how the principles of universalisability and reversibility can be used to apply Kant's deontological theory.
5. Explain Mill's Greatest Happiness principle and also how you would go about applying it to a specific situation.
6. Looking at all three of the theories discussed in this chapter, what do you regard as their respective strengths and weaknesses?

Bibliography

Harris, CE, Pritchard, MS, & Rabins, MJ. 2005. *Engineering ethics: concepts and cases*, 3rd ed. Belmont (CA): Wadsworth.

Kant, I. 1929. *Fundamental principles of the metaphysics of ethics* (translated by TK Abbott). London: Longman.

Mill, JS. 1965. *Mill's ethical writings*. New York: Collier.

Tredennick, H (tr). 1976. *The ethics of Aristotle* (translated by JAK Thomson (1953), revised by H Tredennick), Rev ed. London: Penguin.

4

Ethical decision-making

Deon Rossouw

Outcomes

After working through this chapter, you should be able to do the following:
- Identify the importance of making ethically-sound decisions in business
- Generate options for consideration in the decision-making process
- Consider the legality of decisions
- Assess whether decisions are in accordance with organisational ethical standards
- Determine the possible impact of decisions on stakeholders
- Apply the disclosure test to decisions.

Overview

The decisions that we inevitably have to make in any work or profession have a variety of consequences. One of the consequences our decisions may have is ethical, because they can be either beneficial or detrimental to the interests of other people. In this chapter, we focus on how we can proactively ensure that we take decisions in a morally-responsible manner.

The decision-making procedure that is introduced consists of assessing whether a business decision meets a set of normative criteria. The criteria against which a decision has to be assessed to judge its moral soundness are the following:
- Is it legal?
- Does it meet company standards?
- Is it fair to all stakeholders?
- Can it be disclosed?

In this chapter, each of these criteria will be discussed in order to arrive at a professional decision-making process.

These criteria are then applied to a case of downsizing in an accounting firm. By applying these criteria to the case at hand, we learn how to ensure that the decisions we make are morally sound.

Introduction

Professional people typically have to exercise their professional discretion and therefore have to make decisions in their work on a daily basis. These decisions have many implications, which often include ethical ones. Accountants and auditors are well trained to deal with the financial implications of their decisions, but often lack the ability to deal adequately with the ethical implications of their decisions.

> The ethical challenge that all professional people in business face is to ensure that they avoid or restrict the negative impact that their decisions have on other people.

The ethical challenge that all professional people in business face is to ensure that they avoid or restrict the negative impact that their decisions have on other people. Positively stated, it means that professionals need to make decisions in a manner that will ensure that the interests of all affected parties are covered.

In the next chapter we will deal with a different type of ethical decision-making, namely making decisions when we are faced with **moral dilemmas**. In Chapter 1 we said that a moral dilemma occurs when an ethical evaluation of a situation produces two or more conflicting judgements. This, however, is not the kind of ethical decision-making that we will consider in this chapter. The focus is instead on the **ethical consequences** of business or professional decisions. We will explore a decision-making procedure that can ensure that business and professional decisions are made with ethical sensitivity towards all who are affected by the decision.

> A moral dilemma occurs when an ethical evaluation of a situation produces two or more conflicting judgements.

This procedure consists of assessing whether a business or professional decision meets the set of normative criteria previously mentioned. The criteria against which a decision has to be assessed to judge its moral soundness are the following:

- Is it legal?
- Does it meet company standards?
- Is it fair to all stakeholders?
- Can it be disclosed?

In the remainder of this chapter, each of these criteria will be discussed in more detail. In applying these criteria to business or professional decisions, one does not first have to complete a decision and only then start to apply the criteria for ethical decisions. On the contrary, it is preferable that these criteria form a constant mindset that becomes an integral part of the normal business or professional decision-making process. It should therefore become almost second nature to keep these criteria in mind when making ethical decisions.

A case study will first be introduced, after which the above decision-making procedure will be discussed. Each aspect of the decision-making procedure will then be applied to the case study and to the ethical challenge that Jane Peterson is facing in this case study.

> ### Case study: Jane Peterson's downsizing assignment
>
> Henry Peterson started a small accounting firm in Pretoria 20 years ago. His strong insistence on professional service to clients and respect for staff served the firm well. After the first few lean and difficult years of building a steady client base, the firm grew steadily to the point where Peterson and Associates now employs 250 staff members in total.
>
> Although the client base of Peterson and Associates is quite diverse, a substantial number of their clients is linked to the agricultural sector. That is the reason that, apart from their headquarters in Pretoria and their city offices in Cape Town, Durban and Johannesburg, Peterson and Associates also had offices in Bothaville, Lephalale and Bela Bela.
>
> With the recent recession in the agricultural sector, their offices in Bothaville, Lephalale and Bela Bela had started running into financial difficulties. At the last meeting of the partners of Peterson and Associates, they came to the conclusion that they had no option but to close their offices in Bothaville, Lephalale, and Bela Bela. At the same meeting, they also decided to explore the viability of opening new offices in Windhoek (Namibia) and Gaborone (Botswana) instead.
>
> Jane Peterson, a senior partner in the firm that her father started, was put in charge of the process of closing down the three offices. Jane was somewhat overwhelmed by her assignment. She could still remember all the excitement that had gone with opening the offices in Bothaville, Lephalale, and Bela Bela.
>
> Twelve years ago, when she was an accounting student, she would never have dreamed that closing down offices and laying off people would one day be part of her job as a chartered accountant. But now it is, and she has to deal with it.

Making ethical decisions in business or the profession

The decision that has led to Jane's assignment looks like a straightforward business decision, caused by the recent recession in agriculture. However, the fact that the decision is informed by business considerations does not mean that it does not have a very distinct ethical dimension as well. It is a decision that affects many people in different ways. The financial position of the company will be enhanced by the decision to close down the three offices. In that sense, the decision can be considered a good and vital one for the firm. However, closing down three offices is likely to be to the detriment of those employed in the affected offices. The remaining employees of the firm at the offices not affected by the closures may benefit financially from the closure of the three offices, but psychologically, they may feel less secure than before. It is therefore a decision that is good for some people but bad for others, and both good and bad for still some others.

For the purposes of our discussion, we will assume that the decision taken by the partners of Peterson and Associates is irreversible and unavoidable. Consequently, we will focus on the decisions that Jane will have to make in implementing the decision that was already taken at the last partners' meeting of Peterson and Associates.

> A decision-making process consists of identifying possible solutions and then considering which of these possibilities has the best potential of solving the problem at hand. To find an optimal solution for a problem, it is important to explore as many options as are practically possible.

A decision-making process consists of identifying possible solutions and then considering which of these possibilities has the best potential of solving the problem at hand. To find an optimal solution for a problem, it is important to explore as many options as are practically possible, because different options have different implications and therefore different potential for solving the problem.

Let us suppose that in the process of generating options Jane identified the following three possible options:

- Terminating the contracts of all affected employees according to accepted fair labour practice.
- Terminating the contract of all affected employees according to accepted fair labour practice, but also offering them assistance in finding alternative employment.
- Delaying the process of closing down the offices and accelerating the investigation into the opening of new offices in Gaborone and Windhoek in order to determine whether existing staff in the three offices that are about to be closed can be redeployed to the new offices.

In order to ensure that the ultimate decision taken is ethically sound, the various options identified above have to be assessed against a set of four criteria. They have to pass the legal test, the company or firm's standards test, the fairness test, and the disclosure test.

Is it legal?

> The first criterion that a business decision has to meet in order to be considered ethically sound is that it should be legal. In an ideal world, the law lays down a standard of acceptable behaviour which all citizens need to abide by in order to ensure a safe and just society. Since businesses are corporate citizens of the societies within which they operate, they have an obligation to ensure that they abide by the laws of their societies. The fact that businesses have to make a profit or that they are engaged in fierce competition with their business rivals does not hand them a licence to operate outside the law. It is therefore imperative that as decisions are being made in business, this first criterion of ethical decision-making should be kept in mind.

Determining whether a planned business decision is legal can range from a fairly uncomplicated process to an extremely complicated one. In many, if not most, work environments, the legal standards that apply to a specific work environment are common knowledge. Human resource personnel, for example, are usually familiar with the standards of labour law that govern recruitment, retirement and dismissal; civil engineers are familiar with legal standards of safety for construction and design; and accountants are familiar with legal standards for reporting and disclosure in accounting. When one operates in such an environment where legal standards are common knowledge, the application of this first criterion is straightforward. If a decision is in conflict with the law, it should be abandoned, unless there are exceptional circumstances, which will be discussed later on in this section.

When the legal standards that apply to a specific work environment are not common knowledge among staff, it may be because the staff have been inadequately trained. In such situations, this can be rectified by training interventions that will equip them with the required legal common knowledge that pertains to their work environment. There are, however, circumstances where legal standards are simply unclear. This happens, for example, in fast-developing fields such as information technology, where the law is unable to keep up with the speed of technological innovation. Consequently, existing legal standards are vague and ambiguous, and there is often no common knowledge about legal standards. In such environments, applying the first criterion of ethical decision-making becomes a complicated process. The same holds for doing business in other countries with different legal jurisdictions. In cases where legal standards are not common knowledge, it is advisable to call on internal or external legal advice to settle the question on whether a decision under consideration is legal or not.

The fact that legal standards are sometimes unclear is one of the reasons that the legal criterion can never be the only criterion in determining the ethical soundness of a decision. Another reason that the legal criterion on its own is inadequate for determining the moral soundness of business decisions is that in some cases, the law may be morally flawed. It has been said above that in an ideal world, the law lays down a standard of acceptable behaviour which all citizens need to respect in order to ensure a safe and fair society. However, as we are all well aware, we do not live in an ideal world, and therefore we do from time to time and in certain circumstances encounter laws that are flawed and unfair.

Anyone who is familiar with the apartheid laws in South Africa or the media laws in Zimbabwe under the Mugabe regime would intuitively sense that legality does not always equal morality. It is exactly for this reason that the legal test for ethical decision-making needs to be supported by the tests implied by the remaining three criteria for ethical decision-making in business and professions.

> In an ideal world, the law lays down a standard of acceptable behaviour which all citizens need to respect in order to ensure a safe and fair society. However, we do not live in an ideal world, and therefore we do from time to time and in certain circumstances encounter laws that are flawed and unfair.

Application to Jane Peterson's assignment

When the three options that Jane is considering are subjected to the legal test, it is clear that legal considerations have already played a significant role in determining her options. From the way in which she formulated her options, it is clear that she wanted to avoid breaking any laws, because she made it clear that her actions should be 'according to accepted fair labour practice'. We can safely assume that she was determined not to contravene any laws in closing down the three offices. All her options therefore pass the legal test.

Does it meet company standards?

The second criterion against which decisions need to be tested is the ethical standards of the company or accounting firm. These standards are usually formulated in a set of company values or in a code of ethics or in policy statements dealing with specific issues, such as procurement, expense accounts, or the giving and receiving of gifts. Since these documents are intended to prevent irresponsible behaviour or to promote responsible behaviour, it is clear that they should play a central role in determining the ethical soundness of business and professional decisions.

Applying the company or firm's standards test to business or professional decisions can be a fairly simple and straightforward process when the relevant ethical standards are formulated very clearly and precisely in either a detailed code of ethics or in policy documents that deal in detail with specific matters. The company or firm's standards test is somewhat more difficult to apply when these standards are formulated in the form of core values that stipulate general standards of behaviour, such as honesty, transparency and respect, without spelling out what such standards imply in business or professional practice. Applying the test is also difficult when a code of ethics or a policy is vague and too general.

> Ethical standards are usually formulated in a set of company values or in a code of ethics or in policy statements dealing with specific issues, such as procurement, expense accounts, or the giving and receiving of gifts.

The above observations should, however not lead to the hasty conclusion that detailed codes of ethics and policies are preferable to value statements when it comes to making ethically-sound business decisions. Both a rule-based approach (as one would often find in detailed codes of ethics and policy documents) and a value-based approach have their respective benefits and drawbacks when it comes to ethical decision-making. Rule-based standards of ethics have the benefit of being very clear and specific and can therefore provide clear guidance in making ethical business decisions. A strong rule-based approach, however, runs the risk of undermining personal discretion and responsibility for ethical decision-making by cultivating a mentality of 'what is not forbidden is allowed' among employees. The strength of value-based codes, on the contrary, lies exactly in their ability to invoke personal ethical discretion and responsibility in the staff members of a business or firm. However, their drawback lies in their generality, which prevents them from providing guidance on specific issues.

> When the company or firm's standards test is applied and it turns out that a decision clashes with those ethical standards, it is a strong indication that the decision needs to be abandoned. When it is not clear whether a decision contravenes ethical standards or not, it is advisable to discuss the decision with other colleagues in order to see how they interpret the relevant ethical standards with regard to the issue at hand. If the doubt still prevails, it becomes imperative to invoke the remaining two criteria for ethical business or professional decisions that will be discussed in the remainder of this chapter.

There are also two further reasons that applying only the company or firm's standards test may not always be sufficient to ensure ethically-sound business or professional decisions. The same two deficiencies that haunt the law will always haunt company standards as well: first, these standards may be incomplete, as they can never keep up with all new developments that the company or firm has to face; second, these standards may be ethically flawed and, notwithstanding their best intentions, nevertheless give rise to unethical decisions.

Application to Jane Peterson's assignment

Peterson and Associates being an accounting firm, the relevant values and standards that would apply to the firm are the professional codes and standards of the accounting profession and the ethical values and standards of the firm itself. Since the professional codes and standards of the accounting profession do not deal explicitly with staff lay-offs, Jane will have to look at the ethical standards of the firm for guidance. Although Peterson and Associates do not have a formal code of ethics, it is clear from the case study that the firm places a high value on professional service to clients and respect for staff. These two core values of the firm have not been translated into a set of guidelines for conduct that would tell Jane how to deal with the situation that she now faces. Nevertheless, the value of 'respect for staff' does place a moral obligation on her to respect the interests of all staff members who are affected by the closing of the three offices. Following fair and due labour process in laying off the affected staff members (her option one) would certainly be part of respecting their interest, but the strong emphasis on 'respect for staff' that characterises Peterson and Associates most probably will compel her to move beyond the mere adherence to fair labour process and to give greater weight to options two and three, which are aimed at softening the negative impact of the office closures on the affected employees.

Is it fair to all stakeholders?

> Making ethical decisions in business or professions amounts to ensuring that the interests of all parties likely to be affected are considered and respected.

Making ethical decisions in business or professions amounts to ensuring that the interests of all parties likely to be affected are considered and respected. In order to ensure that such decisions are ethically sound, the fairness test needs to be applied. This means that one has to consider the possible impact that a decision may have on those who are likely to be affected by the decision.

Applying the fairness test requires more creativity on the part of the decision-maker than applying the legal and the company standards tests that we discussed above. It requires that one should determine how the decision that one is considering taking will be perceived and experienced by those whose lives will be affected by the decision. The two most important ways of discerning the possible impact of decisions on the interests of others are through **moral imagination** and **stakeholder engagement**.

Moral imagination, within the context of the fairness test, refers to the ability to think beyond one's own perspective and to speculate about how the decision may be perceived and experienced by all other parties who stand to be affected by the decision. It first of all involves identifying all those who may be affected, and then putting oneself in their shoes in order to get an idea of how the decisions would be experienced from their perspective.

Stakeholder engagement, within the context of the fairness test, refers to the process of interacting with persons and parties who are likely to be affected by the decision in order to determine how they foresee that the decision is likely to impact on them. It means that stakeholders are being given the opportunity to voice their concerns and to tell what the decision looks like from their vantage point.

> Stakeholder engagement refers to the process of interacting with persons and parties who are likely to be affected by the decision in order to determine how they foresee that the decision is likely to impact on them.

What both moral imagination and stakeholder engagement have in common is that both methods assist one to move beyond one's own or the company immediate self-interest and to discover how other persons and parties may be affected by such decisions. Should one discover via these ways of applying the fairness test that the company will benefit at the expense of other stakeholders, then the red lights of an unethical business or professional decision are clearly flashing, and the decision should best be reconsidered or abandoned. Should one sense, however, that the decision would be fair to all stakeholders, and is in accord with the law and company standards, one could feel confident that the decision would be ethically sound. It would, however, be prudent also to test the decision against the one remaining criterion, which is the disclosure test.

Application to Jane Peterson's assignment

The fairness test requires Jane to determine the potential impact of each of the three options that she is considering on those who stand to be affected by them. We will take the options one by one and consider their potential impact on affected stakeholders.

Option one: Terminate employee contracts
Should the employment contracts of all employees be terminated according to accepted fair labour practice, they will each receive a severance financial package that will leave them better off in the short run, but without a steady income in the long run. They might therefore have sufficient financial means to cope for the first weeks or months after they have been dismissed, but thereafter, they would be worse off than before, unless they have already accumulated sufficient wealth to cope without the steady income that they will no longer be receiving from Peterson and Associates.

The firm itself might be worse off in the short run, because of the severance packages they have to pay to their staff in the three offices that will be closed. In the long run, however, the firm would be better off financially: it will no longer suffer the financial losses that were incurred by the three offices that were in financial difficulties.

A third group that might potentially be affected by this option are the employees of Peterson and Associates who work in the remaining offices of the firm. They might suffer from 'survivor syndrome' (Horton and Reid, 1991; Mumford, 1995). This is the guilt, insecurity and lack of confidence that often prevails among the staff who remain after an organisation has gone through a downsizing. Although they might at first not seem to be directly affected by the closure of the three offices, the potential psychological harm to them also needs to be taken into consideration.

Option two: Terminate contracts and assist in finding new employment
If this course of action is followed, the employees who are being retrenched will suffer the same fate as indicated in the first option. However, because of the assistance being offered to them in finding new jobs, they might soon find themselves in new jobs where they will once more enjoy a steady income. If this option can be implemented successfully, the detrimental impact on the employees would be substantially softened.

This option might cost the company even more financially than the first option, because apart from paying severance packages, the firm will have to fund the cost of assisting employees to find alternative employment. Both these expenses are, however, temporary, and in the long run, the company most probably will still be in better financial shape.

The remaining employees of Peterson and Associates might benefit from exercising this option, because their experience of 'survival syndrome' is likely to be less acute. They will experience the firm as caring for the plight of those who have been retrenched. It will provide

CHAPTER 4 ETHICAL DECISION-MAKING

them with the security of knowing that if they find themselves in similar situations in future, they can expect the firm to do the same for them.

Option three: Redeploy employees to new offices
For many employees facing the financial hardship that might result from the pending termination of their employment contract, this option is likely to hold the most promise. Although they will have to cope with the inconveniences associated with relocating to another town and country, they will at least have a secure income again in a firm with which they are well acquainted. One might assume that there could be some employees who might prefer not to make use of this option, but they are likely to be the ones who have alternative employment options or the ones who have accumulated sufficient wealth to be no longer dependent on the income that they receive from the firm.

For the company, this third option will obviously have an immediate financial implication in the sense that they will have to keep their offices in Bothaville, Lephalale, and Bela Bela running at a loss for two, three, or even more months longer than they had initially intended. However, if the firm is able to accommodate most of the employees affected by the closure of the three offices in the new offices in Windhoek and Gaborone, it will save on the cost of paying financial severance packages to these redeployed employees. At the same time, they will also save on recruitment costs for new staff in the new offices. On top of that, the other employees of the firm will be spared from experiencing 'survival syndrome', as no substantial retrenchments will occur.

The application of the fairness test will most probably convince Jane further that options two and three are ethically the soundest solutions to her problem as they would both soften the negative impact on those who are worst affected by the decision to close the three offices.

Can it be disclosed?

The disclosure criterion assesses whether one would be comfortable in accounting publicly or privately for the decision that one has taken. If one is comfortable about explaining and defending one's decision to significant persons in one's life or on a public forum, it is a good indication that the decision is ethically sound and justifiable.

The disclosure test should preferably be applied in two ways. The first version of the disclosure test is the public one. In the public version of the disclosure test, you should ask yourself whether you would be morally comfortable if the decision and (consequent action) is reported in a newspaper, on TV or the Internet (or for that matter in any other medium that is publicly accessible). The purpose of the first form of the disclosure test is to determine whether one would be willing and able to provide in public good and socially-acceptable reasons for taking a specific decision. Should one cringe in the face of such a prospect, the ethical alarm bells should sound.

> The disclosure criterion assesses whether one would be comfortable in accounting publicly or privately for the decision that one has taken. If one is comfortable about explaining and defending one's decision to significant persons in one's life or on a public forum, it is a good indication that the decision is ethically sound and justifiable.

The second version of the disclosure test is the private disclosure test. It adds a more personal and emotional element to the disclosure test. In this version you should ask yourself whether you would feel morally comfortable disclosing your decision to the most significant person(s) in your life. For this purpose, you should identify one or more persons who matter most to you, like your best friends, your parents, a special colleague, or the person with whom you are in a romantic relationship. Once you have identified the most significant person(s) in your life, ask yourself the following question: Would I feel morally comfortable if this person(s) should know what I am about to do?

Should one feel confident about disclosing and defending a decision both in public and in private, it is a strong indication that the decision is ethically sound.

Introducing the disclosure criterion to the ethical business decision-making process adds an important dimension that has not come to the fore in the other three criteria, namely the personal conscience dimension. It emphasises the importance that our business decisions should be in accord not only with the law, company standards and stakeholder interests, but also with our own moral consciousness. When all four these concerns match, one can feel confident about the ethical soundness of one's business decisions.

Application to Jane Peterson's assignment

In applying the public version of the disclosure test, Jane will have to imagine herself, for example, reading in big black bold letters on the front page of the local newspaper the headlines of a report on the decision by Peterson & Associate to close their local office. The report will not only carry the story of the decision to close the offices, but will also detail the firm's history and values, its justification for the decision, the impact on the affected staff and the measures that the firm has taken to assist the staff members who have been worst affected by the decision. Jane will then have to ask herself which of the three options that she is currently considering she would be most comfortable reading about in this newspaper article.

> In applying the public, and especially the private, version of the disclosure test, Jane will be bringing her own personal values into play. As an individual, she will have to live with the decision that she has made. For this reason, she needs to be personally convinced that what she is about to do is right and good and therefore the best ethical alternative in her situation. The relevant question that she needs to pose to herself is: which of the options that she is considering will contribute most to her sense of what is fair and good? If she is not able to align her decision with her own values, she is likely to suffer feelings of guilt and may end up experiencing alienation towards her firm and her profession.

Conclusion

As professionals we make decisions that impact on the wellbeing and interests of other people. It is part of our professional ethos to care about how our professional activities affect other people as well as the community. Consequently we should take the necessary care to ensure that our business and professional decisions are ethically sound. Using a disciplined approach, such as has been outlined in this chapter, will assist in giving due consideration to the ethical implications of our professional and business decisions.

When one applies the above tests to the options that one is considering, the ethical soundness of the various options should become clear. The ethical dimension of the decision is only one of the dimensions of that decision. The decision also has other dimensions, such as, for example, financial and reputational dimensions. The ethical dimension of the decision needs to be aligned with the other dimensions of the decision in order to ensure that in addition to being ethically sound, the decision is also financially sound and will enhance rather than detract from the company's reputation.

There is always the possibility that a decision that is being considered passes some of the tests, but fails the others. It is, for example, possible that a decision may meet the legal requirements and also the criteria required by the standards of the company or firm, but fails the fairness and disclosure criteria. In such cases, a situation develops where a decision can be justified morally on some grounds, but also rejected morally on other grounds. Whenever that happens we are faced with a moral dilemma. Resolving moral dilemmas requires a different decision-making approach from the one that has been discussed in this chapter. In the next chapter a procedure for resolving moral dilemmas will be introduced.

Questions for discussion

1. Why is it important to generate a variety of possible options for consideration in the decision-making process?
2. Why is it important to engage stakeholders in the process of making ethical decisions?
3. What is the role of moral imagination in the process of ethical decision-making?
4. Which professional code(s) would you consult as part of appraising your available options against relevant ethical criteria?
5. What tests would you apply to check whether a decision is ethically sound and justifiable?
6. What decision would you have taken if you had been in Jane Peterson's shoes? And how would you have justified your decision to an audience of sceptical journalists?

Bibliography

Horton, RT & Reid, PC. 1991. *Beyond the trust gap: forging a new partnership between managers and their employers*. Homewood, IL: Business One, Irwin.

Mumford, E. 1995. 'Contracts, complexity, and contradictions: the changing employment relationship'. *Personnel Review*, 24(8):54-70.

5

Resolving ethical dilemmas

Deon Rossouw

Outcomes

After working through this chapter, you should be able to do the following:
- Distinguish between personal and social ethical dilemmas
- Ggain insight in how ethical dilemmas could be resolved despite moral dissensus
- Apply the RIMS process for resolving ethical dilemmas
- Evaluate the suitability of arguments for inclusion into the RIMS process
- Identify positive and negative concerns in ethical dilemmas
- Generate creative solutions for moral dilemmas.

Overview

Moral dilemmas arise in situations where we are confronted with contradicting moral choices, but are not certain which option is the right or best one to follow. In this chapter, we first explore the nature of both personal and social dilemmas. Then, we look at the Rational Interaction for Moral Sensitivity (RIMS) strategy for resolving such dilemmas. To make sense of the RIMS strategy, one should understand the basic assumptions upon which it is premised. After these assumptions have been introduced, the three steps of the RIMS strategy will be discussed. The RIMS strategy will then be applied to a case study about a social dilemma that developed in an organisation around management monitoring employees' email messages. The concerns of both management and employees will be analysed and addressed via the various steps of the RIMS strategy. Finally, we will show how this strategy can be used to generate solutions to this dilemma that are sensitive to the moral concerns of both parties to the dispute.

Introduction

A dilemma occurs when one is confronted by a situation in which one has to choose between two or more options, without being sure which option is the right one. It is almost like travelling on an unfamiliar stretch of road and then reaching a fork in the road, but with no road sign to indicate which of the two roads is the correct one to take. From time to time we encounter dilemmas in just about all spheres of our lives. In ethics we also have to deal with dilemmas from time to time, and when such dilemmas occur, they are notoriously difficult to resolve.

> Whenever a clash of convictions about the right thing to do emerges between individuals or groups, we are dealing with a social ethical dilemma.

In ethical matters, we deal with the challenge of finding the right thing to do. Because individuals have different values and priorities, they often differ from one another about what the right thing to do is in a specific situation. Whenever such a clash of convictions about the right thing to do emerges between individuals or groups, we are dealing with a **social ethical dilemma**. In such social dilemmas both parties believe that their view is the morally correct one. Dilemmas do not only occur between persons, but can often be internal as well, i.e. occur within an individual. Sometimes we find ourselves torn in two when we need to make a decision. We are then no longer sure which of the options we are facing is ethically correct. Whenever we encounter such ethical dilemmas in ourselves, we are faced with a **personal ethical dilemma**.

Resolving ethical dilemmas should be distinguished from the process of ethical decision-making that we discussed in the previous chapter. In Chapter 4, we focused on the ethical implications of ordinary business and professional decisions in an attempt to ensure that such decisions are ethically sound and justified. In this chapter, however, we focus on *personal and social clashes* that can develop around ethical issues and how to resolve such conflicting moral judgements.

> There are no obvious solutions to ethical dilemmas. We need to draw on our resources of imagination and creativity to find solutions to moral dilemmas. In this chapter, we will introduce an ethical dilemma resolution strategy. We will demonstrate how it can be applied in a workplace setting. The strategy is called **Rational Interaction for Moral Sensitivity** or **RIMS** for short. The purpose of the RIMS strategy is to structure a process of rational interaction between rival points of view in a moral dispute that will result in morally-sensitive decisions.

Assumptions behind the RIMS strategy

Before outlining the RIMS strategy in detail, we first need to understand the assumptions upon which it is based.

Assumption one: Dissensus does not equal defeat

The RIMS strategy starts from the assumption that **moral dissensus** is an inescapable feature of our culture (Macintyre, 1985:6). Moral dissensus is the opposite of moral consensus. The fact that we live in a diverse multi-cultural and multi-religious society inevitably leads to a situation where individuals operate according to different sets of values. In such a situation, it is not surprising that people would look at the same situation and make different judgements about what is ethically right in that situation. Some people look at this situation of clashing value judgements and then conclude that it is impossible to find consensus in such a situation of moral dissensus. The RIMS strategy, however is based upon the assumption that moral dissensus does not spell defeat. Although moral dissensus is accepted as a given, the RIMS approach assumes that interaction between people having rival moral viewpoints is not only necessary, but is also an important source of creativity that can assist in finding morally sensitive resolutions to dilemmas.

> The RIMS strategy is based upon the assumption that moral dissensus does not spell defeat.

Assumption two: Dialogue can produce solutions

The RIMS strategy assumes that, through dialogue, conflicting moral views can be creatively harnessed to produce morally sensitive solutions to moral dilemmas. The preconditions for such a dialogue are that:
- the reality of moral dissensus is understood and accepted by all participants
- participants commit themselves to finding solutions within this context of moral dissensus.

Once these pre-conditions have been satisfied, moral decision-making is no longer frustrated just because differing moral positions exist. Instead, the moral differences become a creative resource that allows us the opportunity to find more inclusive and morally-sensitive solutions to problems than any one moral viewpoint can achieve on its own.

Assumption three: Focusing on motives is futile

A further assumption is that focusing on the motives underlying moral viewpoints cannot solve moral dilemmas in a situation of moral dissensus.

If we accept that our moral judgements are ultimately based on subjective commitments to certain basic ethical values, focusing on these subjective ethical commitments underlying the various moral standpoints cannot solve moral problems. At most, focusing on the underlying motives can provide us with a deeper understanding of why people opt for their specific moral viewpoints, but it cannot overcome the rivalry between conflicting viewpoints. For this reason, the RIMS strategy advises that motivations underlying moral views should not dominate the process of ethical decision-making. The focus should rather be on finding solutions that can accommodate the concerns of all parties in the dilemma.

Assumption four: Only moral arguments are allowed

Only moral arguments can be included in the dialogue. That is, only arguments that meet the minimum requirements of a moral argument will be allowed. To qualify for inclusion in the RIMS process, an argument should display a concern and respect for others and not be merely selfish. It therefore excludes any sociocentric or egocentric arguments. It is only on the basis of ethical considerations that one can expect to arrive at ethical decisions.

The RIMS strategy

The RIMS strategy begins with 'rational interaction' (Habermas, 1993). This is a rational debate between two or more rival views on the moral issue under discussion. In such a debate, the rival points of views should be presented, analysed, and discussed in a rational and tolerant way. 'Rational' in this context means that points of view are based on reasons that will make them understandable to others. These reasons are not restricted to empirical evidence, but could also include values, culture, religion, and emotions, which can provide support for a point of view. Rational arguments of this type are the only valid means of persuasion permitted.

All parties to a dialogue should exercise tolerance and respect all points of view. If there is tolerance, parties will recognise these points of view as valid perspectives that can contribute towards the resolution of the problem. Parties have to allow one another freedom to express their points of view as well as opportunities to counter and criticise these views. Participants in such a dialogue are not required to give an account of the specific moral tradition to which they belong or the moral theory, if any, to which they subscribe. Such a qualification would lead to only an elitist conception of dialogue that would exclude vast numbers of people who could make valuable contributions.

> The RIMS strategy begins with 'rational interaction'. This is a rational debate between two or more rival views on the moral issue under discussion.

The RIMS strategy for moral decision-making can be summed up in three basic steps:
1. Generate and evaluate all points of view.
2. Identify implications.
3. Find solutions.

Step one: Generate and evaluate all points of view

Any moral point of view that satisfies the following three criteria should be taken into consideration in the decision-making process:
- It should be a moral argument and not selfish.
- It should be clear and intelligible to all.
- It should be factually correct.

Step two: Identify the implications

The focus should not be on the motives behind the various points of view. Instead the focus should be on identifying the positive and negative implications articulated in the different points of view.

Step three: Find solutions

Participants should co-operate in finding solutions that will keep negative implications to a minimum, while retaining the positive implications as far as possible (Rossouw, 1994).

The above strategy can be used for resolving both social and personal dilemmas. In the case of social dilemmas, the different points of view are likely to be presented by different parties. It therefore makes sense in social dilemmas to use a competent facilitator to guide and structure the process according to the RIMS strategy. In the case of personal dilemmas, the different points of view will be articulated and mediated by the person confronted with the dilemma. The individual will therefore have to structure his or her thinking according to the steps of the RIMS strategy as outlined above. Let us now apply the RIMS strategy to a social dilemma in an accounting firm.

Case study: The email dilemma

FFAF is a large auditing firm with offices in all provinces and major metropolitan areas in South Africa. Given their wide geographical spread across the country, their email facilities not only provide an essential function in their internal communication, but have also proved to be a very cost-effective and efficient mode of communication. From an analysis of the email traffic flow in FFAF, it is also apparent that email communication is playing an ever-increasing role in FFAF's communication with its clients.

A recent incident, however, cast a shadow over the use of email in the company. Recently Lindy, a junior accountant at FFAF, sent confidential information about one of FFAF's clients in a personal email to a friend from her work email address (Lindy@FFAF.co.za). The friend, in turn, shared the content of the email with someone else. Eventually, the information came into the hands of a journalist, who wrote an article that embarrassed FFAF's client. The client was most upset and threatened to terminate its long-standing relationship with FFAF. Decisive action was taken and Lindy was fired for breaking the confidentiality clause of FFAF's employment contract.

The incident made it clear that although the use of email has obvious benefits for FFAF, it also exposes the firm to some risks. It was therefore decided that a proper risk analysis on email usage in FFAF would be done. The risk analysis revealed that Lindy's abuse of the email facility was not an isolated incident. It was found that:

- On average, employees send a substantial number of personal email messages.
- Sensitive and even confidential information is sent by email to unauthorised recipients.
- Email messages with abusive racist and sexist content are distributed by employees.

FFAF's management is very concerned about the abuse of the company's email facility. They decide to take immediate and decisive action to prevent further abuse. They want to prevent further abuse by randomly monitoring the content of email messages. This will enable them not only to identify those employees who abuse the firm's email, but also to take immediate disciplinary action against such employees. Management justifies their proposed action by indicating that computers are the firm's property and are therefore intended only for work-related emails. They also argue that it is their moral duty as managers to ensure that employees use the firm's facilities to the benefit and not to the detriment of the firm.

Some members of the firm are enraged when they learn about management's decision to monitor the content of their email messages. They regard it as an invasion of their privacy. They believe that employees have a right to privacy and that management should respect that right. Furthermore they believe that this decision by management will

> destroy the internal trust within FFAF. They are also concerned that the monitoring of email content will result in poorer communication both internally as well as with clients, since employees will shy away from email communication.

Resolving the email dilemma: RIMS at work

It is apparent that a social and ethical dilemma has erupted at FFAF. On the one side of this dilemma is the management team. Management believes that the right thing to do is to monitor the email content of members of the firm (the pro-monitoring position). On the other side of this dilemma are some employees of the firm who believe that such monitoring will be unethical and to the detriment of the firm (the anti-monitoring position). We will now apply the three steps of the RIMS strategy to this dilemma to see whether this dilemma could be resolved in a manner that is sensitive to the moral concerns expressed by both parties to this dispute.

Step one: Generate the moral points of view

The first step in the process of resolving this moral dilemma is to bring all the moral arguments of the pro-monitoring and the anti-monitoring groups to the surface and to ensure that they meet the requirements for inclusion in the moral dilemma resolving process. Starting with the pro-monitoring position taken by the management team, their argument is as follows: the moral thing to do is to monitor actively the content of email messages generated by staff. They ground their conviction in the following considerations:

- They have a duty to protect the confidentiality of their clients' information.
- They have to protect the facilities of the firm against abuse.
- They have to ensure that facilities of the firm are used for the sole benefit of the firm.

The anti-monitoring position can be outlined as follows: it is immoral to monitor the content of emails generated by members of the firm. Their conviction is based on the following considerations:

- Monitoring email content constitutes an invasion of privacy.
- Monitoring email content will destroy internal trust in the firm.
- Monitoring email content will hamper effective internal and external communication.

> Now that the arguments have been extracted from the social dilemma, they need to be checked against the criteria stipulated in the first step of the RIMS strategy, which states that arguments should meet the following criteria:
> - They should be moral in nature and not merely selfish.
> - They should be clear and intelligible to all.
> - They should be factually correct.

When the above arguments are tested against these criteria, it is clear that they all meet the criteria. The arguments are not merely selfish, but articulate concerns that seek to serve the greater good of the firm and the people who work for it. All the arguments are also clear, intelligible, and contain no factually incorrect information. We can therefore recognise all arguments as valid moral points of view which need to be included and taken seriously in the process of resolving this dilemma.

Step two: Identify the implications

In the case of both the pro- and anti-monitoring positions, the respective parties indicated certain things that they wanted to avoid and/or other things that they wanted to protect. Those things that they wished to avoid can be called their negative concerns, while the things that they wanted to protect can be called their positive concerns.

The second step in the RIMS process requires that we isolate the negative and positive concerns of the respective parties in this dilemma.

Starting once more with the pro-monitoring group, their positive concerns are the following:
- Protecting the confidentiality of client information
- Ensuring appropriate use of the firm's email facility.

The second step in the RIMS process requires that we isolate the negative and positive concerns of the respective parties to a dilemma.

The negative concern of the pro-monitoring group is:
- Avoiding abuse of the firm's email facility.

The anti-monitoring group only expressed negative concerns. The things that they wish to avoid are:
- Invasion of personal privacy
- Destruction of internal trust
- Ineffective internal and external communication.

The above two sets of positive and/or negative concerns can now be combined into one set of positive and negative concerns that apply to the situation as a whole.

Table 5.1 Summary of the positive and negative concerns that apply to the email dillemma

Positive concerns	Negative concerns
• Confidentiality of client information • Appropriate use of email	• Abuse of email • Invasion of privacy • Destruction of trust • Ineffective communication

With the list of positive and negative concerns now clearly isolated, we are ready to move on to the final step in the RIMS process.

Step three: Find solutions

At this point in the RIMS process, all the existing thinking about the dilemma has been presented and analysed. The challenge posed by the third step in the RIMS process is to move beyond the existing thinking and to create solutions that will be able to minimise or eliminate the negative concerns, while retaining the positive concerns expressed above. All participants in the RIMS process should therefore be urged to generate creative proposals that will achieve this objective.

We will keep the positive concerns in the back of our minds, while we first try to find ways of eliminating or minimising the negative concerns. Once we have generated sufficient proposals for avoiding the negative concerns, we will then revisit the positive concerns to ensure that they have not been compromised in the process of eliminating the negative ones. We will address the negative concerns in the same sequence as listed in the table above.

Abuse of email

The first negative concern that needs to be minimised or eliminated is the abuse of email by employees. Since we already know that monitoring employees' email content was the cause of the current dilemma, we deliberately have to look for other means of preventing email abuse by employees. A number of proposals each of which can contribute towards preventing email abuse are listed below.
- *Proposal one: develop and communicate policy on email use:* The firm could start by clarifying any misunderstanding that might exist regarding the use of email by issuing a clear policy directive on the use of email in the firm. This policy position can even be included in the code of conduct of the firm whenever the firm's code is revised again. This policy directive should be communicated to all members of the firm. Communication by email will ensure that the correct target audience will be reached. However, it also needs to be communicated by other means such as meetings, posters, and the internal newsletter of the firm.

- *Proposal two: train staff on proper email use:* The abuse of email in the form of either personal use or the leakage of confidential client information can be further countered by training staff on the proper use of email in the firm.

  Such training could emphasise that the email facility is intended exclusively for serving the objectives of the firm. The importance of protecting the confidentiality of client information must be stressed. During training, employees should also be made aware of the fact that all emails sent by members of the firm could be accessed via the email administration system. Employees should also be made aware that their emails are not as private as they may believe. The recent case of Lindy, who was fired for the improper use of email and the leakage of confidential client information, can be used as a case study in training to illustrate the dangers inherent in email abuse for both employees and the firm.
- *Proposal three: personal email accounts:* Employees can also be encouraged to open their own personal email accounts with independent email service providers. It should be made clear in both the above-mentioned policy directives and in the training that using email for personal messages should be restricted to a minimum or, better yet, avoided altogether. Should employees need to send personal emails from work, they should access their personal email accounts with their independent service providers and use their personal email accounts to send such messages.

Invasion of privacy

An objective of all the above proposals is avoiding email abuse without invading the privacy of employees. The firm could allay any fears of invasion of privacy by opting for a different kind of monitoring system that will steer clear of monitoring the content of email messages. This alternative approach to monitoring email usage is captured in the next proposal.

- *Proposal four: monitor usage patterns rather than content:* Instead of opting for monitoring the content of email messages, the firm could implement software solutions that rather focus on frequency and patterns of usage. Such software is able to detect not only the frequency of email use by specific staff members, but also the frequency at which messages are being sent to people who are not clients of the company. It could also collate information on how often employees access independent email service providers. When such statistics suggest that an employee may be guilty of irregular or improper use of email, the statistics can then be fed back to the specific staff member with a request to explain why such patterns and frequencies occurred. In this way, the firm can still monitor the use of email without reading the content of messages and therefore also without invading the privacy of staff members.

Destruction of trust

It is clear that the members of the firm who were alarmed by management's initial decision to monitor the content of email messages perceived it as an attempt by management to spy on them. Monitoring was interpreted by the employees as an indication that management did not trust them and therefore saw the need to monitor them. Proposal four above represents a clear move away from monitoring the content of email, but it still retains an element of monitoring as it monitors frequencies and patterns of email usage. Although this kind of monitoring is less invasive than the monitoring of email content, it can still be perceived as a sign of distrust by management towards members of the firm. One therefore needs to think of proposals that can counter the perceptions of mistrust that might accompany any system of employee monitoring. The next proposal might minimise such perceptions of distrust.

- *Proposal five: a value-based approach:* The entire intervention regarding the prevention of email abuse could be premised on a value-based rather than a rule- or compliance-based approach. Management could communicate to employees that they have deliberately moved away from a system of monitoring email content to an approach that relies on the integrity and responsibility of each member of the firm. The fact that the core of the intervention revolves around developing an email policy and training members of the firm, indicates that management relies on staff to adhere to policy guidelines and to use email facilities responsibly. It should further be communicated that monitoring frequencies and patterns of email usage is similar to monitoring expense accounts and telephone usage – both forms of monitoring that already occur in the firm as part of the normal operational risk management of the firm. The monitoring that will occur should therefore not be perceived as a motion of distrust in staff but rather as a necessary safety net to protect the company against the risk that is posed by the inappropriate use of email.

Ineffective communication

The five proposals above will allay the fear that introducing a system of email content monitoring might lead to ineffective internal and external communication. The anti-monitoring group believed that ineffective communication would be a consequence of employees' fears that their privacy might be invaded and their perception that monitoring represented managerial distrust towards them. Since the above proposals are geared towards eliminating or minimising both the fear of invasion of privacy as well as distrust, one can assume that the conditions that might have led to reluctance to use the firm's email facilities have effectively been taken care of. There is therefore no need to generate any further proposals that deal directly with ineffective internal and external communication.

All the negative concerns of the parties in this moral dispute have now been either eliminated or minimised through the above proposals. What remains now is to determine whether the positive concerns of the parties have been retained in the process. In Table 5.1, which lists the concerns of the parties to the dispute, two positive concerns have been raised. Let us attend to each of them now.

Confidentiality of client information

At least three of the proposals above are geared towards protecting the confidentiality of client information. The proposal on the development of a policy on email use, the proposal on training, and the proposal of a value-based approach all emphasise the importance of responsible use of the firm's assets. The responsibility that will thereby be engendered in members of the firm will make them more careful about how they treat not only the email facilities of the firm, but also its confidential client information.

Appropriate use of email

Each of the five proposals listed above is intended to encourage responsible and appropriate use of the firm's email facilities. The abuse of email has been countered by a value-based approach that consists of policy directives and training and the additional safety net of a frequency- and pattern-monitoring system for email use. Encouraging staff to open and use private email accounts to send and receive their private emails will further prevent the abuse of the firm's email facilities. We can therefore conclude that this last positive concern has been protected and retained through the above proposals.

Conclusion

At the beginning of this chapter, we stated that because of the nature of ethics, moral dilemmas are always likely to arise. What this chapter has demonstrated is that such dilemmas are no reason for despair. On the contrary, dilemmas can be creatively resolved by engaging constructively with them on the basis of a proper dilemma-resolving strategy. Harnessing the conflicting views in a moral dilemma through a process of creative engagement not only resolves dilemmas, but also leads to more morally-sensitive organisations.

Questions for discussion

1. What is the difference between ethical decision-making (as discussed in Chapter 4) and resolving ethical dilemmas (as discussed in this chapter)?
2. How do social ethical dilemmas differ from personal moral dilemmas?
3. Explain the purpose of the RIMS strategy as well as the steps that it consists of.
4. What are the requirements that an argument should meet before it can be accepted into the RIMS process?
5. What is meant by positive and negative concerns respectively in the RIMS process?
6. Formulate one (or more) further proposals that can be used to resolve the ethical dilemma discussed in this chapter.

Bibliography

Habermas, J. 1993. *Justification and application: remarks on discourse ethics* (translated by Cronin). Cambridge, UK: Polity Press.

MacIntyre, A. 1985. *After virtue: a study in moral theory*. London: Duckworth.

Rossouw, GJ. 1994. 'Rational interaction for moral sensitivity: a post-modern approach to moral decision-making in business'. *Journal of Business Ethics*, 13(1):11-20.

6

Case study using ethical skills and insights

Martin Prozesky

Outcomes

After working through this chapter, you should be able to do the following:
- Relate professional and business activity to key ethical concepts
- Use the three philosophical theories about ethics to judge the morality of professional and business opportunities
- Link relevant value systems to professional and business decisions
- Use the RIMS method of resolving ethical dilemmas
- Know how to reach sound ethical decisions in connection with professional and business decisions.

Overview

The previous chapters are brought together in this one, with an emphasis on how to handle tricky moral dilemmas in the business and professional worlds in which members of the accountancy profession operate, whether directly, on the part of those employed in commerce and industry, or indirectly, as with those who work in accountancy firms and as registered auditors. The chapter is based on the detailed case study in the introductory chapter. We focus in this one on the moral dilemma facing Rob Abrahams and his wife Miriam, about whether or not to accept the lucrative position being offered to him in connection with the new national lottery in the fictitious Black Sea country of Larnia. We then draw on the various conceptual and practical resources outlined in Chapters 1 to 5 to show how they can assist the couple to reach an ethically-correct decision. In doing so we introduce a new character to their story in the person of an expert in applied business and professional ethics, who helps them to understand and use those conceptual and practical resources to reach their own decision.

Introduction

We return now to the story told in the introductory case study to this book, and especially to the quandary in which Rob and Miriam Abrahams found themselves at the end of that story. Should Rob accept the very lucrative job being offered to him to head the new lottery operation in Larnia, a country rife with corruption but also with an immense need for development finances, even if these finances were to come from a lottery – or should he decline precisely because of all that corruption and the other ethical problems involved?

As we saw at the end of that case study, Rob, normally an impulsive decision-maker, could just not decide what the right thing to do would be.

The preceding chapters provide a wealth of knowledge and insights as well as skills for making ethical decisions and resolving moral dilemmas. We will use those resources in the present chapter by linking them to the decision Rob has to make as soon as possible.

Case study: Using ethical skills and insights

Miriam's brainwave

As they walked home from the Camps Bay restaurant where they had debated whether Rob should take the job in Larnia or decline it, Rob put in words what they were both thinking. 'What do we do now? I've been to Larnia. We both know the serious ethical challenges the job will entail. We know it will make us a good deal of money quite soon. And we both want to be sure that we do the right thing. It must be ethical. And we are still not sure whether taking or refusing the job will be the right choice. So what do we do now?'

At this moment Miriam had an idea. 'I think we need somebody to guide us. Somebody who knows much more about ethics than we do.'

Rob nodded. 'Good idea', he replied. 'As soon as we get home I will go on to the Internet and see what I can find on the university's web site.' He was referring to the campus of Helderberg University, where he had studied accountancy. Situated an hour's drive away, it would be easy to visit if there was an ethics expert there who was willing to help.

Rob's Internet search quickly paid dividends. He entered the word 'ethics' in the search box of the Helderberg University home page, and was led swiftly to Professor Daniel East, Director of the university's Centre for Practical Ethics, a recent addition to the campus. The Centre's home page seemed to promise exactly what Rob and Miriam needed, and included Professor East's email address. Calling out to Miriam, Rob passed on the news and immediately sent off an email requesting a meeting as soon as possible with the professor, giving the gist of their problem.

Daniel East and his wife lived in a seaside house at Gordon's Bay, not far from the university campus. Fortunately for Rob and Miriam Abrahams, he was still at his desk when Rob's email popped up in his inbox. He replied at once, suggesting that they meet him at a small nearby restaurant for lunch at noon the next day.

The first meeting

It was just before noon that Rob and Miriam entered the restaurant and asked the waiter for Professor East. They found him at a table with a spectacular view of the sea. He rose as they arrived, greeted them warmly and invited them to take their seats. The usual small talk followed, drinks were ordered and lunch selections made.

'Thanks for getting in touch', began the professor. 'Please tell me more about your problem, and then I'll see what I can suggest. And remember, what you tell me remains with me just as much as if I were a priest hearing a confession, or a doctor hearing from a patient about a health matter.'

And so Rob and Miriam told him about the job offer, giving as many details as they could without mentioning names or revealing anything confidential. By the time the waitron brought their lunch, they had finished the story.

Professor East nodded and suggested that they enjoy the meal and return to business over coffee when they had finished eating. So for the next half hour, as they ate, they chatted about the usual topics – the economic situation, politics, sport, campus life, and even the weather, also discovering that they shared a passion for hiking in the mountains – and for cricket.

Over coffee the professor returned to business. 'Here is what I suggest', he said. 'You are caught up in a moral dilemma and must make your decision very soon. Fortunately, there is a way of resolving such dilemmas. It's called the RIMS method – short for Rational Interaction for Moral Sensitivity.' He paused and noted the interest on their faces.

'Ethics is often about good teamwork, and the RIMS method calls for a small team of those involved in the dilemma and, if possible, a facilitator. Why don't we form a small team – the two of you, with me as a facilitator? I won't ever tell you what to do. What I can offer is knowledge and skills designed to help people – and organisations – to make the right decisions. We'd need to meet again for much longer, possibly two or three hours one morning when we are fresh and creative, as soon as we can find a suitable date. We have a small but comfortable meeting room at my Ethics Centre where this can take place.'

Rob and Miriam nodded their acceptance enthusiastically. Diaries were consulted and a time and date fixed for a few days hence.

The next meeting

Professor East began the meeting by suggesting that they use first names and explaining a few introductory points about ethics. He pointed out that ethics, or morality – noting that he and many others in ethics use these two terms interchangeably – is about doing what is right and good in ways that benefit the person concerned as well as those affected by his or her actions. The same applies to business deals. Ethics is therefore about living and working unselfishly, while at the same time not neglecting one's own legitimate interests.

Rob and Miriam nodded their agreement, and Miriam then asked the professor to clarify whether ethics and values were the same thing.

'No, they aren't,' he replied. '"Values" is a much broader concept, referring to whatever we treat as important or desirable, like friendship, success, safety, satisfying work, money and love. As such, our values definitely influence our choices, because all of us tend to go for whatever we regard as important and desirable. Our values can therefore differ, depending on our cultural backgrounds and personalities.' Daniel, or Dan as he preferred to be called, paused and asked the couple if they were following him.

'Yes,' said Rob. 'And I think I can see where values and ethics differ. We can value things in ways that harm others, in which case they would be morally wrong, like exploiting others in a selfish quest for money.'

Ethics and business

Given that Rob's decision involved a business organisation, he asked the professor to give him and Miriam some guidance about ethics in the business world. After repeating his earlier point that in business as elsewhere, ethical practice means acting in ways that yield benefit to others and not just for oneself or one's business, Daniel East explained that it is very helpful to bear in mind that the business world operates at three main levels, and that Rob needed to be clear which of these were at issue in the decision he had to make.

He explained that there are entire economic systems, which we can call the macro-level, such as multi-party trade agreements, or even the entire free enterprise system of capitalism. Then there is a middle level, which many who work in business ethics call the meso-level, involving whole organisations and their relationships with the rest of society. The third level, the micro-level, concerns what goes on within organisations, where the main concern is the impact that the activity of a business has on the people who work in it.

Having given this explanation, the professor asked Rob to link it to the lottery situation in Larnia.

'Certainly, Dan, the lottery would involve the meso- and micro-levels,' replied Rob. 'A very big concern about any lottery is what it does to the society where it is permitted. Does enough money flow from it to help enough worthy causes, or is it just a way for the shareholders to get richer? That would be a meso-level ethical issue. But there is also the impact which the organisation running the lottery has on those who work for it, and that would be a micro-level issue. Are their salaries and other terms of employment fair? Is sexual harassment suitably punished, and so on?'

'What about the macro-level?' asked Professor East. It was Miriam who answered, saying that she believed there were also large-scale, macro aspects of the situation. As an example, she mentioned the widespread acceptance of bribes and nepotism in Larnia. These are not, she added, merely within or between organisations but about the whole of society and its values, or lack of them. Rob and the professor agreed.

Ethics, law, professionalism and value systems

The next clarification was about ethics and law. Having grown up under apartheid with its many evil laws, both Rob and Miriam needed no persuading that ethics and law were not the same thing. While the ideal is for the laws of a country to be expressions of ethical values like justice, dignity and equality, sometimes they are not. So you can't assume that if something is legal it is also ethical.

At this point Professor East addressed a different aspect of ethics. Mentioning Rob's profession, namely his being a Chartered Accountant (SA), he urged Rob to keep his moral obligations as a CA (SA) in mind. Rob readily agreed, adding that this obliged him to act in ways that would meet the five core ethical values of the profession, which he named as integrity, objectivity, competence and due care, confidentiality and professional behaviour.

One final clarification followed. 'Your dilemma, Rob,' said the professor, 'involves a situation with different cultures. Larnia is a Black Sea country, quite different in many ways from the South Africa you know. It has a significant Muslim minority, so Islamic ethics is a factor there, bigger than here, because our Muslim community is far smaller both in numbers and as a percentage of the total population. Like us, Larnia has many Christians, but they are mostly Eastern Orthodox, unlike ours, and it also experienced strong communist influences in the days of the former Soviet Union. You two probably grew up under the dominant influence of values stemming from the west. So bear in mind that these other value systems in Larnia could all be ethically relevant to your decision and a real factor there if you were to take the job.'

Step 1 of the RIMS method

With these clarifications out of the way, Dan steered the discussion to the RIMS method, explaining first that it relies upon clear, rational discussion using facts and logical arguments about the moral issues facing Rob and Miriam, and involves three steps. The first step, he told them, requires that they generate and evaluate all relevant ethical points involved in the decision about going to Larnia.

'All right', said Rob, 'there are just two options here. Either I accept the lottery job, or I decline it.' Miriam and the professor both nodded in agreement. The latter then took this first step in the method a stage further by asking his visitors to identify the grounds on which these two options were based. He suggested that Miriam identify the grounds for accepting the job and Rob for declining it.

Table 6.1 The structure of the RIMS method

Steps	Option 1 Accept the lottery job in Larnia	Option 2 Decline the lottery job
1. Generate and evaluate all ethical points		
2. Identify positive and negative concerns in both options		
3. Find solutions that retain the positive concerns and reduce or eliminate the negative ones		

Grounds for accepting the job

Miriam thought back to the recent discussion she and her husband had had in the Camps Bay restaurant and quickly identified the following grounds for accepting the position in Larnia:

- They would benefit greatly in financial terms.
- The lottery would have real potential to help with much-needed social upliftment and therefore bring benefit to a very needy sector of Larnian society.
- The new president, being committed to sound values, would need the support of morally-committed people like Rob in combating corruption.

- A man with a conscience, such as Rob, would be able to resist corruption in the lottery.
- If Rob declined the job, it could be accepted by somebody with less respect for moral values.

Evaluating the grounds

At this point the professor interrupted and questioned whether these grounds, and especially the first one, met the requirements of the RIMS method. Were they moral in nature and not just selfish? Were they clear? Were they factually correct? He pointed out that if the desire for personal financial benefit was the real reason for taking the job, then it seemed to him to be a selfish reason, and thus unethical. To this Miriam replied that she didn't see it that way, but rather as a just and fair reward for a very difficult assignment, far away from home in an extremely challenging environment. Professor East nodded his acceptance of her argument, and advised her to reword that point as a rich but just reward for the difficult work involved.

The other grounds in Miriam's list were all, the three of them agreed, ethical arguments and not merely selfish motives, because all of them involved some or other real benefit to people other than Rob and Miriam Abrahams. They also agreed that each of those grounds rested on fact, or were valid inferences from known facts, such as Rob's integrity.

Grounds for rejecting the job

Rob then listed the grounds for rejecting the job:
- Both he and Miriam had doubts about the morality of gambling.
- Therefore it would be wrong to enrich themselves through it.
- Larnia is so corrupt that it is unlikely that its new lottery could be run ethically, even with the backing of an honourable president.
- The corruption could taint Rob, possibly even suck him into it.
- Rejecting the job would ensure that Rob's ethical reputation would remain beyond reproach.
- The South African business partners to this venture, with their involvement in highly questionable arms deals, could not be trusted to be ethically-reliable business associates.

Evaluating the grounds for rejecting the job

Once again the little group checked whether these grounds met the three criteria of the method. The grounds were certainly clear, and each one involved issues of right and wrong and was therefore ethical in nature. But were they all factually correct, or at least based very firmly and logically on fact?

They quickly agreed that there might be objections here to the third and fourth of Rob's grounds, about Larnia being too corrupt for the lottery to be run ethically and therefore being able to taint Rob and perhaps even corrupt him, too. Wasn't this more an apprehension and surmise rather than a fact? Is there really no room for ethically-committed people to work for change in situations marked by serious wrongs such as endemic corruption? What about those who struggled against the evils of apartheid or Hitler's Germany?

'Let's pause here,' said Professor East, 'and dig a bit deeper. In ethics you must consider not just the individuals involved but also the context – not just the apples, but also the barrels in which they are stored. And a dirty barrel will spoil even the healthy apples placed in it. And so will any rotten apples also placed there. Larnia is the dirty barrel. Some of the senior people Rob met there are the bad apples. The new president and Rob are the good apples.'

'That certainly seems to support Rob's third reason for rejecting the job,' he added, 'but is this in fact so? Let's probe this a bit more deeply, because thoroughness is part of ethical responsibility and of the CA's duty to practice due care.'

The group agreed that it would be a mistake to pre-judge Larnia as so irredeemably corrupt as to defy the ethical efforts even of an honourable new president, and it would also be wrong to assume that Rob would quite possibly be tainted by working there, let alone be sucked into the corruption. But they also agreed that nobody is so morally strong that he or she can be guaranteed never to do something seriously wrong, given enough pressure or temptation. Just possibly, Rob could be ethically compromised. To be sure, people are quite unlike apples, in that they can think and act creatively to change the problems they encounter. But they are like apples in that they too are affected by the contexts in which they live and work, and they too can be tainted, even made rotten, by evil contexts.

Dan therefore summarised their discussion of this particular issue by suggesting that while the third and fourth of Rob's grounds were certainly not obvious facts, they did arise from the reality of a very corrupt society and did generate justifiable moral worries. Therefore they should be retained, though with less force than a moral concern of a clearly factual kind.

Gambling and the value systems

Next, the professor turned to another issue. 'Why are you worried about gambling?' he asked Rob.

'We both are,' said Rob. 'Though neither of us is actively religious, we come from value systems – mine is Christian and Miriam's is Jewish

– which make us worry that lotteries can cause poor people to try their luck rather than buy bread, and so on. And we know that Islamic ethics forbid gambling altogether. With its substantial Muslim community, this is bound to be a serious problem for many Muslims over there in Larnia. But, at the same time, neither Miriam nor I see controlled gambling as a clear and outright evil, like theft or child abuse. It makes us hesitate and think again, but it obviously isn't something we find morally unacceptable, otherwise we wouldn't even have considered this job opportunity.'

Step 2 of the RIMS method

Satisfied by Rob's reply, the professor next explained that Step 2 in the RIMS method requires them to isolate the negative and positive concerns involved in both of the options, the positive ones being the things Rob and Miriam wish to support and the negative ones being those they want to avoid or oppose.

A useful way of dong this, he added, is to group the positive and negative concerns in both options in a simple table, and he sketched one for them on his notepad.

Table 6.2 Summary of the positive and negative concerns relating to Rob's dilemma

Positive concerns	Negative concerns
• Obtaining a deservedly large financial recompense	• Contending with corruption in the new lottery
• Supporting an honourable president	• Possibly having an unscrupulous person taking the job if Rob refused
• Helping to keep Larnia's national lottery free of corruption	• Benefiting from gambling
• Supporting something that will benefit the needy	• Rob perhaps being drawn into corrupt activity
• Protecting Rob's reputation	• Rob being linked with morally-dubious business partners

At this point Daniel East suggested that they take a short break and enjoy some refreshments which his personal assistant had arranged for them. Excusing himself to make a phone call, he left Miriam and Rob to talk between themselves as they stretched their legs and helped themselves to coffee and sandwiches. They both strongly agreed that the meeting had already helped them understand the complexities of their dilemma far better, and that they were looking forward to the third step in the RIMS method.

Step 3: Finding solutions

When Professor East returned and the meeting resumed, he explained that they were now in a position to use their creative imaginations to seek ways of eliminating or at least reducing the force of the negative concerns just identified while retaining the positive ones.

They began with the problem of corruption already threatening the new lottery. Was there a way of dealing with this, short of Rob refusing the job and therefore losing the benefits it promised for him and others? Could Rob perhaps accept the job on conditions which included the stipulation that the new lottery would be run on ethical lines with no hint of corruption, with a suitably-qualified ethics committee and an enforceable code of ethical practice to be set up as further conditions?

But what if these stipulations were refused? Would Rob then not be honour bound to decline the job? That might conceivably open the door to somebody with less commitment to ethical business practice than his. Would that not be too high a price to pay for declining the position?

'Since your objections to gambling are not so strong as to rule this job out completely, how would you deal with your worry that there is still something wrong about receiving such a handsome financial benefit from gambling?' asked the professor.

Rob and Miriasm looked at each other, before the former responded to Dan by saying that he could always reduce the income he had negotiated, or better still, donate the amount of the reduction to a charity in Larnia.

Professor East chuckled and said, 'Yes Rob, and the amount of the reduction would be a very good measure of just how strong your conscience is about gambling as a source of wealth for you. After all, a reduction of a mere 10 per cent, for example, wouldn't put too much of a dent on your earnings.' Neither Rob nor Miriam was deaf to the element of moral challenge in that comment. Both felt uncomfortable, and Rob immediately said so.

'Good,' replied Dan, 'that admission shows just how honest you are, and honesty is central to moral integrity.'

Grateful for those words, Rob continued the search for creative ways of countering the unacceptable side of the job he had been offered. He looked at Miriam and said, 'You know me better than anybody. Do you believe that, with your support and perhaps also an ongoing link with the professor here, I would be ethically strong enough to avoid falling for any temptation the job might bring to accept any bribes, or fall for anything else that would be morally wrong? You know I want to keep my nose clean, but would I be strong enough in that bad barrel over there in Larnia?'

Marion did not hesitate at all before saying, 'Of course you will be strong enough, because you have a conscience and you already know that you won't be alone in such a situation. You know I will be there to support you. The same holds for the fact that taking the job means that you will have business links with people from South Africa who continue to make money from arms deals. If you make your ethical principles clear when accepting the job, they will know that it is a waste of time trying to tempt you into dicey deals. And perhaps we can also have Dan's support.' Both of them looked at the professor and smiled with relief when he nodded.

'So,' he said, 'it looks as if there are creative ways of at least reducing the force of those negative concerns of yours, and the only positive concern that this would affect is the size of your financial benefit from the job. That is not something to be discussed here. It is between the two of you and your conscience. But you may also decide that even if you keep the whole amount, the job still has more going for it, ethically, than against it.'

Guidance from moral philosophy

Professor East then added a further set of suggestions, taking them through the philosophical foundations of ethics. For example, Rob and Miriam might agree with virtue ethics that the right course of action is whatever helps build and strengthen moral character. In their situation, what would do more to foster virtues like generosity, helpfulness towards others, fairness and honesty, accepting the job or declining it? As he listened, Rob sensed that the job in Larnia would call for virtues like integrity, perseverance and courage, far more so than any other work he might do instead.

Or they might like to think about a second philosophical theory about ethics. This one goes back to the great German thinker of the 18th century, Immanuel Kant. He held that the hallmark of moral behaviour is having a sense of duty to obey objective standards of behaviour. Very simply put, what he called his 'categorical imperative' stipulates that whatever you propose to do, ask yourself if you would be comfortable if everybody did the same. In another version of that principle, Kant held that we must never treat other people as mere stepping stones to the achievement of whatever we want, but as also having interests of their own which we must respect.

Rob and Miriam had been listening carefully, with Miriam making a few notes as the professor spoke. As Dan paused, Rob asked him if he was right in understanding Kant's view as an ethic of respect for others which should guide everybody's actions at all times. The professor nodded.

'In that case, Kant's view lines up very neatly with what I gather is a hallmark of African ethics, at least here in southern Africa, namely respect, above all for those with long experience and wisdom like older people,' said Rob.

'Yes, indeed,' replied Professor East. 'And I think you will find, if you do go to Larnia, that the new president will appeal to the principle of respect as he sets out to foster genuinely democratic values and fight corruption, because corruption means exploitation, the very opposite of respect for others. Respect is not just part of the traditional African value systems of southern Africa or of Kant's ethics, but also occurs in Larnia.

The discussion then moved on to a third philosophical approach to ethics, the utilitarianism of John Stuart Mill and others like him. Professor East summarised it as the principle of choosing whatever action will lead to the greatest happiness for the greatest number. Would taking the job maximise happiness more than diminishing it? Miriam voiced the hesitation that they both felt at this point – how could they be sure about the consequences of either option, given the uncertainties of the future and the complexity of the situation in Larnia?

The professor nodded, but also pointed out that in life generally we often take decisions that involve expectations about the future. When we do so, we know that unforeseeable events such as accidents can play havoc with those expectations, but that doesn't mean that utilitarianism can't help us with our moral dilemmas. 'For example,' he added, 'you will benefit financially by taking the job, and that in itself is likely to make you happier than you would otherwise be. By giving moral support to the president of Larnia, you will make him happier, and so on.' The two visitors glanced at each other and both nodded. They sensed real, practical value in taking utilitarianism seriously.

Ethical decision-making

It was time for another break. Professor East suggested that they take a walk across the attractive Helderberg campus to the university's staff club for some lunch. As they walked, he took them through a final set of guidelines for ethical decision-making.

'You must now decide what Rob should do, bearing in mind all that we have explored today. I know this isn't easy, but fortunately, there are some helpful considerations that can help you reach finality. First of all, ask if whatever you decide to do is legal. As far as I can see, this is easily answered because neither of your options breaks any laws. A second test is whether you would conform to the standards of the organisation you work for, or those of your professional association, by taking the job. As you are an independent business consultant, there wouldn't be any company standards involved. But Rob is a CA (SA), so the question of professional ethical standards definitely comes into the picture.' He paused and waited for Rob to respond.

'There are indeed basic ethical values in the profession,' Rob said in reply to Dan. 'Integrity comes first, meaning that we must never compromise our duty to be straightforward and honest in our professional and business relationships. Next there is objectivity, which means not to compromise our professional or business judgement because of bias, conflict of interest or the undue influence of others. And then there is competence and due care – which requires the maintenance of professional knowledge and skill, and acting diligently in accordance with applicable professional standards in the performance of our work. Next, I must respect the confidentiality of client information, which I would of course do, and lastly I must behave like a true professional. I strive to do that already and can't see myself violating this duty in Larnia.'

The professor responded by suggesting that if Rob had any uncertainties about whether the ethical standards of the profession were at risk if he were to take the Larnia job, he could always discuss the situation with a respected fellow CA (SA) or with the ethics officer at SAICA.

Two further tests were explained, the fairness and disclosure tests. The former offers a person like Rob an opportunity for creative thinking by using his moral imagination, which is the skill of thinking beyond one's own perspective and imagining how one's decision would be seen by those affected. That means noting who they are and, by an exercise of empathy, trying to understand how things look from their standpoint. Would they feel they were being fairly treated?

'So, Rob,' said the professor, 'you need to ask yourself if taking the Larnia job is fair to all who are affected, and especially to Miriam. I suggest that when you get home, you two make a list of those affected, note their situations, and check each one for possible unfairness towards them if you take the job. Then do the same for if you were to decline it – unless you are already sure that there would be no unfairness.'

Dan then mentioned that the fairness test can also be applied by means of stakeholder engagement. This would require Rob to ask those who would be affected either way by his decision how they thought the decision would affect them. Since doing this meant that those stakeholders would have a chance to respond, this was clearly a very fair step to take. And if it resulted in no negative responses, or none that could not be overcome, then the decision in question would be a fair one.

The remaining test of whether a decision is ethical or not is the disclosure test. Dan explained that it has both a public and a private or personal aspect. 'Ask yourselves,' he said to his visitors, 'how you would feel if your decision and subsequent course of action appeared on the front page of a newspaper or on TV. If that were to make you uncomfortable, even cringe, then you know there is an ethical problem about that option. Or maybe you need to ask yourself which option would make you feel more comfortable than the other one.'

As they neared the staff club, Miriam turned to the private aspect of the disclosure test. 'I suppose this means checking how Rob would feel, and I too for that matter, when telling close friends or trusted workplace colleagues what we had decided. Would either option make us feel awkward or embarrassed, or might one decision do so but not the other? And would we feel able to justify the decision, both in private and in public, on moral grounds?'

'Precisely so,' replied Professor East. 'And now that we have worked our way through everything I can offer, how do you feel? Is a decision beginning to emerge as the morally right one?'

'We can't thank you enough,' said Rob. 'And yes, I think we know what we are going to do. And now, please would you let us host you as we have something to eat and drink in the staff club?'

Questions for discussion

1. Put yourself in Rob Abrahams' position and say, with full reasons, what you think he and Miriam should chose as the ethically-correct decision about the job in Larnia.
2. Rob is a member of the South African Institute for Chartered Accountants. Assume that he takes the job in Larnia. Check the SAICA web site at <www.saica.co.za> to see whether that decision complies with its Code of Professional Conduct.
3. Corruption is a broad term. What activities does it refer to, and why are they morally and legally wrong?
4. Make contact with a few fellow students and lecturers from different cultural backgrounds, and ask them whether their value systems regard gambling as immoral and if so, why?
5. Consider each of the three philosophical theories about ethics and state, with reasons, which of the options facing Rob Abrahams – whether to accept the job in Larnia or to decline it – each theory indicates as being the right one, or at least ethically preferable.
6. If you were Rob and had decided to accept the job in Larnia, and wanted a personal code of workplace ethics, what would you include in it, and why?

Part 2
Business ethics

The business world is the most important source of wealth. Sustainable success in that world is therefore of key interest for all members of society and is certainly vital to the accounting profession. The majority of clients for auditing firms will be from the business world, for example, and therefore constitute a good source of income for auditing firms. It also provides employment for the many members of the profession who work in commerce and industry. Part 2 of this book provides readers with essential knowledge and guidance in relation to business and its ethical challenges, starting with wide-ranging economic issues and proceeding to more specific and practical matters.

Macro-ethics is the subject of *Chapter 7*. We firstly investigate the moral justification and the key features of capitalism as an economic system. Thereafter, such aspects as property rights, free markets, competition, profit, and the role of the corporation are dealt with. In the last part of the chapter, the question of economic justice is discussed further.

We turn in *Chapter 8* to the ethical responsibilities of the most powerful structure in today's business world, the modern corporation, reviewing two influential theories about shareholders and stakeholders respectively. It emerges that a very clear shift has occurred over the last decades. Corporations are now recognised as moral agents (or corporate citizens) with moral obligations towards society. Although shareholders still enjoy a privileged status in corporations, the interests of a range of other stakeholder groups have gained prominence. These changes have also had profound consequences for the way in which corporations have to account for their economic, social, and environmental performance.

Corporate governance and the *King III Report of (2009)* are the focus of attention in *Chapter 9*. We discuss governance structures such as the double agency construct to explain the relationship between the various parties. Various crises and stumbling blocks in governance practice are analysed, and we then look at stakeholder management as an alternative approach to governance. The impact of the King Reports is discussed, and finally we look at the crucial role of the auditing profession in ensuring the integrity of full corporate disclosure.

How to achieve best ethical practice is a key management issue. This is the subject of *Chapter 10*. Using a corporate governance framework, it sets out a four-step process of effective ethical management applicable to both business and accounting.

Part 2 ends with practical case studies in *Chapter 11*. Case studies that deal with a wide variety of ethical business issues are presented. We also provide guidelines for analysing and discussing the case studies. The chapters in Part 2 lay the foundation for Part 3, which focuses directly on ethics in the world of accountants and auditors.

7

Macro-ethics

Minka Woermann

Outcomes

After working through this chapter, you should be able to do the following:
- Demonstrate the relation between macro-ethics and business conduct
- Present a normative critique of capitalism
- Compare capitalism to statism
- Describe the evolution of capitalism
- Critically explain the key features of capitalism
- Demonstrate knowledge of critical challenges facing the future of capitalism
- Demonstrate the relation between capitalism and distributive justice
- Describe and assess the utilitarian, egalitarian and libertarian theories of distributive justice.

Overview

Although the study of ethics is concerned with an evaluation of the moral desirability of individual and group actions, these actions can only be properly understood within the **contexts** in which individuals and groups operate. This is because these unique contexts determine the **rules of the game**; and, therefore, the types of actions that are deemed appropriate or not within a given setting. The rules of the game change over time and are themselves subject to ethical scrutiny. Typically this latter activity falls under the domain of what is termed **macro-ethics**. More precisely, macro-ethics is the study and evaluation of the social, economic, political, environmental and cultural contexts (and the interrelations between these contexts) that shape our practices. This is an important task since these contexts **constrain and enable** individual and group behaviour. Although many themes fall under the domain of macro-ethics, in this chapter we shall restrict ourselves to exploring the capitalistic system in which business operates, as well as to different conceptions of distributive justice that either supports this system or that can be employed to critically evaluate capitalism.

Introduction

Capitalism is undoubtedly an empirical fact of today's world. Indeed, with the fall of socialism, capitalism has no strong contenders, and is so pervasive today that many commentators are talking of a **globalised capitalism**. Although it is important to take cognisance of both the historical rise of capitalism, and the key features that define capitalism, what is of greater concern for business ethicists are the values upon which the capitalistic system is premised, and the social issues that capitalism gives rise to. In other words, we are interested in examining capitalism as a **normative**, rather than a descriptive, system.

> Capitalism has no strong contenders, and is so pervasive today that many commentators are talking of a globalised capitalism.

As with any normative evaluation, it is important to critically assess both the strengths and weaknesses of the subject under study. The capitalistic system has undoubtedly led to many **advances** in our society, most important of which include incentivising development and innovation in fields such as science, technology, transportation and medicine; increasing choices between available products and services; and facilitating the development of a global trade and finance community. Furthermore, capitalism has also increased the general wealth of society, as argued in a recent article entitled 'How to save capitalism'. In this article, TIME reporter Michael Schuman (2012: 32) cites the following noteworthy statistics in support of this point: '[the] global GDP increased by a factor of seven over the first 1,820 years of the common era; since then – during the two centuries dominated by modern capitalism – it surged more than 70 times.' Whilst we cannot deny the benefits of capitalism, not all the assumptions on which capitalism is based, or the consequences arising from capitalism, are positive.

Despite capitalism's strengths, it has also contributed to the steady increase in **socio-economic inequality**. Capitalism is premised on the **homo economicus** view of the human, which is grounded in the assumptions that we are **rational beings** who seek to maximise both monetary and non-monetary **utility**. Although very influential in economic theory, this view only accounts for the self-interested dimension of human nature and translates into a description of human beings as acquisitive, materialistic, and individualistic. These characteristics are, in turn, reinforced in the way that capitalism is practiced. Furthermore, one of the golden rules of capitalism is that one needs to invest money in order to make money. It therefore stands to reason that the poor are unlikely to benefit from a system that advances the wealthy and rewards self-interested behaviour. Empirical evidence supports this argument, and in this regard, Schuman (2012: 32) cites a 2011 report by the *Organisation for Economic Co-operation and Development*, in which it is stated that the level of income inequality of its 22 member states increased by 10% since the mid-eighties accompanied by declining conditions in 17 of the member states. Indeed, if we look at income disparity in South Africa (as measured by the gini-coefficient, where a score of 0 represents no inequality, and a score of 1 represents maximal inequality), we see that South Africa scored 0.66 in 2008. As Trevor Manual (2010: 22), the former minister of finance of South Africa, argued in the *2010 Development Indicators Report*, this level of inequality severely undermines the constitutional mandate of '[h]uman dignity, the achievement of equality and the advancement of human rights and freedoms'. Although many factors contribute to this appalling state of affairs (not least of which is South Africa's Apartheid Legacy), the socio-economic system's contribution to economic inequality cannot be ignored. Therefore, despite all the benefits that capitalism holds, the system also raises some very important questions concerning **distributive justice**.

As will be explained in more detail further on in this chapter, questions regarding distributive justice centre on the criteria and principles according to which societal burdens and benefits should be distributed. These are by no means easy questions, since rival criteria and principles exist. Some of the common criteria evoked in debates on distributive justice include **effort, merit, need, and social contribution**. It is easy to see how any of these criteria can serve as a good basis for determining the distribution of resources, however the problem is that many of these criteria are also incompatible. In other words, one cannot simultaneously claim that resources should be distributed on the basis of superior effort and need, since those in dire need often have not had the opportunity to undertake extensive training or study (i.e. exert superior personal effort), in order to secure an economically advantageous position in society. Similarly, although effort and merit coincide in ideal situations, there are many situations where effort is not acknowledged due to the fact that the product of one's efforts does not merit reward (for example, most of us can think of a situation where we scored low on a test or a project even though we worked very hard; whereas a friend, who hardly put in any effort at all, received a good mark).

In a nutshell, distributive justice hinges on the question of what would constitute a **fair** allocation and division of benefits and burdens. Although this is a difficult question to answer, certain divisions seem intuitively unfair. For example, the fact that 'CEOs at large U.S. firms earned, on average, $10.8 million in 2010, a 28% increase from the year before, while the average worker took home $33, 121, a mere 3% more' – as Schuman (2012: 32) reports – strikes us as grossly unfair; as does the fact that 'the richest 1% of adults alone owned 40% of global assets in the year 2000', as reported by the *World Institute for Development Economics Research of the United Nations University*. The fact that capitalism makes such inequalities possible necessitates that we critically evaluate our current day economic system, in order to challenge the status quo. Given the recent financial crisis and the near global economic recession that followed, it is particularly imperative that we undertake this task, so as to promote a more sustainable form of capitalism for the future.

This may seem a daunting and even futile task, and it is reasonable to ask what difference we, as individuals, are capable of making. Although we may be limited in our power to shape the world, we would nevertheless do well to remember the response of one of David Mitchell's protagonist's in the excellent novel 'Cloud Atlas' to the statement that his life 'amounts to no more than one drop in a limitless ocean'. He retorts with the question: 'Yet what is an ocean but a multitude of drops?' (2004: 510), meaning that every life *can* make a difference, and so too can every critical voice. As with all things, however, it is firstly necessary to acquire sufficient knowledge of one's subject matter before attempting a critical assessment, and it is to capitalism's history, evolution, and key features that we turn next.

The rise of capitalism

Capitalism versus Statism

Capitalism operates on the basis of a market system in which production and distribution is privatised. The purest form of capitalism is *laissez faire* capitalism, which loosely translates from French as 'let do' or 'let things alone'. This form of capitalism was espoused by **Adam Smith**, the father of modern economics, and author of *An Inquiry into the Nature and Cause of the Wealth of Nations* (1776). According to Smith, the market will be more efficient if we allow the market mechanism to function with minimal interference from the state. The gist of his argument is captured in his concept of **the invisible hand of the market**, which is the mechanism through which the market is regulated, as explained below under the section entitled 'Competition'. Furthermore, Smith also extolled capitalism because it brings about a **division of labour** and **specialisation**. As regards the division of labour, Smith uses the example of the pin-maker to illustrate how dividing the manufacturing of pins into distinct operations can lead to an increase in the quantity of work performed. In other words, a team in which different people take charge of specific functions in the production process will work a lot more effectively than one person who attempts to make a product from scratch. The division of labour will also lead to specialisation as labourers become more dexterous and proficient in their specific tasks, and as labourers begin to explore readier and easier methods of performing work. Smith (2008: 165) argues that the division of labour thus allows for 'the great multiplication of the productions of all the different arts' and consequently 'a general plenty diffuses itself through all the ranks of society'.

The antipole of capitalism is statism, which found its most significant expression in **market socialism**. Socialism is characterised by the public ownership of property and a state-controlled economy. The father of this doctrine is **Karl Marx**, and he develops his ideas in the *Communist Manifesto* (1848), which he co-wrote with Friedrich Engels. Marx's critique of capitalism centers on the **alienation** and **exploitation** of the workforce, brought about by capitalism. Briefly, he argues that capitalism creates hierarchies which allows for the exploitation of workers. This is because the working class or **proletariat** have no bargaining power, and are forced to work for the capitalist class or **bourgeoisie** for a meager wage. This results in **surplus value** for the capitalist, where surplus value is defined as the difference between the labour market and the commodity market, or the difference between what it costs to employ the worker and what he can produce. This further serves to heighten the inequality between the worker and the capitalist, since the worker becomes poorer the more wealth he produces. Not only is the worker exploited through forced labour, but he is also alienated from his labour. This is because his labour is externally-imposed, which means that his work does not belong to him, and therefore does not fulfill him. His labour thus becomes a means towards an end and is not seen as valuable in itself.

To understand the implications of Marx's argument, one need only imagine the dehumanising effects that dedicating one's life to performing one distinct repetitive action in the manufacturing of pins can have. Marx (2008: 167) argues that '[t]he *devaluation* of the human world increases in direct relation with the *increase in value* of the world of things'; and, because of the unsatisfactory outcome of this situation, he predicted that the capitalistic order would be reversed through a **communist revolution**. According to his prediction, workers would rise up against the system and institute a more egalitarian order, in which the working class would run the economy collectively to the benefit of the majority.

History belies Marx's predictions. Not only did the communist revolution never take place, but socialism as such has failed to prove a worthy alternative to capitalism, and was dealt its death blow by the fall of the Berlin Wall and the end of the Cold War. However, many of the specific measures introduced by Marx and Engels have been implemented, such as the institution of a minimum wage and occupational health and safety laws to protect workers. The Great Depression of the 1930s also legitimised state interference in the economy, and most countries have instituted policies and regulations that help to mitigate the destabilising impact of market cycles. In other words, most economies therefore sit somewhere between *laissez-faire* capitalism and statism, although the degree of market intervention is context and time specific.

> Most economies sit somewhere between *laissez-faire* capitalism and statism, although the degree of market intervention is context and time specific.

The dynamic nature of capitalism

Whereas Western economic systems are characterised by a market-orientated capitalism, China practices state capitalism. In terms of the Western paradigm specifically, the USA is more pro-market than Europe (West, 2006; Demirag, 2005). The **Anglo-American model** is geared towards a shareholder model, which is characterised by a single-tiered board that gives primacy to shareholder interests; a dominant role for financial markets; a corresponding weak role for banks; and, little or no industrial policy involving corporations cooperating with government. In contrast, the **European model** is characterised by a stakeholder model. Here we see that a two-tier board structure (which also accommodates stakeholder interests) is prevalent; the share market is less developed than in the USA; banks traditionally play a more dominant role in the economy; and, industrial policies is employed to regulate the business environment. Although **South Africa** tends towards the Anglo-American model, especially as concerns board structure and the role played by the financial markets and banks, the evidence is mixed with regard to industrial policy. Whilst state assets are being privatised and competition promoted (for example, through the issuing of additional licenses in the telecommunications industry), we see a fair amount of government intervention in labour markets, especially in terms of the Employment Equity Act (1998) and the Broad-based Black Economic Empowerment Act (2003).

Not only do we see different degrees of state intervention in the economy across contexts, but also over time. Schuman (2012) argues that the never-ending dance between the state and the market is responsible for all the historical transformations of capitalism, and will continue to inform debates about the future of capitalism. With regard to these historical transformations, Schuman (2012: 32) writes that:

> The never-ending dance between the state and the market is responsible for all the historical transformations of capitalism, and will continue to inform debates about the future of capitalism.

> [Capitalism] has survived and thrived because it has reformed, again and again, in response to the ills of the moment. The suffering brought on by the Great Depression sparked a movement to make capitalism more equitable and stable, which led to greater government protection and regulation – the New Deal and the European welfare state. Then, to overcome the stagflation of the 1970s, capitalism had to be more productive and innovative. Ronald Reagan and Margaret Thatcher ushered in an era of deregulation, free trade and free flows of capital that spawned a global economic boom. Today, amid the protracted downturn, capitalism has reached another inflection point. The world's financial sector remains so unsound, and the pain inflicted on the average family has been so great, that capitalism needs to morph again, to become more inclusive and balanced and less prone to recurrent meltdowns. The question is not whether capitalism must be reformed. It is how.

At the 2012 meeting of *World Economic Forum* (held annually in Davos, Switzerland), the future of capitalism was the central topic of discussion. According to TIME business correspondent Roya Wolverson (2012), there was however very little consensus as to who should accept responsibility for the myriad problems that we are currently facing. On the one hand, union representatives felt that **powerful corporations** should accept responsibility for the failure of capitalism, since their greed has led to inequality and to the inability of the man-in-the street to fuel a global recovery. On the other hand, corporate executive officers argued that capitalism has lifted millions out of poverty, and that the real culprit is **government**. This is because governments (specifically Western governments) issued a number of competing regulations that caused confusion and limited job creation, and did not promote sound educational policies to properly skill the future workforce. At any rate, finger pointing will not help to solve our current day problems. Rather, what is needed is greater cooperation between business and government, in order to overcome these problems.

Key features of capitalism

Despite substantial differences in the way that capitalism is, and has been, practiced, a number of key features have nevertheless emerged over time. Many theorists attempt to define capitalism in terms of these key features, and although there are contesting views on what constitutes a comprehensive list of features, William Shaw (2011) argues that the rise of the corporation, private property, the profit-motive, and competition are especially significant in understanding the core of capitalism.

Corporations

The word 'corporation' derives from the Latin word 'corpus', which means 'body [of people']', and refers to the incorporation of a group of people who act as a single entity in pursuing a common objective. During the early days of capitalism, capitalists financed (and also took responsibility for the losses of) their individual enterprises. However, as the power and size of business grew, it became impossible for individual financiers to underwrite business activities. The solution was to **pool capital** through the incorporation of business enterprises – a process which was initially authorised by a governmental charter, but which now takes place through **public registration**. This allowed a group of investors to share the risk and potential gains of their business activities.

Modern day corporations have three outstanding features. Firstly, theoretically-speaking, the corporation has a **perpetual lifetime**. The corporation can continue to exist beyond the lifespan of its individual members (although corporations can, of course, be dissolved or liquidated). Otherwise stated, the identity of the corporation is not contingent on the identity of its founders. If this were not the case, corporations would cease to exist once the founding members retired. Secondly, the corporation has a **legal identity**; and, in the eyes of the law, corporations are viewed as artificial beings. As with natural beings, corporations enjoy certain rights and privileges, but also have corresponding duties and responsibilities. This means that the corporation can sue and be sued as an entity. Thirdly, because of the size and power of corporations, it is often impossible for its individual shareholders to shoulder corporate losses. As a result, the concept of **limited-liability** was introduced, which means that, as a shareholder, one's liability (or responsibility) for corporate debt equals the amount of one's investment.

Many corporations today operate across national boundaries and wield enormous **socio-economic power**. Indeed, in many cases, the annual revenue of multinational corporations exceeds the gross domestic product (GDP) of a number of countries. For example, for the fiscal year 2010, Wal-Mart reported revenue of $421.849 billion, Exxon Mobile's revenue was $370.125 billion, and Royal Dutch Shell's revenue was $368.056 billion. In contrast, South Africa's GDP for the year 2010 was $525, 806 billion, and according to the *International Monetary Fund (IMF)*, South Africa ranks as the world's 25th largest economy. From the IMF's list of the 183 economies, 155 reported a lower 2010 GDP than Wal-Mart's 2010 revenue. What this example shows is that the corporation is a force to be reckoned with, and the rise of the modern corporation has led to a concentration of economic power that equals, or even surpasses state power. This fact alone serves as a strong justification for the significance of business ethics, since proper ethical scrutiny can serve as an important check on corporate power.

> In many cases, the annual revenue of multinational corporations exceeds the gross domestic product (GDP) of a number of countries.

Private property

The modern corporation gave rise to diverse patterns of shareholding, and this phenomenon has (in part) challenged our traditional understanding of private property. In the past, however, private property was mostly associated with tangible assets; and, it is with this understanding in mind, that the British philosopher, **John Locke**, defended both our **natural right to property** and capitalism (which he viewed as the outcome of this right). Locke's justification for our natural right to property is tied to his understanding of human labour. He argues that when we mix our labour with the natural world, we are entitled to the product of that labour on the condition that we leave enough and as good for others, and that we do not squander our resources. For example, if I plant a number of apple trees and water them regularly, and they bear fruit, I am entitled to those apples. However, I can impossibly eat more than 50 apples per week. Picking more than 50 apples would be a waste of limited resources and thus wrong.

Locke lived in the 17th century, and since his time, we see that property has become a much more complex concept. Today, private property consists of both **tangible assets** (such as factories, offices, computers, ground and other physical resources) and **intangible assets** (such as shares, bonds, warrants, and futures), and most property is not the outcome of mixing one's labour with the natural world. Although Locke's argument is unconvincing in today's world, private property is nevertheless a core feature of capitalism. In order to grow business and make money, it is essential to reinvest capital back into the business, and private property is thus both an indication of our present wealth and of our future potential for generating wealth.

> Private property is both an indication of our present wealth and of our future potential for generating wealth.

The profit motive

Corporations and private property both serve as means to generating profit, and the profit motive is the **lifeblood** of the capitalistic system. Profit is defined as the residual income left for the owners of capital once all claims against the corporation have been settled. The amassment of individual wealth through profit distinguishes capitalism from the earlier guild systems of Western Europe, in which craftsmen filled out orders on a needs basis, thereby making enough money to secure a decent living, but not to advance their station in life. The profit motive is also absent in market socialism, which (as defined above) is based on the public ownership of property, and in which the goal is to distribute wealth on the basis of one's contribution to society.

Unlike natural resources, there is no limit to how much wealth a single person can accrue. The profit motive is the **incentivising force** behind capitalism, since without it entrepreneurs would have little reason to risk their time and money on new ideas and businesses. Indeed, one of the most prominent reasons for socialism's failure is that it provided no incentives for the individual, because wealth was collectively owned. In other words, and as Smith points out, the profit motive speaks to our desire to maximise our own utility, as underscored by the view of the individual as *homo economicus*.

> The profit motive is the incentivising force behind capitalism, since without it entrepreneurs would have little reason to risk their time and money on new ideas and businesses.

Competition

Although the economy is driven by profit, it is regulated by competition (which acts as **the invisible hand of the market**), as explained by Smith in *The Wealth of Nations*. Capitalism works because everyone is free to pursue their own interests, but since everyone is motivated by the same interest (i.e. profit), competition arises. For example, if (hypothetically-speaking) I was the inventor of cell phones I would initially make a lot of money. The reason being that due to the high **demand**, I can charge exorbitant prices for my product. Soon, however, other people will catch on that manufacturing cell phones is a very profitable enterprise and will also enter into this market. In other words, I am now competing with a number of other manufacturers, which means that there is an increase in the **supply** of cell phones. The consumer can now choose from whom he wishes to purchase his cell phone, and the obvious choice is the manufacturer who sells a quality product for a lower price. Hence, the increase in supply leads to a decrease in price, as manufacturers try to undercut their competitors. This process continues until we reach **economic equilibrium**, which means that the product supply is equal to the consumer demand. If supply outstrips demand, then the market becomes over-saturated, and it will no longer be profitable to manufacture cell phones. According to Smith, the beauty of the invisible hand of the market is that it directs private, **self-interested behaviour** in a way that **benefits society as a whole**. In this regard, Smith (1985: 223-225) writes that:

> According to Smith, the beauty of the invisible hand of the market is that it directs private, self-interested behaviour in a way that benefits society as a whole.

> Every individual is continually exerting himself to find the most advantageous employment for whatever capital he can command. It is his own advantage, indeed, and not that of society, which he has in view... [But] by directing that industry in such a manner as its produce may be of the greatest value, he [is]... led by an invisible hand to promote an end that was no part of his intention... By pursuing his own interest he frequently promotes that of society more effectually than when he really intends to promote it.

One assumption on which Smith's theory is based is **perfect competition**. In other words, the relation between the buyer and the seller must be equal. As soon as one party is in a stronger position, **price manipulation** can take place. This happens when there is a concentration of resources in the hands of single firm, such as is the case with Eskom (which functions as a **monopoly**), or in the hands of a number of firms such as is the case with the oil and petroleum exporting companies (OPEC) (which function as an **oligopoly**). Another example is that of illegal **cartels** (where a number of firms collude to artificially inflate the prices within a certain industry). In fact, there are very few examples of perfect competition, with the result that the greater welfare of society has not always been promoted by capitalism.

Theories of justice

> Issues pertaining to justice inevitably arise in a world dominated by an economic system which results in certain individuals having more opportunities in life to advance their station, more resources at their disposal for realising their dreams, and more socio-economic power for facilitating the achievement of their goals.

Issues pertaining to justice inevitably arise in a world dominated by an economic system, which results in certain individuals having more opportunities in life to advance their station, more resources at their disposal for realising their dreams, and more socio-economic power for facilitating the achievement of their goals. These justice issues concern the fair acquisition, distribution, and use of limited resources. The way in which we frame issues of distributive justice also have a profound effect on how we view the nature of capitalism and the consequences arising from capitalism, and can thus be employed to assess the strengths and weaknesses of capitalism. However, before turning to specific conceptions of distributive justice, it is important to firstly try to define the term 'justice'.

Defining justice

According to Plato, the four cardinal virtues on which our moral life is based are **prudence, temperance, courage and justice**. However, André Comte-Sponville argues in *A Short Treatise on the Great Virtues: the Uses of Philosophy In Everyday Life* (1996) that of these four caridnal virtues, justice is good in itself, whereas the other virtues only lead to good consequences if the will of the doer is good. For example, a murderer can take great personal risks and thereby show great courage, but will not be a virtuous person. In other words, if the will is good, prudence, temperance and courage are instrumental in creating, sustaining and promoting the moral life; but if the will is not good, these qualities take on a different value. Whilst a murderer may be prudent, courageous, or tempered, he can never just. Hence, justice is what Aristotle refers to in the *Nicomachean Ethics* as a 'complete virtue'.

Following Aristotle, Comte-Sponville argues that there are two common conceptions of justice, namely justice as respect for state **legality**, and justice as respect for **equality** amongst individuals. With regard to the first conception, justice demands consistency and impartiality before the law, meaning that like cases should be treated alike. The symbol of the judicial system namely, a blind-folded lady balancing the scales of truth accurately represents this conception of justice. In order to act consistently and impartially, one should also recognise the fundamental moral equality of all people. In other words, before the law, everyone deserves equal respect and equal moral consideration. The problem however is that the legal system is a human institution, and is prone to failure. The Apartheid regime serves as a good example of where justice as respect for state legality fundamentally contradicted the view of justice as respect for equality amongst individuals. In a perfect world, the **fact** of justice (i.e. law) would coincide with the **value** of justice (i.e. equality). However, since we don't live in a perfect world, justice should not amount to a form of **legal positivism** (where we equate the law with justice), but should rather involve a never-ending critical engagement with our practice. In the words of Comte-Sponville: 'justice does not make just people; just people make justice'.

> Justice does not make just people; just people make justice

The fact that justice does not have any clear, substantive definition means that there are competing ideas of how justice should be conceptualised and achieved. With regard to distributive justice, there exists a number of rival views on which principles should inform a theory of distributive justice. Three influential views on distributive justice in social and political philosophy are the utilitarian, egalitarian, and libertarian justice theories, and in the sections that follow, these three theories will be discussed and evaluated.

The utilitarian theory of justice

As explained in chapter 3, utilitarians use the **'greatest happiness principle'** as the yardstick for determining the morality of our actions. To recap: the greatest happiness principle constitutes the idea that an action is right to the degree that it promotes happiness, and wrong to the degree that it produces unhappiness, for everyone affected by a given situation (Mill, 1965). The main proponent of this view is **John Stuart Mill**, a British social and political philosopher. Mill employed utilitarianism in order to critique 19th century societal institutions (such as the prison system), and his philosophy is therefore associated with societal reform.

> For Mill, distributive justice should be based on the principle of social utility.

For Mill, distributive justice should be based on the principle of **social utility**. In other words, an action would be deemed just if it promotes overall societal welfare. Using the yardstick of social utility can help to resolve the problem of competing criteria (mentioned in the introduction). Deciding if benefits and burdens should be distributed on the basis of equality, need, personal effort or merit is contingent on which actions will maximise social utility. For example, merit should be rewarded higher than effort if talented workers are able to make a greater contribution than industrious workers to the overall welfare of society. Whether this truly is the case, is a context-dependent question. This means that deciding on the distribution of benefits and burdens depends on the social, economic, and political consequences that will arise from different resource distributions. This is of course not so easy to determine since the impact of our actions on an array of societal structures and institutions needs to be considered.

Although a utilitarian theory of justice has the benefit of providing a uniform yardstick for determining the justness of a certain action, conceiving of justice in terms of utility alone can also be dangerous, since – according to this perspective – **condemning or sacrificing innocent individuals is justifiable,** if done to promote social utility. In other words, the rights of individuals are always secondary to the maximisation of societal utility. For example, according to utilitarians, it is perfectly justifiable to institute a land redistribution policy, if such a policy increases long-term net societal utility. Dennis Masaka (2011) argues along this line in a paper on Zimbabwe's land reform policies, in which he claims that these policies are morally justifiable from a utilitarian point of view, since they stand to benefit a large number of disenfranchised Zimbabweans whose ancestral land was violently appropriated during colonialism. However, since these policies have undermined the sustainability of Zimbabwe's agricultural sector, he argues that the Zimbabwean government should rethink the manner in which land is redistributed, in order to ensure that land reform policies also hold long-term benefits for Zimbabweans. Note that Masaka is critical of Zimbabwe's land reform policies because they have failed to contribute to societal welfare, and not because they violate individual property rights. A number of people would however find these policies unjust, and would take issue with the utilitarian justification of these policies. Comte-Sponville (1996: 62) is one such a person, and he follows Kant and Rawls in arguing that '[j]ustice is superior to and more valuable than well-being or efficiency; it cannot be sacrificed to them – not even for the happiness of the greatest number.

> Utilitarians are critical of our current capitalistic system, which contributes to a situation in which 31.2% of the world's population lives below the poverty line (CIA World Factbooks, 2003 – 2011). The poverty line is defined as 'the monetary threshold under which an individual is considered to be living in poverty' (Investopedia), and is currently fixed by the World Bank at $1.25 per day (Ravallion, Chen and Sangraula, 2009). Utilitarians would support any policies that would lead to a more equal distribution of resources, since societal welfare will undoubtedly be improved if everyone has enough resources to secure a decent living.

The egalitarian theory of justice

If justice cannot be sacrificed to well-being or efficiency, which principles should inform our understanding of justice? **John Rawls**, an American philosopher, offers an alternative to utilitarianism in his influential book, entitled *A Theory of Justice* (1971). Herein, he argues that justice should be understood in terms of **fairness**, and that the only way in which we can ensure fairness, is to hypothesise an **original position of equality**. Rawls attempts to resist the **genetic lottery**, whereby we are born into a unique set of circumstances that influences our opportunities in life (for example, a child born in an informal settlement to an HIV positive mother and an alcoholic father is unlikely to have the same opportunities in life, as is a child who is born to middle-class, healthy parents). Since the genetic lottery is the outcome of chance, Rawls argues that we should actively work against the inequalities that arise as a result of the genetic lottery. This can be achieved by undertaking a **thought-experiment**, whereby we choose the principles of justice that will regulate society.

> Rawls attempts to resist the genetic lottery, whereby we are born into a unique set of circumstances that influences our opportunities in life.

Rawls's thought experiment asks of us to hypothesise the so-called original position (which forms the basis of many contract theories). In Rawls's original position we are placed behind a hypothetical **veil of ignorance**, which means that we find ourselves in situation where we are ignorant of our personal circumstance in life, including our class or position in society, our economic status, our abilities, intelligence, strengths, and so forth. From this position, we must then choose the **governing principles** of society, which will necessarily be just – the reason being that because we are unaware of our unique circumstances in life, we will be unable to campaign for principles that promote our specific ends. Rawls (1994: 72) explains as follows:

> For given the circumstances of the original position, the symmetry of everyone's relations to each other, this initial situation is fair between individuals as moral persons, that is, as rational beings with their own ends and capable, I shall assume, of a sense of justice. The original position is, one might say, the appropriate initial status quo, and thus the fundamental agreements reached in it are fair. This explains the propriety of the name "justice as fairness": it conveys the idea that the principles of justice are agreed to in an initial situation that is fair.

Rawls (1994: 73) further argues that parties in the original position should be viewed 'as rational and mutually disinterested'. In other words, when choosing the governing principles of society, Rawls postulates that, behind the veil of ignorance, the **rational choice** for each person will be to act **conservatively**, and not gamble with his future (for example, I will not choose for a division of resources that will only benefit ten percent of the population, since my chances of finding myself as a member of this privileged class once the veil of ignorance is lifted are very small). Furthermore, each person will act in **self-interest**, choosing for principles that are likely to benefit him personally; and since everyone thinks the same, we are able to agree on the principles of justice. Rawls is critical of utilitarianism, since utilitarianism requires that, at least in some circumstances, we forego our own interests in trying to promote a greater net balance of utility. Rawls (1994: 73) thus concludes that 'the principle of utility is fundamentally incompatible with the conception of social cooperation among equals for mutual advantage.'

Given this thought experiment, which principles for regulating society would we choose? Rawls argues that because we are rational and self-interested, we will be led by the **maximum principle** in our deliberations. In other words, we will choose for a division of resources that maximises the minimum; because, in ignorance of our stakes in life, and in fear that we will end up at the bottom of the socio-economic hierarchy, we would want those who are worst-off in society to be in the best possible position (when compared to alternative societal arrangements). As such, Rawls (1994: 73) postulates that we will settle on two governing principles:

> [T]he first requires equality in the assignment of basic rights and duties, while the second holds that social and economic inequalities, for example, inequalities of wealth and authority, are just only if they result in compensating benefits for everyone, and in particular for the least advantaged members of society.

Rawls first principle guarantees **moral equality** between people, which is a grounding condition for a just society. Each person should therefore have an equal right to the most comprehensive set of basic freedoms that are compatible with a reciprocal system of freedom for all. Rawls's second principle (also called the **difference principle**) states that **social and economic inequalities** will only be justified if they **benefit the worst-off** in society, and if they are attached to **positions and offices open to all**. To understand this second principle, consider the following example: imagine two socio-economic distributions in society – one in which resources are equally divided between different societal classes (D1), and another in which resources are unequally divided between different societal classes (D2). According to Rawls's egalitarian theory, D2 will only be justifiable if the activities that gave rise to the inequality also increased socio-economic benefits by a big enough factor to ensure that the worst off in D2 are still in a better position than they would have been had they received an equal share of socio-economic benefits under D1. To put substantive content to this example, imagine a fishing village in which everyone lives on a subsistence basis and is similarly well-off (D1). A big factory is destined to open soon. The factory is bound to cause inequalities, since a percentage of the local population will now work for competitive wages, and two of the community members have been recruited as factory managers, and will earn a large salary (D2). According to the egalitarian theory, the factory's opening can only be justified if the worst-off in the village are better-off under D2 than under D1. The worst-off villagers under D2 are those villagers who have not been employed by the factory and who continue to survive on a subsistence basis. However, the factory owners have also pledged to build and sponsor a school in the village, since this will help to ensure that the future labour pool is sufficiently educated and will also bolster the image of the company. Most of the unemployed villagers are young families with children. As a result of factory's opening, these parents no longer have to worry about money for education or for transporting their children to a school in a faraway village. In other words, the economic inequalities caused by the factory are offset by the compensating benefits that villagers can now enjoy as a result of the factory's operations. These benefits are also to the advantage of the worst-off members of society, and for this reason, the factory's presence is morally-justifiable from an egalitarian viewpoint.

Note that Rawls's principles do not prescribe to us what a just society would look like in substantive terms. Rather, the principles should be viewed as norms for deciding on societal resource allocations and evaluating existing divisions of resources. Furthermore, Rawls (1994: 78) argues that the **first principle holds priority** over the second principle. Greater social and economic advantage cannot serve as justification for moral inequalities. Hence, Rawls (1994: 78) adds this proviso to his egalitarian theory of justice:

> Rawls's principles should be viewed as norms for deciding on societal resource allocations and evaluating existing divisions of resources.

> The distribution of wealth and income, and the hierarchies of authority, must be consistent with both the liberties of equal citizenship and equality of opportunity.

> Egalitarians are critical of policies that promote economic growth at the expense of the poor, such as providing tax breaks for businesses and wealthy individuals. Although proponents argue that the poor will indirectly benefit from policies aimed at stimulating economic growth, opponents argue that such policies only increase socio-economic inequality under the guise of benefiting the poor. The current global levels of poverty and inequality certainly attest to the fact that economic policies and programmes have not always been developed in line with Rawls's difference principle.

The libertarian theory of justice

The American Philosopher, Robert Nozick's book entitled *Anarchy, State, and Utopia* (1974) is both a response to Rawls's *A Theory of Justice* and the most well-known expression of libertarianism to date. Although Nozick agrees with Rawls that a utilitarian theory of justice is indefensible on the ground that it denies our basic rights, he is also critical of Rawls's egalitarian theory of justice, specifically his difference principle. This principle demands an evaluation of economic inequalities and in some cases may even lead to state-sanctioned redistribution policies, which according to Nozick, results in an infringement of our individual rights. In the preface to *Anarchy, State, and Utopia,* Nozick (1974: ix) writes that:

> Individuals have rights, and there are things no person or group may do to them (without violating their rights). So strong and far-reaching are these rights that they raise the question of what, if anything, the state and its officials may do. How much room do individual rights leave for the state?

> **Libertarians support a philosophy of personal freedom, in which individuals can exercise their own choices on the condition that they also do not interfere with other people's freedom.**

Nozick's answer to the above question is 'Not much!' For libertarians, freedom or **liberty** is the highest value and justice should be conceived of in terms of a certain ideal of liberty, namely the ideal of letting people live as they wish, without any interference. Libertarians thus support a philosophy of personal freedom, in which individuals can exercise their own choices on the condition that they also do not interfere with other people's freedom. As regards the state, libertarians argue for minimal state interference, and thus prefer a **night-watchman state** whose functions are limited to **enforcing contracts** and **protecting citizens** from arbitrary infringements of their freedoms through theft, violence, or fraud. State interference would definitely not extend to deciding on a just allocation of benefits and burdens as presupposed by Rawls's difference principle. In fact, Nozick (1974:82) explicitly states that '[t]he minimal state is the most extensive state that can be justified. Any state more extensive violates people's rights.'

This argument however raises questions regarding the basis for resource allocation in society. For Nozick, this resource allocation must be the outcome of a **voluntary exchange**:

> In a free society, diverse persons control different resources, and new holdings arise out of the voluntary exchange and actions of persons. There is no more a distributing or distribution of shares than there is a distributing of mates in a society in which persons choose whom they shall marry. The total result is the product of many individual decisions which the different individuals involved are entitled to make (1974:149-150).

Nozick follows **Locke** in arguing that each person possesses **natural, negative rights**. A natural right is a right that we posses independently from any social or political institutions, whereas a negative right obliges inaction or non-interference. Locke identifies **life, liberty and property** as our three fundamental natural rights, with which no one may interfere. Nozick draws specifically on Locke's view of our natural right to property, in order to defend his entitlement theory of economic justice. According to this theory, you are entitled to your belonging (i.e. your private property), as long as you acquired it **without violating anyone's moral rights**. Once you have legitimately acquired your belongings, you are entitled to do with them whatever you wish, and you are furthermore under no obligation to help the less fortunate.

According to Nozick, there are two ways in which property can be legitimately acquired: firstly, through the **original acquisition** of property; and secondly, through the **valid transfer** of property. Regarding the original acquisition of property, Nozick writes that property is justly acquired if you claim something that belongs to no one else, or if you create something new through your own labour in a manner that does not infringe on anyone else's rights. Here, Nozick again draws on Locke's view of our natural right to property, arguing that anyone is entitled to a thing whose value he has created through labour. However, Nozick does not subject his view of property rights to the conditions or provisos laid down by Locke, namely that we should not squander that which we acquire, and that we should leave enough and as good for others, as these provisos run contrary to the workings of the market system, in which each person should ultimately be free to pursue their own ends without restraint. Regarding the transfer of property, Nozick writes that property acquired through sales, gifting, exchange, or inheritance is deemed a valid transfer, whereas property acquired through theft, force, or fraud constitutes an invalid transfer. Having laid down the conditions for the legitimate acquisition of property, Nozick (1974:151) concludes that:

> If the world were wholly just, the following inductive definition would exhaustively cover the subject of justice in holdings.
> 1. A person who acquires a holding in accordance with the principle of justice in acquisition is entitled to that holding.
> 2. A person who acquires a holding in accordance with the principle of justice in transfer, from someone else entitled to the holding, is entitled to the holding.
> 3. No one is entitled to a holding except by (repeated) applications of 1 and 2.

It should be clear from the above exposition of Nozick's entitlement theory that distributive justice does not extend beyond articulating the conditions for a just acquisition of property to include an assessment of the consequences that arise from actual resource holding patterns. In order to explain why a respect for liberty cannot translate into a more far-reaching

> Nozick's view of distributive justice does not extend beyond articulating the conditions for the just acquisition of property.

theory of distributive justice, Nozick draws on an example featuring **Wilt Chamberlain**. Chamberlain, who played basketball during the 1960's, is described by the NBA as 'basketball's unstoppable force, the most awesome force the game has ever seen.' Nozick asks us to imagine two distributions, namely a distribution based on a non-entitlement theory (D1) and a distribution based on the entitlement theory (D2). Imagine that under D2, spectators are asked to drop 25 cents into a special box marked with Chamberlain's name. Since fans are eager to watch Chamberlain play, they freely oblige and willingly give the 25 cents directly to Chamberlain. If over the course of the basketball season, a million spectators come to watch Chamberlain play, he will receive $250 000 dollars more than the other players. In other words, D2 upsets the initial distribution pattern D1. However, Nozick believes that this is completely justifiable, since the spectators are entitled to spend their money as they see fit, and they freely chose to give a percentage of this money (i.e. 25 cents directly to Chamberlain). Thus, the distribution of resources between the players – although not equal – is perfectly just, according to the entitlement theory. Yet, Nozick pushes the case even further, arguing that imposing a distributional arrangement such as D1 'forbid(s) capitalistic acts between consenting adults' (1974:163), thus interfering with people's liberty. Nozick (1974:163) explains as follows:

> The general point illustrated by the Wilt Chamberlain example... is that no end-state principle or distributional patterned principle of justice can be continuously realized without continuous interference with people's lives... To maintain a pattern one must either continually interfere to stop people from transferring resources as they wish to, or continually (or periodically) interfere to take from some persons resources that others for some reason chose to transfer to them.

Although Nozick makes a compelling argument, he has been criticised for misunderstanding and over-emphasising property rights as something which precedes all social relationships, and therefore as something that we cannot regulate or manage through law. Non-libertarians argue that property is a function or consequence of social and economic arrangements within society, and should therefore also be subject to social and moral critique.

> Since libertarians are against any form of market regulation, they would oppose all forms of taxation, since compulsory taxes violate our right to our justly acquired capital. Libertarians would thus also find the recent governmental bailouts in the banking industry completely unjustifiable.

Conclusion

An overview of the key features, the evolution, the strengths and weaknesses, and the future challenges of capitalism were presented in this chapter. It was further argued that capitalism inevitably gives rise to question concerning distributive justice, which pertains to the allocation and distribution of society's benefits and burdens. The exposition on influential but contesting theories of distributive justice certainly helps us to better formulate and systematise our own views on the matter, and also draws attention to the difficulties inherent in deciding which principles should inform our understanding of distributive justice. Whilst those who benefit from the current capitalistic system might be more drawn towards an entitlement theory of justice; those who are keenly aware of, or directly experience, the socio-economic inequalities that arise from the current day market system, may be more drawn towards an egalitarian or even a utilitarian theory of justice. At any rate, the myriad socio-economic problems that define today's world, necessitates that we continue to ask critical and challenging questions regarding the future of capitalism, and the appropriate means for thinking about distributive justice.

Questions for discussion

1. Provide a justification of capitalism at the hand of Adam Smith.
2. Provide a critique of capitalism at the hand of Karl Marx.
3. Critically assess the relation between capitalism and distributive justice.
4. Is the distribution of benefits and burdens in South Africa just? Motivate your answer.
5. Is the distribution of benefits and burden in the world just? Motivate your answer.
6. What does the concept 'justice' entail?
7. Are fossil fuels a public resource? In other words, should government regulate the use and ownership of fossil fuels or do the fossil fuels belong to those who own the land in which they are found?
   - How would Mill respond to the above question?
   - How would Nozick respond to the above question?
   - How would Rawls respond to the above question?

Bibliography

Aristotle. 1925. 'Nicomachean ethics'. In *The works of Aristotle translated into English*, vol. 9, trans W.D. Ross. Oxford: Oxford University Press.

CIA World Factbooks (2003 -2011) [Online]. Available: <https://www.cia.gov/library/publications/the-world-factbook/> [Accessed 29 February 2012].

Comte-Sponville, A. 1996. *A short treatise on the great virtues: the uses of philosophy in everyday life*. London: Metropolitan Books.

ExxonMobil 2010 Summary Annual Report [Online]. Available < http://www.exxonmobil.com/Corporate/Files/news_pubs_sar_2010.pdf. [Accessed 16 February 2012].

International Monetary Fund (IMF), World Economic Outlook Database [Online]. Available from: < http://www.imf.org/external/pubs/ft/weo/2011/02/weodata/index.aspx. [Accessed 16 February 2012].

Investopedia [Online]. 'International poverty line'. Available: < http://www.investopedia.com/terms/i/international-poverty-line.asp#axzz1nlURASzx> [Accessed 29 February 2012].

Manuel, T. 2010. 2010 *Development indicators report* [Online], The Presidency, Republic of South Africa. Available: <http://www.info.gov.za/view/DownloadFileAction?id=137217> [Accessed 16 February 2012].

Masaka, D. 2011. 'Zimbabwe's land contestations and her politico-economic crises: a philosophical dialogue'. *Journal of Sustainable Development in Africa*, 13(1): 331 – 347.

Marx, K. 2008. 'Alienated labour'. In Donaldson, T. and Werhane, P.H. (eds.). *Ethical issues in business*, 163 – 167. New Jersey: Pearson Education.

Mill, J.S. 1965. *Mill's ethical writings*. New York: Collier.

Mitchell, D. 2004. *Cloud atlas*. New York: Random House.

NBA.com: Wilt Chamberlain summary [Online]. Available: <http://www.nba.com/history/players/chamberlain_summary.html> [Accessed 16 February 2012].

Nozick, R. 1974. *Anarchy, state, and utopia*. New York: Basic Books.Ravallion, M., Chen, S. and Sangraula, P. 2009. 'Dollar a day'. *The World Bank Economic Review*, 23(2): 163 – 184

Royal Dutch Shell Annual Report 2010 [Online]. Available: <http://www-static.shell.com/static/investor/downloads/financial_information/reports/2010/shell_2010_annual_report_20f_03.pdf> [Accessed 16 February 2012].

Schuman, M. 2012. 'How to save capitalism'. *TIME*, January 30, 2012: 30 – 39.

Sevic, Z. 2005. 'Corporate governance models: international legal perspectives'. In Demirag, I. (ed.). *Corporate social responsibility, accountability and governance*, 248 – 260. Sheffield: Greenleaf Publishing.

Shaw, W.H. 2011. *Business ethics* (International Edition). Boston, MA: Wadsworth, Cengage Learning.

Rawls, J. 1994 'Justice as fairness'. In Daly, M. (ed.). *Communitarianism: a new public ethics*, 71-78. Belmont, California: Wadsworth.

Smith, A. 2008. 'Benefits of the profit motive'. In Donaldson, T. and Werhane, P.H. (eds.). *Ethical issues in business*, 167 – 172. New Jersey: Pearson Education.

Smith, A. 2005. *The wealth of nations*. New York: Modern Library.

Walmart 2011 Annual Report [Online]. Available: < http://walmartstores.com/sites/annualreport/2011/financials/Walmart_2011_Annual_Report.pdf> [Accessed 16 February 2012].

West, A. 2006. 'Theorising South Africa's coporate governance'. *Journal of Business Ethics*, 68: 433 – 448.

Wolverson, R. 2012. 'The TIME at Davos debate: Is capitalism working in the 21st century?'. *TIME Business*, January 25, 2012 [Online]. Available:< http://business.

time.com/2012/01/25/the-time-at-davos-debate-analyses-capitalism-and-corporations/> [Accessed 16 February 2012].

World Institute for Development Economics Research of the United Nations University [Online]. 2006. 'The world distribution of household wealth'. Available: <http://www.mindfully.org/WTO/2006/Household-Wealth-Gap5dec06.htm> [Accessed 16 February 2012]

8

The modern corporation and its moral obligations

Deon Rossouw

Outcomes

After working through this chapter, you should be able to do the following:
- Explain why the moral status and obligations of corporations have become prominent
- Provide arguments for and against corporate social responsibility
- Articulate what corporate moral agency entails
- Discuss different strands of stakeholder theory.

Overview

Modern corporations exert substantial influence on the societies in which they operate. This fact has given rise to theoretical reflections on the moral obligations of the modern corporation. In this chapter, a number of influential contributions to this debate will be explored. We will start with the contribution by Milton Friedman, who argued that corporations have no social responsibilities other than making profit for their shareholders and obeying the law. Two reactions to Friedman's position will then be discussed. One is Christopher Stone's view, which rejects Friedman's position, while also making a strong case for corporations to take responsibility for their impact on society. The other reaction is that of Peter French, who argues that not only individuals but also corporations should be regarded as moral agents with moral obligations. Finally, Edward Freeman's notion of stakeholder theory will be introduced. He asserts that corporations have moral obligations not only towards their shareholders, but also towards a wide range of other stakeholders. Kenneth Goodpaster's view that a distinction needs to be drawn between a corporation's obligations towards stakeholders and shareholders respectively will be discussed as a critique of Freeman's version of stakeholder theory.

Introduction

Since the emergence of multi-national corporations, we are no longer surprised when we find that the annual budgets of some of the larger multi-national companies exceed those of a considerable number of national economies. But with size comes power and influence. Modern corporations exert a significant influence on society. The *King Report on Corporate Governance for South Africa II* reminds us that 'in many respects companies have become a more immediate presence to many citizens and modern democracies than either governments or organs of civil society' (IoD, 2002:8).

The power and influence that modern corporations yield in society inevitably also introduces the issue of the responsibilities of modern corporations. Their impact on society, culture, and the environment has raised many concerns in recent years. This has resulted in many critics rethinking the role and responsibilities of the modern corporation. In this process, many questions have been raised:

- Do corporations have a social responsibility towards society or do they only have a responsibility to make a profit?
- Should corporations be regarded as moral **agents** with moral obligations?
- For whose benefit should corporations be managed?

In attempting to answer these questions, a number of theories on the modern corporation and its moral obligations have emerged over the last few decades.

These theories of the modern corporation are of special significance for accountants and auditors, who work within and often run or direct modern corporations. They therefore need to understand the role and obligations of the corporations that they manage or direct. In their role as management consultants, they also need to have a profound understanding of the modern corporation in order to provide sound advice to their clients. The move from single to **triple bottom-line reporting** provides a further reason for accountants, auditors, and **management consultants** to have a proper understanding of the modern corporation and what it is society expects from the modern corporation.

Triple bottom-line reporting developed in the wake of the considerable power that modern corporations exert over both society and the environment. A need developed for companies to be held accountable not only for their financial (or single) bottom-line performance, but to start accounting additionally for their social and environmental performance, together with financial performance (triple bottom-line). Accountants, because of their experience in financial accounting, were called upon to take the lead in social and environmental accounting. But with accounting comes auditing, and therefore auditors were called upon to audit social and environmental accounts. Furthermore, consultants with an accounting and auditing background were expected to advise their clients on how to go about preparing and disclosing social, environmental, and sustainability reports.

In order to make sense of these new types of accounting, auditing, and reporting, professionals in the accounting and auditing profession need to understand the intellectual context that gave rise to these new phenomena. The theories of the modern corporation and its moral obligations provide exactly that intellectual context.

In this chapter, we will take a look at some of the more influential theories on the modern corporation and its moral obligations. We will first look at the **social responsibility** of corporations. Then we will move on to the question of whether corporations could be regarded as **moral agents**. Finally, we will look at different versions of **stakeholder theory**.

> Do corporations have moral responsibilities only towards their shareholders, or do they also have responsibilities towards the societies within which they operate?

Corporate social responsibility

Do corporations have moral responsibilities only towards their shareholders, or do they also have responsibilities towards the societies within which they operate? This question became prominent in 1970 with the publication of an article in the *New York Times Magazine* by Nobel Prize winning economist, Milton Friedman.

Milton Friedman

> In his famous article 'The Social Responsibility of Business is to Increase its Profits', Milton Friedman (1993) denied that business has any social responsibilities other than making profits for its shareholders. He reacted strongly and negatively to frequent references to corporate social responsibility which business executives were making at the time. He regarded such talk as short-sighted and foolish, and accused business executives who talk about corporate social responsibility of 'preaching pure and unadulterated socialism' (Friedman, 1993:162).

Friedman believes that the path to clearing up this unfortunate confusion lies in getting clarity on exactly what occurs when business executives engage in acts of social responsibility on behalf of corporations. Business executives are employees of the owners of corporations. In this capacity, they are appointed to serve the interests of their employers, which amounts to 'mak[ing] as much money as possible while conforming to the basic rules of society' (Friedman, 1993:162).

When business executives engage in acts of corporate social responsibility, they act outside their mandate and competence. They have no right, nor any responsibility to do so. As individuals, they have moral responsibilities, some of which may extend to society, but these moral or social responsibilities need to be exercised in their personal and private capacity. They can devote their own time, energy, and resources to moral causes of their choice, but the same is not true of the corporation's time, energy, and resources. Corporations, Friedman believes, are not moral agents in the way that individuals are, and therefore they do not have corporate moral obligations. When business executives spend corporate resources on acts of social responsibility, they are actually stealing company resources to spend on illegitimate objectives.

Apart from the fact of diverting money away from shareholders, employees, and customers, business executives also engage in a political process of taxation for which they are ill equipped. In spending corporate funds on social responsibility, business executives are effectively imposing taxes on the shareholders and other stakeholders of the business who might have benefited from the spent money. Furthermore, in spending this money on what they regard as socially-desirable causes, they also effectively decide how these taxes should be allocated. Both the acts of imposing and allocating tax, Friedman believes, are political processes.

Friedman concedes that when certain conditions are met, corporate social spending can be justified. The first situation arises when the individual proprietor decides to spend money on social responsibility. In that case, the proprietor is merely spending money that belongs to him (as opposed to belonging to the corporation) as he wishes. The second case in which it is legitimate to spend corporate money on social responsibility arises when the corporation stands to profit from such expenditure. This is the case, for example, when a company spends money on education in a local community in order to improve the skills levels of its own employees or to upskill members of the community with the intent of their becoming prospective employees for the company. In this case, the company is not engaging in social responsibility, but is merely acting in its own best interests. This is true even though the company may stand to benefit from its actions (upskilling, in this case) only some time down the line.

> Friedman regards talk about corporate social responsibility by business executives as short-sighted and dangerous, unless it is done exclusively in the interests of the corporation.

In summary, Friedman regards talk about corporate social responsibility by business executives as short-sighted and dangerous, unless it is done exclusively in the interests of the corporation. Friedman's stance on corporate social responsibility evoked strong reactions.

Remaining on the topic of corporate social responsibility, we will turn to one of Friedman's critics, Christopher Stone, who directly opposed Friedman's view.

Christopher Stone

> In his book *The Social Control of Corporate Behavior* (1975), Christopher Stone rejects two claims that are central to Friedman's argument. The first is Friedman's claim that managers have a moral responsibility only to make profits for their shareholders. The second is Friedman's claim that corporations have no moral obligation to society other than obeying the laws of society. Stone's reaction to and rejection of these two claims will now be discussed.

Managers' obligation towards shareholders

Stone refutes on two grounds Friedman's view that managers have an obligation to maximise profits only for shareholders. Firstly, he denies that managers have made an implicit promise to shareholders to maximise their profits. He calls this the *Promissory Argument*. Stone denies that there is such a promissory relationship between managers and shareholders. Such a relationship may exist, for example, between an investor and a broker. But it does not exist between managers and shareholders. Most shareholders never meet the managers of the corporations in which they invest. Consequently, no promises are ever made by management to the shareholders. On the contrary, most shareholders acquire their shares in corporations by buying them from other shareholders, who, in turn, have bought these shares from previous owners of these shares. Stone therefore concludes that 'the manager of the corporation, unlike the broker, was never even offered a chance to refuse the shareholder's "terms" (if they were that) to maximise the shareholder's profits' (1992:439).

Stone denies that managers have made an implicit promise to shareholders to maximise their profits.

Secondly, Stone refutes what he calls Friedman's *Agency Argument*. This argument states that managers act as agents of shareholders. In that capacity, managers have an obligation to look after the interests of their principals, who are the shareholders. Stone rejects this argument, because it is both *de jure* (legally) and *de facto* (factually) wrong. It is legally wrong because courts do not recognise managers as the agents of shareholders. It is also factually wrong, because if it were the case, then one would have expected managers to have determined actively the express wishes of shareholders and to act in accordance with their wishes. This, in Stone's view, is seldom, if ever, the case. Or, to put it in his words, 'it is embarrassingly at odds with the way in which supposed "agents" actually behave' (Stone, 1992:440). Stone denies through these and other arguments that managers have obligations only towards shareholders. Instead, he believes that they have moral obligations towards all stakeholders of the corporation.

> Stone refutes what he calls Friedman's *'Agency Argument'*. This argument states that managers act as agents of shareholders.

Corporations and the law

Stone also rejects Friedman's claim that it is sufficient for a corporation merely to obey the laws of society. He insists that in addition to obeying the law, managers have a further obligation to act with moral responsibility towards society. He raises a number of arguments to substantiate his view. His primary argument in this respect is that a mere reliance on what the law stipulates can lead to grossly irresponsible corporate behaviour. The law, according to Stone, is always reactive. Laws are made only after a certain amount of damage has been done and been proved to be harmful. Only then does the lawgiver lay down laws and regulations to prevent further similar damage from occurring. Should a corporation have a responsibility only to remain within the boundaries of the law, it would be acceptable for them to carry on with harmful and irresponsible behaviour until a law has been passed that prevents them from doing so. Such an attitude would foster and protect irresponsibility by corporations. This is clear when Stone (1992:444) says: 'There is something grotesque – and socially dangerous – in encouraging corporate managers to believe that, until the law tells them otherwise, they have no responsibilities beyond the law.'

Consequently, Stone believes that managers do not merely have a responsibility to increase profits for their shareholders. He also asserts that simply obeying the law is insufficient: adherence to the law needs to be complemented by self-initiated corporate social responsibility.

> The law, according to Stone, is always reactive. Laws are made only after a certain amount of damage has been done and been proved to be harmful.

Corporate moral agency

The claim that corporations are legal persons is not in dispute. As legal persons, corporations have specific legal rights and liabilities. However, it is not clear whether corporations should also be regarded as moral agents who have moral responsibilities in addition to their legal obligations.

In Milton Friedman's article discussed above, he denies that corporations could or should be regarded as moral agents. He argues that only individual biological persons are moral agents with moral responsibilities. In contrast, corporations are not biological persons, but mere artificial legal entities who cannot and should not be burdened with moral responsibilities. Only the individuals who work within corporations are moral agents. It is their inalienable right to exercise their moral agency, but then only in their personal capacity and not in the name of the corporations for which they work. Friedman's view in this respect was challenged and rejected by Peter French.

Peter French

> French agrees with Friedman that corporations are artificial legal persons, but disagrees that this disqualifies them from being moral persons as well. His argument for the moral agent status of corporations is based on his understanding of what the concept of 'moral responsibility' implies.

He analyses the concept of 'moral responsibility' and comes to the conclusion that there are two criteria for moral responsibility:
1. An agent must be linked to a specific event.
2. The event (or action) must be intended by an agent.

Whenever this relationship between an event and the intentions of an actor can be established, the notion of 'moral responsibility' can be applied. In other words, the actor can then be held responsible for the event.

The crucial question now is whether corporations can in any meaningful sense be portrayed as having intentions that result in events (or actions). We cannot deny that corporations have an impact on society and consequently we cannot deny that events emanate from corporations. The issue, however, is whether such events can be ascribed only to individuals in the corporation, or whether they can be ascribed to the organisation as a whole. Peter French believed that corporations can be viewed as having corporate intentions and that their actions can therefore be ascribed to the corporation as a whole. There is a specific mechanism at work within corporations that ensures that corporate actions can be linked to corporate intentions. This mechanism is the **corporate internal decision (CID)** structure.

> There is a specific mechanism at work within corporations that ensures that corporate actions can be linked to corporate intentions. This mechanism is the corporate internal decision (CID) structure.

The CID structure

The CID structure of a corporation consists of two distinct elements. First, there is the organisational flow chart (or organogram) which ascribes specific roles, levels, and responsibilities to the various members of the corporation. Second, there are corporate decision-making rules or policies that determine which decisions are taken and how they are taken within the corporation. These rules on decision-making are intimately linked to the purpose and business objectives of the organisation. The rules and policies ensure that decisions are taken in a manner that will assist the corporation to reach its corporate goals.

When the board of directors of a corporation makes decisions on behalf of the corporation, they normally rely on input from various individuals in the organisation. The board is typically presented with a variety of specialist reports from various sections or departments in the company. Based on the information provided to them and also on their vision for the company, its objectives, and priorities, the board will ultimately come to a decision. This decision is not a subjective choice, but, as indicated, is a corporate act in which many individuals will have participated and which was guided by corporate and not subjective objectives. French (1993:233) says in this regard:

> 'Simply, when the corporate act is consistent with an instantiation or an implementation of established corporate policy, then it is proper to describe it as having been done for corporate reasons, as having been caused by a corporate desire coupled with a corporate belief and so, in other words, as corporate-intentional.'

The CID structure of a corporation therefore transforms decisions made on behalf of the corporation into corporate actions. They cannot be described as mere individual actions. They qualify as corporate actions, because are been intended by the corporation to further or defend its interests and objectives. As these corporate acts carry the weight of intention of the corporation, the corporation becomes responsible for its actions and, therefore, accountable to those affected by its actions. Given French's earlier definition of moral responsibility, it is clear why he regards corporations as moral agents with moral responsibilities in their own right.

Stakeholder theory

Another of Milton Friedman's convictions was challenged when stakeholder theory emerged. This time it was his conviction that corporations exist for the sake of their shareholders and should therefore be run in ways that serve their interests. As agents of shareholders, management should maximise the return on investment for shareholders. This approach is called the **shareholder dominant theory**. It is precisely this conviction that became the target of stakeholder theory, which challenges the belief that corporations should be managed for the benefit of shareholders. The name of Edward Freeman is associated with the emergence of the

> As agents of shareholders, management should maximise the return on investment for shareholders. This approach is called the shareholder dominant theory.

stakeholder theory of corporations. In a number of contributions, which he co-authored with various colleagues, he explored what the backbone of a stakeholder theory of corporations might resemble.

Edward Freeman

In an article co-authored by William Evan, Freeman challenges shareholder dominant theory and critically reviews the question: 'For whose benefit and whose expenses should the corporation be managed?' (Evan and Freeman, 1993:76). They rejected the then conventional answer to the question, which stated that the corporation should be managed for the benefit and cost of the shareholders. This rejection is based on both a legal and an economic argument.

The legal argument

> The legal argument for rejecting the idea that a corporation should be managed solely for the benefit of shareholders is based upon recent legal developments. Evan and Freeman (1993:76) refer to a substantial number of court cases which found that corporations have duties towards stakeholders other than shareholders. In this regard they say: 'The law has evolved to effectively constrain the pursuit of stockholder interest at the expense of other claimants on the firm.'

They refer specifically to legislation and court findings that gave certain rights to employees. Corporate managers have to respect these employee rights, and the pursuit of shareholder interest therefore has to be balanced with the interests of employees. This applies to the interests of both individual employees as well as employees collectively. Employees, for example, have legally-protected rights to bargain collectively. The right to collective bargaining is one such right that management has to respect.

Similar arguments are also made with regard to suppliers, customers, and local communities. Recent laws and court findings acknowledged the legitimate interests of these stakeholder groups and granted them legal protection. This further emphasises the point that recent legal developments effectively constrain managers from pursuing the interests of shareholders at the expense of other groups of stakeholders.

The economic argument

The classic justification of free market capitalism is that in pursuing the interests of shareholders, the greatest good of the greatest number of people will automatically be served. This is often referred to as the 'invisible hand' doctrine. The reality of the modern corporation and its impact on society has undermined the credibility of this doctrine. Evans and Freeman (1993:77–78) point out that this doctrine has lost its credibility because 'since the industrial revolution, firms have sought to internalise the benefits and externalise the costs of their actions'.

By 'externalities' they refer to the side-effects caused by corporate actions. In pursuing their goals, corporations often pollute the environment or disrupt communities. The market mechanism does not automatically correct these negative consequences of corporate activity. For this reason, corporations have to be regulated to ensure that the cost of corporate activity is not shouldered only by taxpayers, and to prevent corporations from imposing extravagant costs on societies. The regulations that have consequently been imposed on corporations owing to the market mechanism's failure to deal with externalities provide further ground for the conviction that corporations are indeed constrained and cannot pursue only shareholder interests.

Based on the legal argument, Evan and Freeman conclude that different stakeholders of the corporations have rights that must be respected by the management of the modern corporation. On the basis of the economic argument, they further conclude that corporations are responsible to various stakeholders for the consequences of their corporate actions.

> The classic justification of free market capitalism is that in pursuing the interests of shareholders, the greatest good of the greatest number of people will automatically be served. This is often referred to as the 'invisible hand' doctrine.

The stakeholder corporation

A further stimulus for stakeholder theory was found in Immanuel Kant's ethics of respect for persons, which states that no person should be treated as a means to an end, but that all persons should be respected as ends in their own right. Based on this principle, Evan and Freeman argue that corporations and their managers may not violate the rights of others in their pursuit of corporate objectives. Violating the rights of stakeholders in the pursuit of shareholder value is immoral and unacceptable. Corporations, they argue, thus have a moral obligation to respect the rights of both shareholders and all their other stakeholders. This is clear from the 'Principle of Corporate Legitimacy' that they formulated:

> 'The corporation should be managed for the benefit of its stakeholders: its customers, suppliers, employees, and local communities. The rights of these groups must be ensured, and, further, the groups must participate, in some sense, in decisions that substantially affect their welfare.' (Evan and Freeman, 1993:82)

Within this version of stakeholder theory, stakeholders are defined as 'those groups who are vital to the survival and success of the corporation' (Evan and Freeman, 1993:79). Various groups would qualify as stakeholders in terms of this definition, but typically shareholders, employees, suppliers, customers, local communities, and managers would be included in its scope. This network of stakeholders is demonstrated in the figure below.

Figure 8.1 The network of stakeholders as defined in Evan and Freeman's stakeholder theory

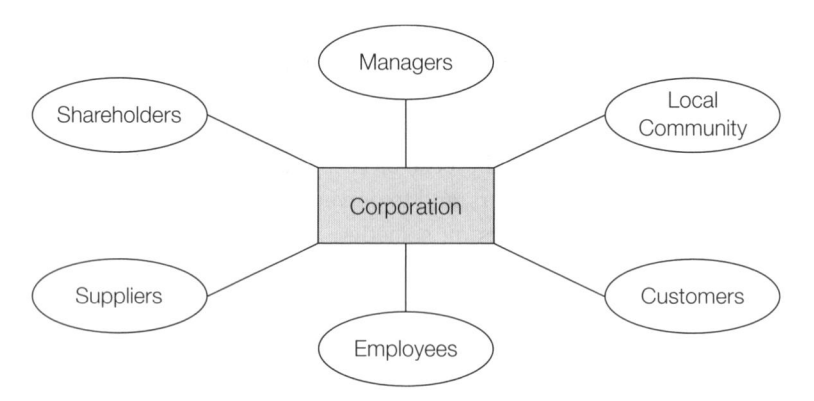

Shareholders have a stake in the corporation because they invest their money in the corporation. Consequently, they expect to earn a return on their investment. Employees invest their knowledge, creativity, and energy in the corporation. Without this investment, the corporation cannot survive. Suppliers provide the company with the raw material that will ultimately influence the quality and price of the company's products or services. They are therefore vital to the survival and success of the company. Customers provide the lifeblood of the company as they provide the income needed to keep the company afloat. In return for what they pay, they expect quality products and good service. Local communities provide corporations with the basic infrastructure and human and natural resources required to run a successful business operation. In return, corporations contribute to the tax base and economies of the communities in which they operate. To maintain this mutually-beneficial relationship, managers of corporations need to respect local communities and act as responsible corporate citizens.

> In the version of stakeholder theory by Evan and Freeman, all stakeholders are treated as equal. No single group's interests are given primacy over those of other groups.

Managers, of course, are also stakeholders of the organisations. They share similar expectations to other employees of the firm, in the sense that they also need to be duly compensated for their contribution to the survival and success of the company.

In the above version of stakeholder theory by Evan and Freeman, all stakeholders are treated as equal. No single group's interests are given priority over those of other groups. This obviously has dramatic implications for how companies are to be run. Among others, it implies that boards of directors need to be constituted in a way that will present the interests of all major stakeholder groups. Opinions among supporters of stakeholder theory are divided on exactly this point regarding equality of all stakeholders. A prime example of someone who subscribes to stakeholder theory without holding that the claims of all stakeholder groups should be treated as equal is Kenneth Goodpaster.

Kenneth Goodpaster

> In an article entitled 'Business Ethics and Stakeholder Analysis', Kenneth Goodpaster takes issue with the Freeman version of stakeholder theory. He believes that stakeholder theory along the lines suggested by Freeman can be detrimental to both business and society.

He describes Freeman's stakeholder theory as a multi-fiduciary stakeholder concept. In this concept, managers of corporations have a fiduciary relationship towards all stakeholders of the corporation. Such a situation, Goodpaster believes, can become intolerable, as the demands of various stakeholder groups can be contradictory and irreconcilable. In fact, it can undermine the very nature of corporations as privately-owned entities with a very specific economic mission. If managers were to accede equally to the claims of all stakeholders, corporations could be turned into public institutions that were no longer geared towards economic value creation for shareholders. This could effectively undermine the freedom and enterprise associated with private corporations. On this score, Goodpaster agrees with Milton Friedman that corporations and specifically their managers have a special duty towards shareholders. As the agents of shareholders, managers have a fiduciary obligation towards shareholders to maximise profits.

This fiduciary obligation by managers towards shareholders does not have to result in a situation where the interests of all other stakeholders are sacrificed for the sake of shareholder interests. Goodpaster contends that apart from the special fiduciary relationship of managers to shareholders, they also have moral responsibilities towards all other stakeholders of the corporation. These moral obligations can never be overridden in the name of shareholder interests. Within the framework of fiduciary obligations to shareholders, managers should find ways to respect their moral obligations to all other stakeholders of the corporation. In this way, corporations can accord due consideration to their moral obligations to all stakeholders without sacrificing the private economic mission of corporations.

> Goodpaster agrees with Milton Friedman that corporations and specifically their managers have a special duty towards shareholders.

Conclusion

The theories discussed in this chapter represent a very clear shift that has occurred over the last decades. Corporations are now recognised as moral agents (or corporate citizens) with moral obligations towards society. Although shareholders still enjoy a privileged status in corporations, the interests of a range of other stakeholder groups have also gained prominence. These changes have not only altered the way in which corporations are perceived, but have also had profound consequences for the way in which corporations have to account for their economic, social, and environmental performance.

Questions for discussion

1. Why have the moral status and obligations of corporations become prominent in recent years?
2. On what grounds does Milton Friedman reject corporate social responsibility?
3. What are Christopher Stone's main objections to Milton Friedman's view of the corporation?
4. Can corporations be regarded as moral agents? Discuss Peter French's view on this question.
5. Who do Evan and Freeman include in their definition of stakeholders?
6. What is Kenneth Goodpaster's objection to Evan and Freeman's version of stakeholder theory?

Bibliography

Evan, W & Freeman, R. 1993. 'A stakeholder theory of the modern corporation: Kantian capitalism'. In Beauchamp, T & Bowie, N (eds.). *Ethical theory and business*, 4th ed. Upper Saddle River, NJ: Prentice Hall.

French, P. 1993. 'The corporation as moral person'. In White, TI (ed.). *Business ethics: a philosophical reader*. New York: Macmillan.

Friedman, M. 1993. 'The social responsibility of business is to increase its profits'. In Olen, J & Barry, V (eds). *Applying ethics*. Belmont, CA: Wadsworth.

Goodpaster, KE. 1993. 'Business ethics and stakeholder analysis'. In White, TI (ed). *Business ethics: a philosophical reader*. New York: Macmillan.

Institute of Directors (IoD). 2002. *Second King report on corporate governance for South Africa*. Johannesburg: Institute of Directors (IoD).

Stone, CD. 1975. *The social control of corporate behavior*. New York: Harper-Collins.

Stone, CD. 1992. 'The corporate social responsibility debate'. In Olen, J and Barry, V (eds). *Applying ethics*. Belmont, CA: Wadsworth.

9

Corporate governance

Jacques Siebrits and Frans Prinsloo

Outcomes

After working through this chapter, you should be able to do the following:
- Understand, and be able to explain, the benefits of sound corporate governance to a company's stakeholders, the company itself and the country.
- Understand, and be able to explain, the relationship between ethics and corporate governance.
- Be able to explain the agency problem in the modern corporation, and how a company's board of directors is supposed to exercise oversight over its management.
- Be able to discuss an alternative stakeholder model of corporate governance, and understand and explain how the King Committee guides this process in South Africa.
- Appreciate the importance of corporate governance disclosures in promoting sound governance.
- Understand the role that the accounting and auditing professions perform in the corporate governance process.

Overview

This chapter deals, as its title indicates, with the important topic of corporate governance, and consists of two parts. The first part provides an introduction to corporate governance theory, and the second part provides an introduction to the King Report on Governance 2009, commonly referred to as "King III". King III is the most important document offering governance guidance in the South African context. SAICA-accredited Accounting programmes typically include a more in-depth look at corporate governance as part of Auditing, but it is also addressed, at an introductory level, in this text because of the connections between ethics and corporate governance.

The importance of the connections between ethics and corporate governance is emphasised in the first chapter of King III, which is headed "Ethical Leadership And Corporate Citizenship". In paragraph 12 of that chapter, it is stated that "[e]thics (or integrity) is the foundation of, and reason for, corporate governance. The ethics of corporate governance requires the board to ensure that the company is run ethically." And in the next paragraph it is stated that "[c]orporate governance is, in essence, a company's practical expression of ethical standards. It follows that all the typical aspects of corporate governance (such as the role and responsibilities of the board of directors, internal audit, risk management, stakeholder relations, and so on) should rest on a foundation of ethical values." The chapter emphasises a principle-driven approach to governance, because it states that "all deliberations, decisions and actions of the board and executive management" should be based on four ethical values, being responsibility, accountability, fairness and transparency. It also lists five moral duties that directors should discharge, namely conscience, inclusivity of stakeholders, competence, commitment and courage.

A further link between corporate governance and ethics is that the board of directors is responsible for ethics management in the company. This is dealt with under Principle 1.3 (headed "The board should ensure that the company's ethics are managed effectively") in King III. Under this principle, an ethics management process that is similar to the one described in chapter 10 of this text is outlined.

Introduction

What does the term "corporate governance" mean? Lee introduces his attempt to define the term as follows: "[C]orporate governance appears to have as many meanings as it has users." Because so many definitions of the term have been proposed, a number of these proposals will be listed, followed by an attempt to flesh out and clarify the concept.

Five proposals:
- Tricker's relatively early (1988) definition: "If management is about running the business, governance is about seeing that it is run properly. All companies therefore need governing as well as managing."
- The definition in the King Report on Governance that was published in 1994 ("King I"): "The system by which companies are directed and controlled."
- Naidoo in *Corporate Governance*: "Corporate governance regulates the exercise of power (that is, authority, direction and control) within a company in order to ensure that the company's purpose is achieved (namely the creation of sustainable shareholder value, the *raison d'être* of most for profit companies)." Note that this explanation makes it sound like corporate governance is only relevant to for-profit companies, but that is not the case – it should also be applied in non-profit entities.

- Monks and Minow in *Corporate Governance* (5th edition): "In essence, corporate governance is the structure that is intended to (1) make sure that the right questions get asked and (2) that checks and balances are in place to make sure that the answers reflect what is best for the creation of long-term, sustainable, renewable value."
- King (of King Reports fame) in *The Corporate Citizen*: "Processes to help directors discharge and be seen to be discharging their responsibilities created by their duties."

To expand on the above definitions: corporate governance deals with the way in which the relationships between the board of directors of an entity, its senior managers and the stakeholders in the entity should be structured and managed to make it more likely that the senior managers will manage the company in the interest of the stakeholders, and not in their own interest. Per King III (in paragraph 6 of chapter 8) "stakeholders can be considered to be any group that can affect the company's operations, or be affected by it", and include "shareholders, institutional investors, creditors, lenders, suppliers, customers, regulators, employees, unions, the media, analysts, consumers, society in general, communities, auditors and potential investors."

It is important that a student who is studying towards becoming an accounting professional should have a good grasp of corporate governance principles, and understand the benefits of sound governance to stakeholders, the company as legal person, and the country. After completion of his/her studies, such a student most likely will work as an:
- External auditor. Per King III the external audit function is an important component of a company's overall governance structure. King III (in principle 3.5) emphasises that an entity's audit committee (an oversight committee consisting of independent directors, which is not to be confused with the company's internal audit function) should ensure that a "combined assurance concept" is applied to provide a coordinated approach to all assurance activities. In a nutshell, this means that the total assurance derived from the responses to risks by the entity's management, internal auditors and external auditors should be adequate, and that their efforts should be coordinated. The external auditor also should be able to assess a company's governance practices as part of the audit risk assessment.
- Accountant. The accountant should understand the importance of high-quality reporting to shareholders and other stakeholders, and how such reporting can contribute to sound corporate governance. He/she may also be involved in drafting the company's specific report on its governance practices.

Also, many students aspire to becoming a senior manager in a large company, in which case he/she will have to understand the role of the senior manager, and the relationship between senior management and the board of directors.

Why corporate governance is important

The post-mortems of many collapsed companies (and far too many companies have collapsed in the last three decades, or have come perilously close to collapse[1]) have shown that the companies were looted by unethical senior managers who were guided by self-interest. This longstanding problem, that managers act in their own interest, instead of serving the interests of shareholders and other stakeholders, is commonly referred to as the "agency problem" (for more on the agency problem, see "Why the increased focus on corporate governance since 1980?" below). The obvious question is why were those managers not kept in check by the companies' corporate governance structures, and more specifically the companies' boards of directors. In this chapter we shall look as this issue, and point out the importance of directors possessing a very high degree of integrity and commitment.

The importance of sound corporate governance to shareholders and other stakeholder groups

Sound governance should make a business less likely to fail, but it does not provide an absolute guarantee against failure. It should also make the company more sensitive and responsive to the diverse needs of its stakeholders.

Furthermore, while much of the information in a company's annual report is historic information, in the sense that the company reports on its performance over an elapsed time period, governance disclosures in such a report provide information that is, to a certain extent, forward-looking. This is the case because the future prospects of the well-governed company would typically be better than those of a badly-governed company. Most listed South African companies now include a comprehensive governance report in their annual reports. For example, the dedicated governance report section in Reunert Limited's first integrated report, for the year ended 30 September 2011, spanned five pages In addition, there was a two-page report by the company's risk committee, and a three-page report by its remuneration committee, making for a total of ten pages of governance-related reporting.

---

[1] International corporate failures or near-failures have included Enron, Lehman Brothers, Worldcom (all US companies), Dutch retailer Ahold, Dutch/Belgian financial services group Fortis and Italian dairy giant Parmalat. SA examples include Leisurenet, Saambou, The Business Bank, Fidentia, and Masterbond.

The importance of corporate governance to the company itself

Sound governance is not only of benefit to the shareholders and other stakeholders in a company; it also benefits the company itself when it wants to raise capital. An oft-quoted McKinsey survey, the results of which were published in 2000, showed that more than 80 per cent of global institutional investors surveyed were willing to pay a premium for the shares of a well-governed company as compared to the shares of badly governed one (on the assumption that the companies perform the same financially). This premium varies depending on the risk profile of the country in which the company operates, with a well-governed company that operates in a more risky country commanding a higher premium (up to more than 30 per cent) than a well-governed one that operates in a less risky country. But sound corporate governance does not only benefit the company when it issues shares; it also benefits the company when it needs loan financing (in the form of a lower interest rate), and makes a company more attractive to private equity investors.

The importance of corporate governance to a country

Naidoo (on p. 11) quotes Arthur Levitt, former chair of the US Securities Exchange Commission, who had the following to say in this regard: "Markets exist by the grace of investors… No market has a divine right to investors' capital… If a country does not have a reputation for strong corporate governance practices, capital will flow elsewhere…All enterprises in that country – regardless of how steadfast a particular company's practices may be – suffer the consequences." Fortunately, South Africa enjoys a good reputation in this regard. In the *Business Report* of 24 February 2012 it was reported (under the heading *SA loses top spot as corruption mars governance*) that "[South African] companies are perceived to have the best corporate governance practices among the 44 countries in the UBS's emerging markets study." It was noted that this very good governance rating contributed to South Africa being regarded as a safe haven for investment in 2011, but that perceptions of increasing corruption were threatening that safe haven status.

A brief history of corporate governance

According to King in *The Corporate Citizen*, governance-related problems and disputes have arisen since the first companies (two early examples being the Dutch East India Company and its British equivalent) were formed in the seventeenth century. In 1856 the modern company form was born when investors in UK companies gained the protection of limited liability, and over the next 150 or so years the importance of the company has grown to such an extent that many now regard it as the dominant institution of our time. But despite the growing importance of the company, corporate governance issues were only dealt with in legislation, and to a limited extent only. The question of how a company should be governed attracted little attention till the 1980s, with the first governance codes being drafted in the early 1990s – the United Kingdom's Cadbury Report and the South Africa's King I, both of which were released in 1992, being two of the earliest codes.

Corporate governance can now be described, without exaggeration, as a hot topic, and you are unlikely to open a financial periodical without finding a governance-related article. And the governance-related topic that gets the most coverage must be the remuneration of senior managers. This attracts much attention, because the remuneration packages of senior managers often increase even when the entity's profits decline, and entities' annual reports typically fail to provide understandable reasons for such increases. Also, many view senior managers' remuneration packages as obscene, particularly in the South African context of severe inequality, and argue that it (further) undermines social cohesion. The importance of this issue is reflected in the space devoted to it in King III – whereas the King Report on Governance 2002 ("King II") contained very little guidance in this regard, more than four pages in King III are devoted to this topic, much of it dealing with how share option schemes should be structured.

> In the Financial Mail of 22 July 2011[2] *inter alia* the following was reported in this regard (all figures relate to South Africa):
> - "R800 000/month is the ballpark top salary in SA, earned by a CEO of a top global company."
> - "R300 000 is what the CE of midsized company [sic] earns monthly."
> - "R1 000/month is the lowest wage level, the legal minimum for a domestic worker and a month-long public works job."
> - "54 times is the average by which a CEO's salary exceeds that of a general worker in a medium-sized firm."
> - "500:1 or more is the wage gap in big global firms in SA."
> - "500 000 people took home a quarter of all the income last year."
> - "R17 500 or more a month puts you in the top 5% of SA earners. That is what an entry-level teacher earns."
>
> Some other concerns that contributed to the focus on corporate governance over the last three decades were so-called "creative accounting" (a euphemism for fraudulent accounting), unexpected

---

2   *Earnings in numbers* by Carol Paton, on p. 26.

> business failures, the role of auditors, and an excessive focus by management on short-term profits, at the expense of longer-term profitability and sustainability.

Why the increased focus on corporate governance since 1980?

There are a two main reasons for this:

The first reason is that ownership and management of businesses are now separated, meaning that managers are not harming themselves or their families when they mismanage a business. Prior to the twentieth century, most businesses were owned and managed by members of the same family. But the "divorce" between ownership and management gained impetus as companies' appetite for capital increased exponentially after the Industrial Revolution, and required the owners to find more investors to help them feed that appetite. The main concern that arises because of the separation between ownership and management is that the managers will make self-serving decisions rather than decisions that are in the best interests of the business owners (and other stakeholders) – the agency problem that briefly was referred to above. But, as pointed out earlier, the agency problem is not a new one. What has changed is that many more people are affected by companies' (mis)fortunes than used to be the case.

For one thing, more people than ever before have stakes in companies, typically via retirement funds. Where in the past stock market investing was confined to the relatively wealthy, it has spread to most people in formal employment, many of whom are participating in stock markets without even being aware of doing so.

Furthermore, the immense size of many companies means that more people are affected by the failure of a single company. Probably the best example of a present-day business behemoth is retailer Walmart, which (at the time of writing) operates in 27 countries, has an annual turnover in excess of US$420 billion and has more than 2.1 million employees. The demise of such a company would adversely affect, without exaggeration, a multitude of people – shareholders (directly, and indirectly through retirement funds), employees, the families of those employees, those living in communities that depend on Walmart stores for their essential grocery shopping, and many others.

The second reason is the number of large corporate failures or near-failures in the last thirty years, many of which resulted from mismanagement. According to Monks and Minow, seven of the twelve largest bankruptcies in United States history were filed in 2002 alone, including Enron, Tyco, Worldcom and Global Crossing. And South Africa has not escaped the carnage: we have seen the collapse of Saambou, Masterbond, Leisurenet, Regal Bank, Fidentia and others.

Superficial corporate governance and substantive corporate governance

As mentioned above, the theory is that sound corporate governance should make mismanagement of an entity less likely, and hence protects the interests of shareholders in the company, as well as other stakeholders. But it is important to note that sound governance practices do not provide an absolute guarantee that a company will not fail, and superficially sound governance provide even less protection. The most often quoted example of superficially sound governance is that of US energy company Enron, which collapsed in 2002 after being, at a time, the sixth-largest (measured by market capitalisation) US company. Enron was a seemingly well-governed company: it had a well-structured board of directors and a fine-looking code of ethics, its CEO proclaimed that it was a company guided by sound principles, it received clean audit reports from respected audit firm Arthur Andersen, etc. But the problem with Enron was that there was a lack of governance substance under the gloss, because its senior managers and directors lacked integrity and/or commitment. On p. 15 of *The Corporate Citizen*, King says the following in this regard: "Good governance will not result from a mindless quantitative compliance with a governance code or rules. Good governance involves fairness, accountability, responsibility and transparency on a foundation of intellectual honesty. One has to employ one's practised abilities and honestly apply one's mind in an unfettered and unbiased manner in making a decision that is in the best interests of the company."

Gillan, during a discussion on integrity in financial reporting (included in Chew and Gillan's *Corporate Governance at the Crossroads*), also highlighted the role of the board in addressing the agency problem: "The board has the power and the duty to hire, fire and compensate managers. From this perspective, the board must set the right 'culture' or 'tone at the top' by hiring the right managers and then holding them accountable for their actions. But to do so the board must be active, informed, and capable of asking the management team probing questions."

Whom should the company's management serve?

The traditional view was that the company's management should serve its shareholders, because they provided the capital to the company. But this is a flawed argument, when looking at present-day circumstances. Today many shareholders are short-term speculators, who buy into the company with the intention to sell out quickly and realise a profit. And most shareholders do not really provide the company with capital – they simply replace an outgoing shareholder, with the company's capital position not being affected in any way.

> Crotty described the situation as follows in the Business Report of 29 July 2009:
> "Occasionally shareholders still do provide funding and so play the traditional investor role. But statistics from equity markets around the globe indicate that these are rare occasions and that over the past 15 years companies have been paying money out to shareholders in the form of dividends and share buy-backs rather than getting money from them.
> Shareholders now do little more than gamble. Shareholder X buys into company A because she believes the share price will appreciate sufficiently to make it a better bet (along with dividend payments) than buying Company B or putting the money in the bank …
> Despite the fact that shareholders are little more than gamblers and equity markets little more than facilities for accommodating those gambles, over the past 30 years any company with a stock exchange listing has steadily become fixated on the equity market and its share price.
> Management teams no longer focus on growing turnover and long-term profit, but in increasing the share price and, what's more, increasing it over the short term.
> Indeed, over the past 15 years or so, as executive pay became tied into share price performance, this tendency moved from a mere "focus" to an obsession."

The obvious question is why such a short-term speculator's interests should enjoy more of a claim to management's consideration than an employee who has served the company loyally for three decades. It is interesting to note that in Eastern countries like Japan the interests of employees, *vis-à-vis* those of shareholders, are regarded as much more important that in Western countries.

While this idea of shareholder supremacy is still the prevailing one in the United States, a more nuanced perspective has become the accepted one in other Western countries. For example, in a number of European countries a trade union representative sits on the upper tier of companies' two-tiered board of directors, which indicates that employees' interests are taken more seriously.

In South Africa, King III declares (in the introduction) that it "seeks to emphasise the inclusive approach of [sic] governance". This approach is then explained as follows:
- It means that "the board of directors considers the legitimate interests and expectations of stakeholders on the basis that this is in the best interests of the company, and not merely as an instrument to serve the interests of the shareholder"; and
- [T]hat...the legitimate interests and expectations of stakeholders are considered when deciding in the best interests of the company. The integration and trade-offs between various stakeholders are then made on a case-by-case basis, to serve the best interests of the company. The shareholder, on the premise of this approach, does not have a predetermined place of precedence over other stakeholders."

So King III clearly states that the directors' primary duty is to serve the interests of the company as a legal person, and that the shareholders are no more important than other stakeholder groupings.

In this regard, South Africa has been at the forefront internationally, through the work done by the King Committee on corporate governance, and these stakeholder practices are progressively becoming part of the governance process in South Africa. In the next section, we will consider the work and the recommendations of the King Committee.

The King Committee

Since the publication of the first King Report in 1994, the King Committee, under the chairmanship of Professor Mervyn King, has acquired a reputation as being a leader in setting benchmarks for best practice in the field of corporate governance. So, for example, the King II Report (published in 2002) was one of the first corporate governance codes to focus on the '**triple-bottom line**' – recognising that investors and other stakeholders increasingly require forward-looking information, addressing the economic, environmental and social aspects of a company's activities.

The King Report on Governance for South Africa 2009 (IoD, 2009b) and King Code of Governance for South Africa 2009 (IoD, 2009a) were published in September 2009 to respond to the Companies Act 71 of 2008 and developments in international corporate governance trends (IoD: 2009a: 4). From a study of these documents it is clear that even greater focus is placed on sustainability and the reporting thereon by way of an 'integrated report'. This will be explored in more detail later.

> The preference of the King Committee in ensuring effective corporate governance (the checks and balances that enable directors to discharge their responsibilities appropriately) is the use of an 'apply or explain' principles-based approach, rather than a legislative/rules-based ('comply or else') approach. The principles-based approach allows flexibility, and recognises that not all entities have exactly the same way of operating. In terms of the principles-based approach, entities can depart from the principles of the King Code of Governance for South Africa 2009 ('the King Code of Governance') should this be in the best interest of the entity and its stakeholders, and full explanations of the reasons for the departures are provided. It is then up to the shareholders and other stakeholders to evaluate the validity of the explanations and to take action should the departures not be considered appropriate.

In contrast, under the legislative approach, any non-compliance is likely to result in criminal action being taken again the entity's management. The Sarbanes-Oxley Act in the USA, promulgated after the Enron and WorldCom scandals, is a good example of legislated corporate governance. In recent years, questions have increasingly been asked about whether the benefits derived from this legislation warrant the costs of compliance – but of course affected companies have no choice but to comply until the legislation is changed.

The advantages of the principles-based approach can be summarised as follows:

- It allows entities to do what is most effective for them in ensuring effective corporate governance, thereby avoiding the incurring of unnecessary costs associated with the implementation of requirements that are not useful or appropriate to the entity. A 'one size fits all' approach, which results from the legislative approach, only really works if all affected entities are similar in nature.
- As all affected entities must comply with the requirements of legislation, a legislative approach tends to be a 'lowest common denominator' of corporate governance requirements, and cannot be aspirational. The focus is likely to be on 'compliance at the expense of enterprise' (IoD: 2009a:5)
- A legislative approach may give rise to actions being taken simply to comply with the 'letter of the law' rather than the spirit.

In South Africa, the Companies Act 71 of 2008 prescribes certain minimum corporate governance requirements for all companies, as well as additional 'enhanced accountability and transparency' requirements for public companies. The principles in the King Code of Governance address those good corporate governance aspects which are not legislated.

Key focus areas of the King III Committee in constructing the King Report and the King Code of Governance were leadership, sustainability and corporate citizenship (IoD: 2009a: 9). As good governance is closely tied to effective *leadership*, boards should direct company strategies and operations with a view to achieving sustainable economic, social and environmental performance. The focus on *sustainability* implies that fundamental shifts in the way companies and directors act and organise themselves are required. Strategy, risk, performance and sustainability have become inseparable – necessitating 'integrated reporting'. The concept of *corporate citizenship* stems from the fact that the company is a juristic person and should operate in a sustainable manner.

The King Code of Governance deals with 'principles' which should be applied by all entities regardless of the manner and form of incorporation (IoD: 2009a:16). In applying these principles, entities should consider the best practice recommendations contained in the King Report on Governance for South Africa.

The principles of the King Code of Governance address *inter alia* the following broad themes:

- *The composition and functioning of boards of directors:* As the board is the body that should assume full *responsibility* for the ethical leadership and corporate citizenship of the company, and must *account for* its actions and decisions to shareholders and other stakeholders, an effective board of directors in any company is vital. Accordingly, the King Code of Governance identifies principles relating to the duties and responsibilities of the board, composition of the board (for example, the chairman, the chief executive officer, the balance of executive to non-executive directors, the role of independent directors), performance evaluation, and appointment of new directors.

    Given that best practice is to have non-executive directors (who are not in the full-time employ of the company) on the board, principles regarding the use of board committees to assist the board in meeting its responsibilities, without abdicating these to the committees, are provided. Important potential conflicts of interest exist in the area of the remuneration of directors, and a number of principles in the King Code of Governance address this.

- *Credible corporate disclosures to stakeholders:* The board should disclose information in a transparent manner that enables stakeholders to make an informed assessment of the company's performance and its economic value. Such disclosures should address all areas of performance (economic, social and environmental). Also, independent assurance as to the credibility of the disclosures is important. An effective and independent audit committee should play a key role in overseeing integrated reporting and the assurance thereof. Principles for these areas are provided in the King Code of Governance and will be addressed in more detail in the next sections.

- *Risk management and internal audit:* A key duty of the board of directors is its responsibility for the governance of risk facing the entity. In order to achieve its objectives, an entity should (using a variety of strategies) manage down the risks to which it is exposed, to a level which is within the risk tolerances set by the board. Excessive risk-taking may manifest itself in large profits in the short run, but in the long run such risks may cause the company to go out of business. The effective internal audit function plays a key role in evaluating the adequacy of the entity's risk management process and identifying and reporting areas for improvement to the audit committee (a board committee). The King Code of Governance provides principles to facilitate the operation of effective risk management and internal audit processes. The governance of risks relating to Information Technology (which today is integral to the functioning and success of most entities) is given specific attention in a chapter of the King Code of Governance entitled 'Governance of information technology'. Risks arising from failure to comply with laws and regulations can also have a significant effect on an entity's sustainability (e.g. through penalties, reputational damage, and, in the extreme, closure of the business) – and a chapter is included in the King Code of Governance to deal with the management of this risk.

A detailed discussion of the principles of the King Code of Governance falls outside the scope of this chapter, but the full texts of the King Report on Governance for South Africa 2009 and the King Code of Governance for South Africa 2009 is available from the Institute of Directors' website (www.iodsa.co.za).

Shareholder activism and the role of the institutional investor

Shareholder activism refers to the idea that shareholders in a company should engage with its board and management if they are unhappy with aspects of the company's corporate governance. This is referred to in the introduction to King III, where it is stated that, under an apply or explain system, "the ultimate compliance officer is not the company's compliance officer or a bureaucrat ensuring compliance with statutory provisions, but the stakeholders." The stakeholder group that one would expect to be most inclined to engage with the company about governance issues is the shareholders, but there are a number of reasons why this does not happen all that much:

- Many shareholders are indirect shareholders by virtue of an investment via a vehicle like a pension fund or a unit trust scheme. These investors often are unaware of the investment vehicle's holdings.
- Many shareholders lack the technical ability to assess a company's governance practices.
- Companies' senior managers and directors tend to be dismissive when a small shareholder wants to engage them about the company's governance practices.

Enter the institutional investor. The term "institutional investor" refers to life assurance companies and other entities, e.g. Old Mutual, Sanlam, and Investec, that re-invest the contributions that many small investors make to pension funds, retirement annuity funds, unit trust funds, etc. A single institutional investor may end up holding, for the beneficial interest of a large number of investors in a number of funds, in excess of 10 per cent of the issued shares in a given company, and this gives that institutional investor much more clout than the individual investor. The tendency, until around 2005, was for these institutional investors to engage with companies "behind closed doors", so it was difficult to assess to what extent they engaged in activism, and about what issues. A notable exception was the largest institutional investor in the country, the Public Investment Corporation, which is responsible for managing state employees' retirement funds. It engaged in public spats with companies (like Sasol and Barloworld) while it was headed by Brian Molefe, who has since moved on to Transnet). But these interventions largely had to do with transformation, typically at senior management and/or board level.

In a 5 October 2009 *Business Report* article headed *Active shareholders shake up management at small firms*, Sanlam fund manager Kokkie Kooyman was quoted as saying that "South Africa's investors have over the last five years become increasingly activist." It was also mentioned, in the same article, that the United States and Europe were seeing increased levels of shareholder activism. Two then-recent local examples of shareholder activism were highlighted in the article, namely the ousting of Afdawn's senior executives, and the resignation of four of Simmer & Jack's directors who had been linked to that company's BEE shareholder.

It must be noted that the South African investment industry adopted, with effect from 1 February 2012, a Code of Responsible Investing in South Africa ("Crisa" for short). Crisa's objective is "to ensure that the powerful institutional investors are doing their bit to...see that good governance is implemented at the companies in which they invest" (per Crotty in a 30 January 2012 *Business Report* article headed *Crisa will give governance a fighting chance*). South Africa is only the second or third (sources differ on this) country in the world to adopt such a code. Crisa is a voluntary code, so there are no penalties for non-compliance. Two important requirements of the code are that institutional investors should disclose the policies that underpin their investment decisions, as well as their voting records.

King III supports activism, particularly by institutional investors. On p. 10 the following is stated in this regard: "Institutional investors should be encouraged to vote and engage with companies...This will ensure that governance best practice principles are more consistently applied."

Integrated reporting

The reporting of financial information to external parties is a well-entrenched practice, with all companies in South Africa having to produce a set of financial statements at least annually in terms of the requirements of the Companies Act 71 of 2008. The financial reporting frameworks in terms of which these financial statements have to be prepared have received attention, with much time and effort being devoted to the development of International Financial Reporting Standards (IFRS) dealing with the recognition, measurement and disclosure of transactions and events pertaining to a company in its financial statements.

The development of 'simplified' standards for smaller entities with less of a 'public interest' has also been receiving significant attention in recent years. Companies listed on the JSE have to comply with IFRS, and their annual financial statements will comprise the following (IAS 1, para 10):

- A statement of financial position (balance sheet) as at the end of the financial year
- A statement of comprehensive income for the financial year
- A statement of changes in equity for the financial year
- A statement of cash flows for the financial year
- Notes to the financial statements, comprising a summary of significant accounting policies and other explanatory information.

Questions about the credibility of the information contained in financial statements have arisen from time to time, given the often large restatements of figures that have been necessary as a result of misstatements owing to error or fraud that were not detected at the time of issuing the financial statements. There has also tended to be an excessive focus on certain components of the financial statements, such as earnings per share (EPS), by certain user groups, thereby creating an incentive for managements to misstate these components. Accountants and auditors who perform roles in the governance process have a key responsibility to respond to these challenges.

Traditionally, financial reporting frameworks have tended to emphasise tangible assets, thereby ignoring the development of the 'knowledge economy'. In the 'knowledge economy', the quality of management, staff, brands and reputation are important value drivers, yet very little information about these aspects is provided in financial statements (White, 2005). Also, given advances in technology, there have been demands by users for more timeous and broader information.

With the increasing recognition that a company must act as a 'responsible corporate citizen' (given that companies do not exist independently from the societies and environments in which they operate), and with boards being responsible for 'triple-bottom line' performance, the reporting of 'broader' information is a logical consequence. In the current environment, it is submitted that failure to provide forward-looking information that will enable a company's stakeholders to more effectively assess the entity's total economic value is likely to detrimental to the company (not least in it incurring higher financing costs).

The King Code of Governance therefore states that '... sustainability reporting and disclosure should be integrated with the company's financial reporting' ' (IoD: 2009a:49). An 'integrated report' is a 'holistic and integrated representation of the company's performance in terms of both its finance and its sustainability' (IoD: 2009b: 121). It puts the financial results in perspective by reporting on 'how a company has, both positively and negatively, impacted on the economic life of the community in which it operated during the year under review and how the company intends to enhance those positive aspects and eradicate or ameliorate the negative aspects in the year ahead' (IoD: 2009a: 4). The integrated report should enable the users to determine whether the organisation is able to create and sustain value in the short, medium and long-run (Integrated Reporting Committee, 2011: 3).

In preparing an 'integrated report', the *Sustainability Reporting Guidelines* v3.0 of the Global Reporting Initiative (2006) may be particularly useful.

> In terms of these Guidelines, three types of disclosures should be included in a sustainability report:
> - *Strategy and profile:* These disclosures provide the overall context for understanding the company's performance and deal with matters such as the company's strategy, key risks and

opportunities, organisational profile (for example, nature of operations), governance structures, and stakeholder engagement.
- *Performance indicators:* The economic, environmental and social performance indicators provide comparable information on the triple-bottom line performance of the company. For example, for the 'environmental' objective, prescribed performance information needs to be provided for 'aspects' such as: materials; energy; water; biodiversity; and emissions, effluents and waste.
- *Management approach:* These disclosures explain how the company addresses the 'aspects' defined under each indicator category in order to provide a context for understanding performance in a specific area.

Governance role of the auditing profession

Executive management, in preparing reports for their company for distribution to shareholders and other stakeholders, are likely to experience significant self-interest pressures to ensure that the reports reflect favourably on their performance. This is because a 'good' report will assist in maximising their remuneration, retaining their positions, and building their reputations. As a consequence, the corporate disclosures may not fairly present the economic, social and environmental performance of the company. In mitigating this threat, accountants and auditors can play a key role – a fact recognised by the King Committee. Specifically, the following role players are identified:
- Audit committee
- External audit
- Internal audit.

Role of the audit committee

In terms of the principles of the King Code of Governance, a company should have an effective and independent audit committee, comprising suitably skilled and experienced independent non-executive directors. These directors will often have a strong accounting and/or auditing background, and in many instances will be professional accountants. With their specialised knowledge, their fairly in-depth knowledge of the company's activities, and the fact that they may have no material interests in the company other than their directorship, the members of the committee can play an important role in facilitating the integrity of corporate disclosures.

Specific duties of the audit committee for the purposes of this section include:
- *To oversee integrated reporting:* The members of this committee have a responsibility to apply their minds when reviewing all corporate communications to ensure the integrity and completeness of reports made available to stakeholders.
- *To ensure that a combined assurance model is applied*: This means that the audit committee should ensure that assurance is received (both from internal and external sources) about the success of the strategies implemented to address all significant risks facing the company.
- *To recommend the appointment of the external auditor and oversee the external audit process:* Given the important role of the independent external auditors (see below) in the reporting to shareholders, the committee must consider carefully the competence and independence of the audit firm before recommending the firm for appointment. Moreover, the audit committee must assist in ensuring the independence of the firm by approving the provision of non-audit services rendered concurrently with the audit, and approving the auditor's remuneration.
- *To be responsible for overseeing of internal audit.*
- *To form an integral part of the company's risk management process* by specifically overseeing the process of identifying and evaluating the financial reporting risks (including fraud and IT risks) and the internal financial controls implemented to respond to these risks.
- *To evaluate the adequacy of the expertise, resources and experience of the finance/accounting function* (responsible for preparing the financial statements).

Role of external auditors

The external auditor's primary duty is to express an opinion on the fair presentation of a company's annual financial statements. The necessity for the audit stems from the fact that users of the financial statements are unlikely to trust the representations made by the directors, given their conflicts of interests explained above. This lack of trust is likely to result in investors and providers of credit finance (for example, banks) being reluctant to provide funds for the company to operate.

By having an independent third party, knowledgeable in the fields of accounting and auditing, who expresses an opinion on the fair presentation of the annual financial statements in terms of an acceptable financial reporting framework (for example, IFRS), users are far more likely to act on the information contained in the financial statements. Traditionally, this audit role has been confined to financial information contained in the annual financial statements. However, principle 9.3 of the King Code of Governance further states that sustainability reporting and disclosure should be independently assured – and it is likely that over time external auditors will play an important role in this area.

Unfortunately, not all external auditors have performed their roles as part of the governance framework effectively. Often they have allowed their own interests (for example, the retention of clients and the maximisation of audit firm revenue) to compromise their expressing the appropriate audit opinion. Examples of such instances, as well as other ethical challenges that the profession has to address, are explored further in Chapters 12 and 13.

Role of internal auditors

In preparing the corporate reports, information needs to be derived from the company's information system. A system of internal control must be implemented by a company's management to mitigate the many risks that may undermine the integrity and completeness of the information system. The company's internal audit function can provide the audit committee/board of directors with assurance about the adequacy of the company's risk management and internal control systems, and recommend improvements to address any weaknesses. In this way, possibilities of fraud or error on the part of the company's employees are minimised, and the integrity and completeness of the information drawn from the information system is enhanced, making for more reliable reporting.

> Accountants and auditors therefore have a key role to play in ensuring effective corporate governance, especially in the area of ensuring the reliability of disclosures made by companies. Without reliable corporate disclosures, corporate governance abuses by boards of directors are likely to go undetected, and shareholders and other stakeholders' trust in the information reported by companies will be eroded.

Conclusion

The key to ensuring ethical conduct is the integrity of the people with the most influence in shaping the behaviour of the firm's employees. The most powerful functionaries, namely the board of directors and management, hold this power to influence. Both these parties experience a regular test of character, as the potential for self-serving leadership often presents itself in the absence of good governance practices. The aim behind the King Report, the King Code of Governance and other governance reforms is to reduce the temptation for misconduct, and to focus corporate leaderships on satisfying the demands of their stakeholders, which include shareholders. The accounting and auditing profession will continue to play an important role in assisting with improvement of the governance process, especially by enhancing the reliability and credibility of disclosures.

Questions for discussion

1. What is an 'executive director', and what are the benefits and drawbacks associated with having executive directors on the board of directors?
2. What is an 'independent director', and why is this independence important?
3. How do we define who the stakeholders of the firm may be, and what strategic opportunities may be derived from a stakeholder management model?
4. How does the King Committee depart from the traditional view of governance?
5. Should the King Committee's recommendations be made mandatory or remain voluntary? What is gained and lost under each alternative option?
6. You are a member of the board of directors of a large listed company. Prepare a motivation to support your proposal to the board to introduce an integrated sustainability report for the company.
7. Comment on the appropriateness of the following statement: 'The external auditors of a company must accept all the blame for errors that are present in the company's audited annual financial statements'.

Bibliography

Burrough, B & Helyar, J. 1991. *Barbarians at the gate: the fall of RJR Nabisco*. New York: Collins Business.

Chew, DH & Gillan, SL. 2005. *Corporate Governance at the Crossroads*. New York: McGraw-Hill.

Clark, RC. 2005. 'Corporate governance changes in the wake of the Sarbanes-Oxley Act: A morality tale for policymakers too'. Working paper, amended December 2005, at Social Sciences Research Network.

Freeman, RE. 1984. *Strategic management: a stakeholder approach*. Boston, MA: Pitman.

Global Reporting Initiative. 2006. *Sustainability reporting guidelines v3.0*. [On-line]. <www.globalreporting.org> [Accessed 9 June 2009].

Institute of Directors (IoD). 2009a. *King code of governance for South Africa 2009*. [On-line]. <www.iodsa.co.za> [Accessed 2 September 2011].

Institute of Directors (IoD). 2009b. *King report on governance for South Africa 2009*. [On-line]. <www.iodsa.co.za> [Accessed 2 September 2011].

Integrated Reporting Committee. 2011. *Framework for integrated reporting and the integrated report: Discussion paper 25 January 2011.* [On-line]. <http://www.sustainabilitysa.org/Portals/0/Documents/IRC%20of%20SA%20Integrated%20Reporting%20Guide%20Jan%2011.pdf > [Accessed 1 August 2011].

Jensen, MC & Meckling, WH. 1976. 'Theory of the firm: Managerial behavior, agency costs, and ownership structure'. *Journal of Financial Economics*, 3:305–360.

King, ME. 2006. *The Corporate Citizen.* Johannesburg: Penguin Books.

Lee, TA. 2006. *Financial Reporting and Corporate Governance.* Chichester: Wiley.

MacAvoy, PW & Millstein, IM. 2003. *The recurrent crisis in corporate governance.* New York: Palgrave Macmillan.

Mittelstaedt, RE Jr. 2005. 'The board's broader role in strategy'. *Directors & Boards*, 1:8–21.

Monks, RAG & Minow, N. 2011. *Corporate Governance.* Chichester: Wiley.

Naidoo, M. 2009. *Corporate Governance.* Durban: LexisNexis.

Sayles, LR & Smith, CJ. 2006. *The rise of the rogue executive.* Upper Saddle River, NJ: Pearson Education.

White, AL. 2005. *New wine, new bottles: The rise of non-financial reporting. A business brief by business for social responsibility.* [On-line]. <www.globalreporting.org/Learning/ JournalArticles> [Accessed 9 June 2009].

Wixley, T & Everingham, G. 2002. *Corporate Governance.* Cape Town: SiberInk.

10

Managing ethics

Deon Rossouw

Outcomes

After working through this chapter, you should be able to do the following:
- Explain why accounting and auditing professionals need a proper understanding of the governance of ethics
- Identify what the process of ethics risk analysis entails
- Distinguish between different kinds of codes of ethics for which companies can opt
- Indicate what the institutionalisation of ethics on the strategic and systems level in organisations should ideally consist of
- Articulate the objectives and principles that should guide socio-ethical reporting.

Overview

The ethical performance of a company cannot be left to chance: it must be managed in an organised manner. Using a **corporate governance** framework, we will show that managing the ethical performance of a company typically starts with a process of **ethical risk analysis**. In such a process, the company engages with its internal and external stakeholders to determine its current ethical reputation amongst stakeholders as well as their ethical expectations of the company. Based on the outcome of the ethical risk analysis, the company can then cast its ethical standards in the form of a **code of ethics**. We will explore a number of vital decisions that need to be made in formulating a code of ethics. A written code of ethics, however, represents only words on paper. A strategy and various interventions are needed to turn the code into organisational practices. Various strategies and means of **institutionalising ethics** in organisations will be discussed. It is a corporate governance requirement that organisations should also account for their ethical performance and report it to the relevant stakeholders. Recent developments in the field of ethical **accounting, auditing, and reporting** will be discussed.

Introduction

There is a growing awareness that business success does not depend on the financial performance of a business alone. It is becoming increasingly evident that the sustainable success of a business also depends on its socio-ethical and environmental performance. This conviction is expressed in the shift from single to **triple bottom-line reporting** that can be seen around the globe.

Whereas the discipline of financial accounting and reporting is well entrenched in business practice, the same cannot be said of the other two aspects of triple bottom-line reporting, namely social and environmental reporting. The challenge facing business in this new era is to infuse discipline in their socio-ethical and environmental performance.

> Accountants need to be trained to add socio-ethical and environmental accounting, auditing, and reporting to their repertoire of professional knowledge and skills.

This challenge has a direct bearing on the accounting profession. As the profession that is responsible for the financial accounting and auditing of organisations, the accounting profession is expected to extend its scope of services to include socio-ethical and environmental accounting and auditing. It therefore does not surprise that members of the accounting profession took a leading role in developing the principles and practice of triple bottom-line accounting, auditing, and reporting. Nowadays, many accounting firms also offer such services to their clients. Also in the consulting business, accountants can be found in the ranks of those who offer organisations advice on triple bottom-line reporting. It is therefore clear that accountants need to be trained to add socio-ethical and environmental accounting, auditing, and reporting to their repertoire of professional knowledge and skills.

The focus of this chapter is on exploring what the governance of the ethical performance in particular of a business should ideally entail. The argument is that governing the ethical performance of a business within a triple bottom-line reporting model consists of these four dimensions:

1. *Determining the ethical risk of the company:* The company needs to determine the current perceptions that stakeholders have of the ethical performance of the company as well as what their ethical expectations of the company are. Based on these perceptions and expectations, the company can then identify ethical dangers that should be avoided and ethical opportunities that can be embraced.
2. *Codifying the ethical standards of the company:* The ethical standards that are needed to avoid ethical dangers and to embrace ethical opportunities have to be written into a code of ethics.
3. *Institutionalising ethical standards in the company:* The ethical standards identified in the code have to be institutionalised in the company. This needs to happen on the strategic and systems levels of the company.

4. *Reporting the ethical performance of the company:* Finally, the company has to keep a record of its ethical performance. This performance must be accounted, independently verified, and disclosed to stakeholders of the company.

Each of these facets of governing the ethical performance of an organisation will be unpacked in this chapter.

Determining ethical risk

It is beyond dispute that boards of directors have an obligation to direct and control the risk of companies. In the UK, the *Turnbull Report* asks directors not only to consider what the significant risks are that face their companies, but also to ensure that there are effective mechanisms for identifying and managing such risks (Garratt, 2003:195). Similarly, in South Africa, the *Third King Report on Corporate Governance* requires directors to take responsibility for the governance of risk (IoD, 2009). To argue that boards should take responsibility for the governance of risk would consequently be superfluous, as it has become accepted practice for boards to do so – at least as far as best practice in corporate governance is concerned.

> Triple bottom-line reporting requires boards to report on companies' economic, social, and environmental vision and performance.

Boards' responsibilities with regard to risk have, however, expanded significantly with the shift towards triple bottom-line reporting. Triple bottom-line reporting requires boards to report on companies' economic, social, and environmental vision and performance. Part of this process of reporting entails that boards should report to their shareholders (and other stakeholders in the case of inclusive corporate governance models) what they perceive as the most significant risks in each of these three areas. They also have to report on the strategies they have adopted for dealing with these respective risks.

Where boards traditionally dealt only with economic (financial and business) risks, they are now expected to deal with a much broader set of risks, which are sometimes referred to as sustainability risks. Although internationally it is increasingly clear that boards should take responsibility for a wider set of risks than they used to do, there is no similar clarity on how boards should go about disposing of this broader responsibility. This also applies to ethical risk. **Ethical risk** is an integral part of the second line of reporting, namely social reporting. Social reporting is usually divided into two aspects: social reporting and ethical reporting. Social reporting refers to the obligations that an organisation has towards its internal and external stakeholders. Ethical reporting focuses on the ethical performance of a business, which is sometimes also referred to as organisational integrity.

> Ethical risk is an integral part of the second line of reporting, namely social reporting.

Risk, in general, can be defined as conditions or behaviour that can affect a company either beneficially or detrimentally. According to Garratt, the concept of 'risk' found its way into the English language via the Italian word *riscare*, which means 'to dare' (2003:194). He claims that risk 'concerns the real, or possible, events that reduce the likelihood of reaching business goals, and increases the probability of losses' (Garratt, 2003:194). This view of risk is, however, unduly negative as risk need not only be associated with losses. On the contrary, risk is often associated with gain. The belief that risk is rewarded with financial gain belongs at the very heart of entrepreneurship and capitalism. Managing corporate risk consequently entails mitigating or avoiding those conditions or kinds of behaviour that can affect companies detrimentally while embracing those that can benefit the company.

> Risk, in general, can be defined as conditions or behaviour that can affect a company either beneficially or detrimentally.

What applies to risk in general also applies to ethical risk. Ethical risk can therefore be defined as potentially detrimental or beneficial outcomes caused by ethical or unethical practices or kinds of behaviour.

In the governance of ethics, the first obligation of the board of directors is to ensure that the negative and positive ethical risks of an organisation are properly gauged. The board will normally delegate this function to one of the functional areas in the organisation, such as internal audit, company secretariat, or human resource management.

Ethical risk assessment

When ethical risk assessment is done, it can be approached in either a unilateral or a multilateral manner. Should ethical risk be identified unilaterally, the board or a delegated function within the company takes responsibility for identifying the ethical risk of the company. The benefit of a unilateral approach to ethical risk identification is that the board becomes actively involved in the process of ethical risk identification. The obvious disadvantage of a unilateral approach is that risk identification is restricted to the perspectives of the board or the delegated function within the company responsible for identifying such risk. In terms of a unilateral approach to risk identification, the perceptions that other internal and external stakeholders have of the ethical behaviour of the company are excluded. It is exactly for this reason that a multilateral approach is regarded as best practice when it comes to ethical risk identification (Driscoll and Hoffman, 2000:46). Through a process of stakeholder engagement, the perceptions that stakeholders have of the ethical reputation of the company is gauged. This process typically starts with the compilation of a stakeholder map in which the company maps out its various stakeholder groups. These stakeholders are then prioritised in terms of the impact that they might have on the company as well as the impact that the company might have on them.

The process of risk identification is essentially a research process. As such, it should comply with the accepted norms of research in terms of reliability and objectivity. A range of quantitative and qualitative instruments can be used to determine the perspectives of internal and external stakeholders (Rossouw and van Vuuren, 2004:209–213). Typical instruments that can be used to determine stakeholders' perceptions of conditions and kinds of behaviour that yield ethical risk are qualitative methods such as personal interviews, focus groups and document analyses, and quantitative methods such as surveys (Driscoll and Hoffman, 2000:51). Through domestic and global benchmarking (i.e. comparing themselves with best practice in their industry), companies can also determine how their industry peers perceive their ethical risks.

> A multilateral approach is regarded as best practice when it comes to ethical risk identification.

A process of risk identification is likely to produce more ethical risks than a company can afford to manage. It is precisely for this reason that the board needs to determine what the most significant risks are. They also need to determine what ethical values and/or kinds of behaviour need to be embraced by the company to avoid the dangers associated with unethical conduct and/or to utilise the opportunities associated with ethical behaviour. These ethical values and preferred kinds of behaviour then need to be codified.

Codifying ethical standards

After having determined the ethical risk factors facing the company and the ethical expectations that internal and external stakeholders have of the company, the company needs to draft (or revise) its code of ethics. The code of ethics identifies the standards of ethical behaviour that all employees need to adhere to in their decisions, actions, and interactions with the stakeholders of the company. As such, the code of ethics is the pivotal point of the company's ethics management intervention, because it provides the standard against which the company has to measure its own performance. Codes of ethics can assume one of two formats. They can be either directional or aspirational (Rossouw and Van Vuuren, 2004:219–220).

> Codes of ethics can assume one of two formats. They can be either directional or aspirational.

Directional codes

Directional codes are very specific in prescribing as clearly as possible what kinds of behaviour are unacceptable and what kinds of behaviour are expected from all employees. The strength of directional codes lies in the fact that they are very specific. They state very clearly what should or should not be done. Consequently, they provide clear guidance to employees and can therefore be enforced in the organisation. This strength, however, also constitutes a weakness in directional codes. Because they are so specific, they leave very little discretion to the individual employee. This often gives rise to a mentality of 'what is not explicitly forbidden is allowed'. When this mentality prevails, organisations need to formulate even more rules of behaviour to cover all forms of misconduct that may affect the organisation. This inevitably results in a proliferation of rules of conduct. When there are too many rules, it becomes difficult to recall them and consequently, the directional code can start losing its force as it is almost impossible to comply with the plethora of ethical prescriptions.

> Directional codes are very specific in prescribing as clearly as possible what kinds of behaviour are unacceptable and what kinds of behaviour are expected from all employees.

Aspirational codes

Aspirational codes are less directive as they identify the ethical values, norms, and principles that should guide employees in their decisions and actions. Rather than being very specific, they provide employees with broad guidelines which they are expected to apply with discretion in their jobs. Because aspirational codes are not very specific, they are fairly short documents and are consequently easy to recall. This enhances the ability of aspirational codes to become living documents that live in the hearts and minds of employees. The major drawback is that they can be perceived as very vague and as providing insufficient guidance to employees. When this happens, they may cease to be relevant to employees and may even be perceived as largely non-binding. They may also be perceived as lacking authority as they cannot prescribe sanctions for specific transgressions.

Irrespective of whether a company opts for a directional or aspirational code of ethics, the board needs to take the responsibility for institutionalising the code of ethics in the organisation.

> Aspirational codes are less directive as they identify the ethical values, norms, and principles that should guide employees in their decisions and actions.

Institutionalising ethics

The commitment to organisational integrity that is demonstrated through adopting a code of ethics has to be translated into organisational practice. In other words, ethics has to be institutionalised. This institutionalisation should occur on both the strategic and systems level in the organisation.

Strategic level

On the strategic level in the organisation, the board has to take the responsibility for committing the company formally to the code of ethics.

The commitment should be reflected in the vision, mission, and identity of the organisation. It should be clear on this level that ethics is ingrained in the way in which the company does its business. This commitment to ethics should be communicated to all relevant stakeholders. It is also the board's responsibility to decide on an appropriate strategy for managing the ethical performance of the company. The strategy that the board selects for managing ethical risk will be largely determined by whether the board merely wants to protect the company from ethical failures or whether it wishes the company to benefit actively from good ethical performance. Two broad strategies for managing ethical performance can be distinguished. They are the compliance and integrity strategies (Rossouw and Van Vuuren, 2004:50–54).

Compliance strategy

> The objective of a **compliance strategy** is to prevent unethical behaviour in an organisation. Companies with a compliance strategy commit themselves to monitoring and managing their ethical performance. They use their code of ethics as the standard against which the ethical performance of employees is measured. Companies with this strategy of managing their ethical performance typically express their intention ensuring that all employees abide by the ethical standards of the company. In order to ensure compliance with the code, they monitor the ethical performance of employees. When employees deviate from the code of ethics, the company takes corrective action by disciplining or penalising the transgressors. Alternatively, the company may opt for not only penalising ethical transgressions, but also for rewarding those who consistently adhere to ethical behaviour. The compliance strategy is thus a rule-based approach to managing ethics.

A compliance strategy may have a number of side-effects that the board needs to take cognisance of when considering this strategy. Firstly, it may breed a mentality of 'what is not forbidden is allowed'. Given the rule-based nature of this approach, employees can rely merely on the existing rules for moral guidance. Secondly, it tends to disempower employees from using their own discretion in making ethical decisions as it requires almost blind adherence to the rules of conduct (Sharpe-Paine, 2002:135). This undermines their ability to cope with issues and grey areas that are not addressed in the code of ethics. Finally, the compliance strategy can lead to a proliferation of ethical rules and guidelines for conduct. In an attempt to provide unambiguous guidance on ethical conduct, more and more ethical guidelines are issued. These rules can grow so numerous that it becomes difficult to keep track of them. Should this happen, it is almost impossible to recall all the directives, and for that reason, they may have very little impact on actual corporate behaviour.

None of these side-effects are insurmountable. They can all be countered with appropriate management interventions. But often, these side-effects prompt companies to adopt an integrity strategy instead.

The integrity strategy

> The **integrity strategy** is a value-based approach to managing ethics. The purpose of the integrity strategy is to raise the level of ethical performance of the company. Instead of merely trying to minimise incidents of unethical behaviour, it proactively endeavours to promote an ethos of ethical responsibility within the company. Companies typically follow this strategy when they realise that ethical performance is of strategic importance to the company or even its competitive edge. In such cases, a defensive approach that protects the company against the damage of unethical conduct is no longer deemed sufficient. On the contrary, a concerted effort in which all members of the organisation take joint responsibility for the ethical performance of the company is required.

Where the compliance strategy is characterised by externally enforcing ethical standards upon the employees, the integrity approach is marked by employees' internalising of ethical values and standards. The integrity strategy works by obtaining the commitment of individual members of the organisation to a set of shared corporate values instead of imposing ethical standards upon them (Moon and Bonny, 2001:26). By ensuring that the locus of control resides within members of the organisation, less external control is required. Therefore, the need for external control is lessened and there is more reliance on employees' discretion to act in a morally responsible way and in accordance with the company's ethical values.

The integrity strategy also has a number of side-effects that the board needs to take cognisance of should they opt for this strategy:

1. The increased discretion granted to employees in an integrity strategy can be abused. This can either lead to an increase in unethical conduct or it can fuel moral disputes in a company.

> Where the compliance strategy is characterised by externally enforcing ethical standards upon the employees, the integrity approach is marked by employees' internalising of ethical values and standards.

> An integrity strategy is usually complemented by a limited form of compliance where a limited number of rules serve as a safety net to protect the company from gross ethical failures.

2. The integrity strategy depends heavily on the leadership of the company for setting both the tone and the example of ethical behaviour. If the leaders in a company do not unanimously endorse the core ethical values in their practical behaviour ('walk the ethics walk'), it can pose a serious challenge to the viability of an integrity strategy.
3. Finally, the integrity strategy presupposes a clear sense of corporate identity and priorities. The individual discretion upon which the integrity approach is premised can be properly exercised only when core ethical values are aligned with corporate identity and priorities. Should there be a lack of clarity about corporate identity and priorities, the viability of an integrity approach may be jeopardised.

Once the board has decided on an appropriate strategy for governing ethical risk, the institutionalisation of ethics on the systems level can commence.

Systems level

In implementing its code of ethics and ethical strategy, the board needs to delegate authority for managing the ethical performance of the company to a specific function within the company. A special office can be created for this purpose, or alternatively, this responsibility can be delegated to an existing functional area within the company, such as the company secretariat or human resource management. The office that receives the responsibility for managing ethics has to institutionalise systems and processes that will ensure that ethical behaviour becomes entrenched in the operational behaviour of the company. The management of ethics within the company can be overseen by an ethics committee which can either be a board committee or at least a committee with close proximity to the board.

> On the systems level, the challenge is to translate the ethics strategy into meaningful ethics management systems.

On the systems level, the challenge for the key role players involved in ethics management, is to translate the ethics strategy into meaningful *ethics management systems*. Designing and implementing such systems are crucial processes in ensuring that the vision and strategy for ethics are realised throughout the organisation. There is a wide range of possible ethics management systems that can be introduced. We will now turn to some of the most obvious ones.

First a **communication system** is needed. An organisation has to communicate its ethical expectations clearly to all stakeholders. Also, every employee has to understand and apply the standards that have been determined for ethical conduct in the organisation. In addition to this, the organisation would want to know what kinds of ethical issues their employees are confronted with, what types of unethical behaviour occurs, what the 'good news' ethics stories are, and so on. Communication about ethics forms the backbone of implementing an ethics strategy. A good two-way communication strategy that enables the organisation to convey ethical expectations and that affords its stakeholders, in particular the employees, opportunities to tell the organisation about their ethical experiences, has to be designed and implemented. Communication systems that can be used to achieve these objectives include ethics awareness programmes, an ethics help-line, a confidential reporting channel for reporting unethical behaviour, and ethics newsletters.

A second system that is required is **a staffing system** that will ensure that the organisation hires and promotes persons of integrity. This implies that distinct ethical criteria should be built into the recruitment, selection, and promotion processes of the organisation.

A third system required for institutionalising ethics is an ethics **induction system**. A new employee induction programme can be a powerful intervention in creating ethical awareness amongst newcomers. New employees are made aware of the organisation's expectations regarding ethical behaviour from the outset. This is also an appropriate time for explaining the code of ethics and how to apply its values and ethical guidelines.

> To reflect the ethical responsibility of employees, their ethical performance should be appraised.

A fourth system that can be used to institutionalise ethics is the organisation's **performance appraisal system**. Ethics is not only the collective responsibility of the organisation as a whole, but also the individual responsibility of each employee. To reflect the ethical responsibility of employees, their ethical performance should be appraised. This can be done by making it a stand-alone key performance area (KPA) for some jobs that require continuous ethical decision-making from their incumbents. At the very least, ethics can be integrated into one or more key performance areas. In this way, employees know what ethical performance is required and the extent to which it will be measured as part of their broader performance appraisal.

A further system that is almost indispensable for the institutionalisation of ethics is an ethics **training system**. A key focus area of organisational ethics training interventions is training employees to understand, interpret, and apply the code of ethics. Training on systems related to ethics such as an ethics help-line, a confidential reporting channel, and the appraisal of ethics as part of the general performance appraisal process of the organisation, both need to be addressed in ethics training.

A sixth system that typically forms part of the institutionalisation process is a **disciplinary system**. In building an ethical organisational culture, there are times when unethical or non-compliant behaviour has to be discouraged through punishment. Organisations have to resort to deterring unethical behaviour by dealing with transgressions, especially serious ones, in a swift and decisive way. This can happen only when the ethical code and policies are linked with disciplinary procedures.

A final system that is required is a **monitoring and evaluation system**. Constant monitoring is vital in actively managing the ethical performance of a company. The ethical performance of the organisation can be gauged and recorded through a variety of interventions. Examples of monitoring are keeping a record of the number of incidents leading to complaints about fraud, corruption, sexual harassment, racism, calls to the ethics helpline, and reports via the confidential reporting system. This information needs to be systematically documented and analysed. External indices that rate companies with regard to reputation, sustainability, or attractiveness to aspirant employees also provide information that can be captured in the monitoring and evaluation system. If ethical performance is included in the performance appraisal system of the company, it also provides feedback to the company on whether levels of ethical performance are improving or declining. The feedback on ethical performance that is gained in this way serves two purposes. On the one hand, it provides the information required for further ethics management interventions. On the other hand, it provides the data required for reporting on the ethical performance of organisations.

> Constant monitoring is vital in actively managing the ethical performance of a company.

Reporting and disclosing ethical performance

The objective of reporting on the ethical performance of a company is two-fold. Firstly, it infuses discipline into the ethics management of a company, as it indicates whether and to what extent a company has reached the ethical objectives it has set for itself. Secondly, ethics reporting satisfies stakeholders that the company actively deals with ethical risks that might have a bearing on the sustainability of the company.

> Ethics reporting forms part of the social reporting of a company. It is therefore an integral part of triple bottom-line reporting.

Ethics reporting forms part of the social reporting of a company. It is therefore an integral part of triple bottom-line reporting. The discipline of social and ethical reporting is an evolving one which is still being experimented with on a global scale. This reality is reflected in the guidelines on social and ethical reporting that are currently being produced. The most significant markers in this evolving standard are:

- The AA1000 standard developed by the Institute for Social and Ethical Accountability
- The guidelines for sustainability reporting developed by the Global Reporting Initiative.

The nature of ethical reporting compels companies to report to what extent they have met specific performance standards that they have set for themselves. The reports should be of such a nature that they provide evidence of what the company has achieved with regard to its objectives over the reporting period. Although such reports should be accessible to a wide group of stakeholders, they should nevertheless adhere to the principles of reporting that have become accepted in financial reporting. These principles include relevance, reliability, clarity, comparability, timeliness, and verifiability.

> The last principle mentioned in the above list, verifiability, implies that other people should be able to assess independently whether the report is a reliable reflection of what the company has achieved with regard to the ethical risks that it has identified.

The discipline of social reporting requires that companies should have their ethics reports independently verified. They need to be audited in a similar manner to financial reports.

Finally, the audited ethics report needs to be disclosed to relevant stakeholders by the board. Social and ethical disclosure differs from financial disclosure in terms of the scope of disclosure. Whereas financial reports are geared towards a select group of financially sophisticated analysts and investors, social and ethical reports should be accessible to a wide range of diverse stakeholders. This poses a number of challenges with regard to both how the report is compiled and how it is disclosed or communicated to various stakeholder groups. In some cases, the traditional glossy printed report may be inappropriate, and, for example, need to make way for a series of community meetings. The latter scenario would come into play when a local community with a high rate of illiteracy turns out to be a relevant and important stakeholder of the company. The practice of disclosing social and ethical reports is also currently in a gestation process which can be expected to yield much new research and experimentation.

Conclusion

The process of governing the ethical performance of an organisation has opened a range of new challenges for boards of directors. It has also done the same for the accounting and auditing profession. These new challenges also bring new opportunities to this profession in all three of its manifestations, in accounting, auditing, and management consulting services. To face these new challenges and to take advantage of these new opportunities, it is essential that the new generation of accounting and auditing professionals' training be extended to incorporate the process of governing the ethical performance of organisations. Accounting and auditing professionals also need to acquire the specialised skills needed for ethics accounting, auditing, and disclosure.

Questions for discussion

1. Why has the governance of ethics become relevant to accounting and auditing professionals?
2. What is the purpose of conducting an ethical risk analysis? And what methods can be used to do an ethical risk assessment?
3. What are the benefits and deficits of directional and aspirational codes of ethics respectively?
4. How do the compliance aproach and the integrity approach to institutionalising ethics differ from each other?
5. Which systems can be used to institutionalise ethics in organisations?
6. What is the objective of ethical reporting, and which reporting principles should guide the process of ethical reporting?

Bibliography

Driscoll, D & Hoffman, WM. 2000. *Ethics matters*. Waltham, MA: Centre for Business Ethics.
Garratt, B. 2003. *Thin on top*. London: Nicholas Brealey.
Institute of Directors (IoD). 2009. *Third King report on corporate governance for South Africa 2009*. Johannesburg: Institute of Directors (IoD).
Moon, C & Bonny, C. 2001. *Business ethics*. London: Profile Books.
Rossouw, D & van Vuuren, L. 2004. *Business ethics*, 3rd ed. Cape Town: Oxford University Press.
Sharpe-Paine, L. 2002. 'Venturing beyond compliance'. In Hartman, LP (ed). *Perspectives in business ethics*. Boston: McGraw-Hill Irwin.

11

Case studies in business ethics

Deon Rossouw

Outcomes

After working through this chapter, you should be able to do the following:
- Identify ethical issues in case studies
- Distinguish morally relevant role players
- Make ethical judgements on ethical issues and dilemmas
- Generate imaginative solutions to ethical problems.

Overview

There is a huge variety of moral issues and dilemmas that can potentially arise in business. It is important that aspiring business professionals such as accountants and auditors familiarise themselves with at least some of these issues. A good way of familiarising oneself with potential ethical dilemmas is by studying business case studies with an ethical dimension. One becomes sensitive to the moral dimension of one's work and also develops the skills to deal with related ethical issues through analysing and discussing cases. In this chapter, case studies that deal with a wide variety of ethical business issues such as cheating, fraud, HIV/Aids, black economic empowerment, gifts and gratuities, affirmative action, expense accounts, and whistle blowing are presented. Guidelines for analysing and discussing the case studies are also provided.

Introduction

In this chapter, we present a number of case studies as well as some questions that can guide the analysis and discussion of these cases. The cases deal with diverse issues that are likely to occur in most industries and professions. Although all these cases are not exclusively focused on the accounting profession, accountants and auditors can expect to encounter these general business ethical issues in their careers.

Analysing case studies requires analytical, independent, and imaginative thinking. You should be able to analyse cases in order to determine the morally relevant issues and role players. Whenever an action, decision, or practice detrimentally impacts on the well-being of affected people, we are dealing with an ethical issue. It is important that such ethical issues should be described as clearly and precisely as possible. Those people or organisations that are responsible for creating the ethical issue or who are affected by it are the morally relevant role players. It is equally important that the contribution of each role player or the way in which they are affected by the issue be identified.

Once a case study has been properly analysed, you should be able to make your own evaluation of the morality of the actions, decisions, or practices pursued by the morally relevant role players. This calls for independent thinking and also for providing reasons to back up your judgement.

Working with cases also requires that you use your moral imagination. Case studies typically confront us with difficult choices that have to be made. You will therefore be expected to be imaginative in order to propose possible courses of action that can be pursued to address or resolve the ethical issues in morally sound ways.

The questions for discussion that are listed at the end of each case study will guide you in analysing and assessing the cases, but will also prompt you to use your moral imagination. You can also apply the previously discussed strategies for ethical decision-making (Chapter 4) and for resolving ethical dilemmas (Chapter 5) to some of the cases.

Cheating

Temptations to act unethically are not confined to professional life. They are present in all spheres of life and also in all stages of individual lives. Student life is no exception. From time to time, students find themselves in situations where they are confronted with the temptation to be dishonest in an effort to improve their marks. This temptation can appear in many forms. It can be in the form of plagiarism, where someone else's ideas or writing are presented as one's own, or it can be in the form of consulting notes or other sources in a test situation, where one is not supposed to have access to such notes or sources. The next case study deals with the latter.

Case study one: Cheating and eating

Charlene is an undergraduate university student and stays in one of the residences on campus. She radiates a lot of energy and drive and has an outgoing personality. She is a very popular person and plays a leading role in her residence, where she serves on a number of residence committees. Charlene has a very busy social schedule and apart from diligently attending all lectures, she finds it difficult to put her studies on her list of priorities. For that reason, Charlene failed Business Management 2 in her second year at varsity. With special permission from the Dean, Charlene was allowed to register for Business Management 3 the next year while repeating Business Management 2.

During March of that year, Charlene was heavily involved in organising the 50-year celebration of her residence. She was so preoccupied with the function that she completely forgot to write her semester tests for both Business Management 2 and 3. Dr Smith, a close friend of the family, issued Charlene with a medical certificate stating she had had severe 'flu and armed with this certificate, Charlene applied to write the sick test. Unfortunately, both sick tests were written on the same day at the same time. Charlene obtained special permission from the Head of Department to write Business Management 3 in a vacant office at the department the next day. She was so occupied with her studies for the Business Management 2 test and with making final arrangements for the residence celebration in between, that she hardly had time to study for Business Management 3. Knowing she would be alone in the vacant office while writing the test, she prepared a few cryptic notes for the test. Everything was going according to plan, but half an hour before the end of the test, the assistant in the department, Carl, walked into the office as Charlene was looking at the cryptic notes on her lap.

'What are you doing?' Carl asked. Charlene knew she had been caught and, in a desperate attempt, she put the cryptic notes in her mouth and swallowed them.

'There is nothing. You have no proof!' Charlene replied.

Questions for discussion

1. Identify all the ethical issues in this case.
2. How would you have handled the situation if you were in Charlene's position when she realised that she had missed the two tests? What ethical alternatives could Charlene have pursued?
3. How would you have handled the Business Management 3 sick test if you were in a similar position to Charlene the day before the test?
4. How wise do you consider Charlene's decision to swallow the notes? What ethical ramifications could her action have?

Qualification fraud

A form of fraud that has escalated upwards in recent years is qualification fraud. This occurs when individuals forge their qualifications. In doing so, they deceive others in order to gain access to positions and privileges that they would otherwise be denied. Advances in electronic communication and duplication technologies have fuelled qualification fraud. The following case demonstrates how qualification fraud can harm a company and cause embarrassment to those responsible for appointing someone with forged qualifications.

Case study two: Credible credentials?

Louis Kriel, the managing director of Retirement Fund Management (RFM), retired in December 2006. RFM, a not-for-profit entity, manages pension and provident funds of about R40 billion on behalf of current and retired employees in a variety of industries. RFM purely administers retirement funds. A distinction is made between the management of a fund (how the money is invested) and the administration of the fund (who the money comes from and to whom it goes).

During the second part of 2006, the board of directors of RFM appointed a selection sub-committee consisting of six members to find and appoint a new managing director to replace Louis Kriel. Given the importance of the job, which involved overseeing one of South Africa's biggest private sector funds, the six individuals who served on the selection sub-committee were senior members of RFM's board of directors. The selection sub-committee nominated four short-listed candidates for the position of managing director, who were interviewed for the position by the six committee members in November 2006.

One of the candidates, Peter Mokebe, had his application prepared by Professional Placement Specialists (PPS), a recruitment agency. Mokebe was, at that time, the managing director of a short-term insurance company and was listed in its annual report as holding a BCom (Law) degree. However, during late 2006, RFM was informed in writing by PPS that they had not been able to 'clear' Mokebe's university degree. This bit of information did not deter the board from appointing Peter Mokebe as the new managing director of RFM with an annual salary of R750 000.

During Mokebe's tenure as managing director at RFM, he was allegedly involved in a highly controversial sexual harassment case. He was found guilty at a disciplinary hearing. However, the board of directors complained about the procedures followed in the disciplinary hearing, and requested a re-hearing of his case. Mokebe was again found guilty at the second disciplinary hearing. He was obliged to go on unpaid leave for a month. At the same time, the women involved laid criminal charges, and Mokebe was arrested. On the day the case was to be heard in a criminal court, the state unexpectedly dropped the case.

When Isaac Owen became the chairman of the board in July 2008, he appointed AWI, a screening agency, to conduct an investigation into Mokebe's BCom degree from the National University of Lesotho. In a letter from the university, they made it clear that the vice-chancellor who had signed the 1986 certificate had assumed office only in 1987. The registrar who had apparently signed the same certificate had also assumed office years after Mokebe's supposed date of graduation.

Source: Adapted from <www.moneyweb.co.za>

Questions for discussion

1. If you were a member of the selection committee at the time of Mokebe's appointment, would you have supported his nomination and appointment?
2. What is the corporate governance responsibility of the board of directors in terms of appointing senior executives?
3. Was there any unethical or negligent conduct by the recruitment agency in this scenario?
4. How should the board of directors act on the report they received from AWI?
5. Should the sexual harassment allegations levelled against Mokebe play any role in the board of director's decision on the future of Mokebe at RFM? Motivate your answer.
6. How could this situation have been avoided in the first place?

HIV in the workplace

The human immunodeficiency virus (HIV) is causing havoc on the African continent with its estimated 5 000 Aids-related funerals per day. HIV/Aids is a highly emotional issue that often leads to irrational behaviour by both individuals and organisations. The economic impact of Aids on businesses and the economy is potentially huge. Businesses therefore have to design and implement strategies for dealing with HIV and Aids in the workplace. As the next case shows, it is often more easily said than done.

Case study three: Aids anxiety

Donny Mabitsela, Chief Financial Officer (CFO) of Execu Image (Pty) Ltd, has to finalise the company's annual budget for the next financial year. Execu Image is one of South Africa's largest manufacturers of corporate wear and uniforms for public servants. The company also supplies security uniforms and camouflage clothing to the security and defence industries, as well as to various private dealers in corporate wear. Although the company is considered a leader in its industry, it nevertheless faces tough competition from its smaller rivals.

Execu Image employs approximately 7 000 people, who are stationed at various warehouses and outlets throughout the country. It has a very proactive Human Resource Development division, and providing ongoing training to its employees is one of the company's key priorities. Execu Image also has an Employee Assistance Programme that aims at improving the general wellbeing of its employees and providing support in matters such as drug abuse, alcoholism, and HIV/Aids.

It is Donny's responsibility to propose how the company's budget is to be spent in order to increase profits while protecting the company against possible risks. He knows that company profits are a top priority and that he will have to make some tough decisions as to how the budget should be spent. In his view, the personal lifestyles of the employees, which could lead to the spread of HIV/Aids, put the company at risk. He starts considering the idea of having all employees tested for HIV.

'If the company invests only in the training of employees who are HIV negative, Execu Image will ensure that it is investing in the development of the right people. No money will be wasted on those who are HIV-positive,' Donny thinks to himself.

After much thought about the social problems facing the country and its effects on Execu Image's performance over the last few years, Donny decides to change his strategy with regard to investment in the training of the employees. In Donny's annual budget speech at the company *lekgotla* (strategy planning meeting), he touches upon the company's strategy on the development of employees and makes the following comment:

'We must ask ourselves what value, if any, nice-to-have units like the Employee Assistance Programme have on our workforce. One of the challenges facing us is the fact that this company is ravaged by the HIV/Aids pandemic. It would be irresponsible of us to talk about investing in our people, while, at the same time, hesitating to address the HIV/Aids issue more directly and firmly. Should we not request all our employees to live their lives more responsibly and productively by having their status determined immediately? Does it make sense for us to sit here and spend all this time planning how best to improve the quality of life and productivity of our employees when they do not care?'

The following week, Manny Pather, head of the Human Resource Development division, calls all the trainers of Execu Image to a meeting where he explains the CFO's new strategy. Manny informs the trainers that he fully supports the CFO's idea that all employees must have their HIV/Aids status determined and disclosed, as well as that the company should not invest in people who test HIV-positive. Manny asks his staff for suggestions as to how this new strategy can be implemented effectively.

Most of the trainers react negatively to this proposal and indicate that the CFO's decision contradicts a number of company policies that are aimed at protecting employees. They are also doubtful as to how their integrity as trainers will be viewed if they train only certain employees while refusing to train others on the grounds of their HIV status. The trainers also feel that many people, other than the employees themselves, would be negatively affected by such a policy, and request that the company's labour relations officer, Darryl Jemane, be invited to the meeting. Manny agrees and summons Darryl to the meeting.

Darryl explains that company policies have to be in line with legislation, such as the Employment Equity Act 55 of 1998, the Bill of Rights in the Constitution of the Republic of South Africa, 1996, the Labour Relations Act 66 of 1995, the Promotion of Equality and Prevention of Unfair Discrimination Act 4 of 2000, the Occupational Health and Safety Act 85 of 1993, and the Basic Conditions of Employment Act 75 of 1997. He expresses his concern as to how labour unions would react to such a policy, since they have to protect the rights of all their members, irrespective of their HIV status. He also mentions that the Skills Development Act 97 of 1998 and the training policy of the company do not make provision for giving preference to certain employees on the grounds of their HIV status. The meeting adjourns with nobody being quite sure whether the new proposal can be implemented, given the picture that Darryl painted for them.

After the meeting, one of the trainers mentions the proposed policy to her colleague, Roderick, who happens to be HIV-positive. Roderick is horrified. He decides to write an anonymous letter to the editor of the company's newsletter. A week later, his letter is published. Part of his letter reads:

'I am expected to compile the budget for one of our company's largest divisions, and recently my supervisor told us that everything must be computerised before the end of the year. The budget has to be done on Excel, but I have never been trained to use Excel. How on earth can they expect me to perform the task, yet they deny me the opportunity to be trained just because of my HIV status? Is this the same company that I have been serving with dedication for over 20 years?'

Roderick also makes an appointment with Mapule Phoku, who heads up the company's Employee Assistance Programme. She is very sympathetic and promises to discuss the matter with the Chief Financial Officer (CFO) at the next management meeting. Roderick makes it very clear to Mapule that he refuses to make his HIV status known to others, irrespective of whether they change their minds on the training issue. He comes from a very conservative background, and if his family members were to know about his HIV status, he would most probably be rejected and despised. Roderick also tells Mapule about his colleague Pieter, who recently had a car accident and was infected with HIV during a blood transfusion.

All of this sets Mapule's mind racing. She wonders whether the CFO realises that all people with HIV do not fit his stereotype of sexual irresponsibility. How would Pieter's case fit into this new policy? She also recalls the case of Itumeleng, an employee who was infected by her husband, a man who often spends his business trips in the company of escort girls. How can denying these employees training opportunities add any value to their already desperate situations? And how will this new policy affect other employees with terminal illnesses such as cancer? Mapule realises that the number of 'risky employees' will shock management, especially if the CFO had to know how many of the so-called 'healthy' employees are frequently on leave owing to temporary ailments.

Mapule uses the first possible opportunity to discuss the new policy with Donny Mabitsela. However, he explains that Execu Image cannot be expected to compete with other manufacturers if the company continues investing in the wrong people, and that its limited resources must be optimised to enhance the quality of its services. Over a cup of tea, he closes the discussion with: 'Surely we all want what's best for the firm?' Mapula leaves Donny's office disheartened. Not only will she have to face Roderick and Pieter, but she also has to give some serious thoughts to the future of the Employee Assistance Programme.

Over lunch, Mapula asks her colleague Doris Williams, a senior personnel practitioner for Execu Image, for advice on the CFO's proposed policy. Doris feels that the company should consider various other implications before implementing a policy of this nature. According to Doris, such a policy would affect not only HIV-positive employees, but also their immediate families. By denying them the opportunity to develop their skills, the company would be denying them any possible opportunities to be promoted. They would, therefore, neither enjoy salary increases that go with promotions, nor would they stand an equal chance of applying for other positions in the company, since they would not be trained in any other fields.

Interpersonal relationships and staff morale within the company would also be affected negatively, since ignorant employees who do not have sufficient knowledge of how the disease is contracted may discriminate against those with HIV. She also foresees problems with the employment contracts negotiated with employees when Execu Image initially appoints a person. These contracts do not require employees to reveal their HIV status, nor do they mention the possible withholding of any company benefits, such as training opportunities. Doris feels that from a personnel point of view, the CFO should be advised not to pursue the matter.

At the annual shareholders' meeting, the CFO is confronted by Sheryl Koumbatis, one of the biggest shareholders of Execu Image. According to Ms Koumbatis, she read a letter in the company's newsletter about a disgruntled employee who complained about a new policy on HIV-positive staff to be introduced in the near future, and insists on having the facts. The CFO explains the new policy to the shareholders and defends it on the basis of his concern for their investments. Ms Koumbatis is clearly dissatisfied. She informs the meeting that the company will experience a drop in productivity if employees are not properly trained. Quantity and quality of production will be affected by such a policy and this would result in financial losses for all its shareholders. Some of the other shareholders share her sentiments.

Despite the resistance that he encounters, Donny Mabitsela includes his by now controversial proposal in his final budget proposal to the Finance Committee. A number of financial managers compliment him and show their support for the idea of investing in employees who at least have some chance of serving the company for a good number of years. Elmon Horwitz praises Donny for having such exceptional vision and expresses relief at the prospect of having savings to cover more important issues. The company had had major expenses the previous year when a number of its warehouses had to be renovated and Elmon sees this as an excellent opportunity to purchase new office furniture for management, as was initially planned.

Tampane Nguveni, one of the accountants, does not share Elmon's enthusiasm about the matter. She feels that the company has not followed a scientific approach in calculating the exact amounts that would be saved if infected employees were not trained. According to her, the savings might be a drop in the bucket, not even worth the fuss made by so many of her colleagues.

The next morning, Donny Mabitsela receives a fax from the *Daily Times*, requesting clarification on the new HIV/Aids policy to be implemented at Execu Image. They expect his comments by midday. He calls for an emergency meeting with Joe Johnson, Execu Image's public relations officer, to discuss the best possible way of dealing with the issue. Joe suggests that they look at all possible options before responding to the press. Donny gives Joe an hour to present him with all possible options that he foresees.

An hour later, Joe is back in Donny's office and presents him with the following options:
- Execu Image continues training all its employees, as has been done in the past, and accepts the fact that some of the funds invested in people who are HIV-positive will be lost.
- All staff will be trained only in the most basic skills required for their jobs. Only those who can prove that they are HIV-negative will be given access to more advanced specialisation courses.
- The company sticks to the proposed policy and asks all of its employees to reveal their status and train only those who are HIV-negative. In order to save time and money on the whole exercise, the company might even consider pre-screening all possible candidates prior to employing them.
- Execu Image considers the possibility of obtaining donor funding for the training of HIV-infected employees, thus lessening the burden on the company's limited resources.

Donny is left with less than two hours to prepare his press release.

Questions for discussion

1. Make an ethical evaluation of Donny's standpoint on HIV/Aids. Indicate the possible implications of his standpoint for both HIV-positive employees and for the company.
2. Identify all the moral arguments against Donny's standpoint that were raised in the case study.
3. Are there moral arguments that Donny could use to bolster his proposal?
4. Do you think that Roderick was morally justified in sending an anonymous note to the company newsletter? Or should he have pursued other avenues to voice his dissatisfaction? What other avenues were open to him?

5. What measures could Sheryl Koumbatis and the other disgruntled shareholders use to voice their concern about the proposed strategy?
6. Do you think that Joe has exhausted all the options for Execu Image in his presentation to Donny? What other options can you think of?
7. Prepare a press release on behalf of Donny for the *Daily Times* in which you morally defend the decision you regard best in this situation.

Black economic empowerment

The objective of the Broad-based Black Economic Empowerment Act 53 of 2003 in South Africa is to address the inequalities which resulted from the systematic exclusion of the majority of South Africans from meaningful participation in the economy in the past. It is hoped that over the long term, the effects of the Act will lead to expanding the economy that will benefit all South Africans regardless of race and gender. The onerous requirements of this law often lead to the phenomenon of fronting, which is an agreement between a white company and a black individual (or individuals) that pretends to be an empowerment company while in effect that is not the case. This is illustrated in the next case study.

Case study four: Black front, white back

Lemon Catering is a private company operating in Gauteng. As the government's black economic empowerment (BEE) policy started kicking in during 2003, Lemon Catering experienced a slowdown in its catering business. As a consequence of BEE, the majority of Lemon Catering's potential customers required a detailed black economic empowerment profile and policy from the company. Other companies in the catering industry with better performance on the BEE scorecard were taking business away from Lemon Catering. The board of directors of Lemon Catering realised that the company was too white to compete successfully in this new BEE environment. They therefore decided to register a subsidiary to serve those customers who required BEE criteria in procurement.

The subsidiary, Ziza Catering Services, has a 51 per cent ownership by a black person, Mr Thabo Ntshabeleng. He obtained his 51 per cent share in Ziza Catering through a loan funded entirely by the holding company, Lemon Catering. To achieve the desired BEE numbers for Ziza Catering Serivices, Lemon Catering transferred all their black employees to Ziza. All Ziza's operating activities were run from Lemon Catering's premises. A mere two months from the start of Ziza's operations, it experienced major growth in new business. A two-year contract with the local municipality particularly boosted its business prospects.

During a routine visit by procurement officers of the Department of Trade and Industry, a meeting was scheduled with Mr Ntshabeleng, the controlling shareholder. The meeting was held on the premises of Lemon Catering in an office which Mr Ntshabeleng pretended was his. The normal occupant of the office, Julia Smith, forgot, however, to remove some of her family photographs from the office walls. The procurement officers smelled a rat and decided to do a proper investigation of Ziza Catering Services. Upon investigation of the company's accounts, they discovered that no separate accounts had been kept for Ziza's apparent operations and transactions. No record could be found of Ziza's assets or systems, and all operations were run from Lemon Catering's premises. Furthermore, the employees of Ziza were being paid from the payroll of Lemon Catering. During the investigation, the employees confirmed that they often drove delivery vehicles bearing the holding company's name.

Source: Moloi, 2005.

Questions for discussion

1. Do you think that Lemon Catering's fronting can be morally justified?
2. What are the ethical consequences of fronting for the company and for society respectively?
3. How do you judge the moral behaviour of the board of directors of Lemon Catering and Mr. Ntshabeleng respectively?
4. Would you only hold the board of directors morally responsible for the fronting or Mr. Ntshabeleng as well?
5. What moral course of action would you advise Mr. Ntshabeleng to follow now that the fronting by Lemon Catering has been exposed?
6. What moral directives can you extract from this case for white companies that wish to meet BEE requirements?

Gifts and gratuities

A gift within the context of business might simply be a way of showing gratitude for good service delivered, but sometimes it may acquire an altogether different meaning in business. It may be used to influence unduly the discretion of those who have to make important decisions. The line between a bribe and showing gratitude can be extremely thin. It is for that reason that some people allege that 'there is no such thing as a free lunch in business'. In the following case, the significance of gifts in the context of business comes under the ethical spotlight.

Case study five: Tempting tickets

Chris has just graduated from university with a degree in Human Resource (HR) Management. He was fortunate enough to get a job as a management trainee in the HR department of TECHNICOR, a medium-sized parastatal organisation that manufactures electronic equipment.

The first item on the agenda for his first day at the office was to fill out several forms relating to his appointment. He found it interesting that, among others, he had to sign a declaration that he would not discuss any of TECHNICOR's business with non-employees, apparently because some of its activities were quite sensitive. After all the paperwork had been completed, he was taken on a tour of the plant. For the rest of his first day, as well as a further day-and-a-half, he attended a voluntary, but quite comprehensive, induction programme. The topics that were covered included HR policies, health and safety regulations, training programmes available in the organisation, employee benefits, disciplinary and grievance procedures, as well as information on TECHNICOR's recreational programmes.

During the induction programme, TECHNICOR's Executive Director gave Chris and his fellow new colleagues a short speech. The speech contained a few words of welcome, whereafter the Executive Director provided some statistics on the organisation's successes during the previous financial year. He also stated to new employees in no uncertain terms: 'I don't care what you have to do in the process, as long as the work gets done. The work has to be done with a cost-cutting mindset,' he emphasised. He then wished them well and hurriedly left to attend a board meeting.

After the induction programme, Chris was introduced to Hickson, his supervisor. Hickson was the manager of the recruitment division in the HR department. His supervisor gave him a hearty welcome and assured him that the HR Department was the best department in the company, even to the extent that other departments were jealous of it.

During his first week on the job, he was asked to work through a pile of CVs of candidates applying for jobs in TECHNICOR's call centre. He was told by his supervisor to eliminate all those candidates who were older than 30 years. When Chris asked why the cut-off was 30 years, Hickson told him that they already had enough 'dead wood' in the organisation. While he was discussing this with Hickson, the phone rang. Hickson spoke to the caller for a few minutes and then put the phone down with a triumphant glint in his eyes. 'I just organised a weekend in a resort for my wife and myself!' he said. 'And it's for free,' he continued. Chris later heard through the grapevine that Hickson's resort trip was sponsored by Finders, a recruitment agency that often did business with

TECHNICOR. Hickson, for example, had made about 60 per cent of all new appointments during the past year through Finders.

Later in that week, Chris received a call from a person called Marvin. Marvin introduced himself as an assistant manager with Finders and told Chris that Hickson had encouraged him to call Chris and meet him. Marvin suggested that they have lunch together on the same day. During lunch, which Marvin paid for, Chris was told by Marvin that he had good relations with the soccer fraternity and that he could arrange free tickets for Chris to all major soccer events. Marvin also suggested that he seriously consider some 'excellent candidates' for the call centre positions whose CVs had been sent through by Finders.

Things started bothering Chris. He felt uncomfortable deep down, but couldn't understand why. He was uncertain how to deal with the issue regarding Marvin. The next day he approached Hickson, who told him that Finders 'always provides the best candidates'. Hickson also told Chris that Marvin had a lot of connections and 'that he a is good guy to know'. Chris, sensing that something was not right, attempted to find out what the company policy was regarding accepting gifts from suppliers and vendors. He was told that there were no specific guidelines in this regard. A supervisor in another department said to him, 'Don't be a stirrer,' and another HR manager advised him, 'Use your gut-feel to deal with uncertainties.' He even phoned the Communications Department, but no-one there could answer his query about accepting gifts. When he got to his office the next day, there were two tickets to the next soccer game in a blank envelope on his desk.

Questions for discussion

1. Identify the organisational factors that contributed to Chris's dilemma.
2. Make a moral evaluation of the CEO's contribution to the induction process.
3. To what extent would you blame Hickson for the dilemma in which Chris found himself?
4. What options would you pursue had you been in the situation that Chris found himself in once he had received the two tickets on his desk?
5. What reforms would you recommend to TECHNICOR to prevent similar situations from recurring?

Employment equity

In an attempt to rectify the consequences of racial and gender discrimination that occurred under the apartheid dispensation, parliament passed the Employment Equity Act 55 of 1998. This Act compels companies to apply affirmative action in recruiting, appointing, and promoting staff. Complying with the requirement of affirmative action often complicates appointment decisions, as the following case illustrates.

> ### Case study six: Promotion problems
> As a partner in an accounting firm, Jane Smith has to deal with promotions regularly. With the firm's commitment to reaching its employment equity targets, promotions have become much more complicated lately. She finds the decision that she has to make within the next two days extremely tough. Three candidates were short-listed for promotion to a managerial position in the firm.
>
> Thandi (black, aged 34, and divorced, with one child) graduated in the lower half of her university class. She has been with the firm for four years and in the industry for six years. Her performance rating thus far has been mediocre, although she is very energetic. She has some difficulties in managing her staff, and on two occasions Jane has received complaints about her management style. Her child suffers from a chronic medical condition, and Jane is aware that the higher salary would help Thandi in meeting ends. She really likes Thandi. Occasionally, she even babysits Thandi's daughter. Thandi would be the first black female manager at this level. Jane is aware, however, that promoting Thandi may create the perception that she promotes her favourite people.
>
> Johan (white, aged 57, and married, with three children) graduated from a top international university in the top half of the class. Johan has been with the firm for twenty years and in the industry for thirty. He has always been a steady performer, with mostly average ratings. The reason Johan had been passed over for promotion before was his refusal to relocate, but that is no longer a problem. Johan's energy level is average to low; however, he has produced many of the firm's top performers in the past. This promotion would be his last before retirement and many in the firm feel he has earned it. In fact, one senior partner stopped Jane in the passage and said: 'Jane, Johan has been with us for a long time and done a lot of good things for the firm. I really hope you can see your way to promoting him. It would be a favour to me that I won't forget.'
>
> Shareen (Indian, aged 27, and single) graduated from a local university in the top three per cent of her class and has been with the

firm for three years. She is known for putting in sixty-hour weeks and for her very meticulous management style, which has generated some criticism from her staff. The last area she had managed showed record increases, despite the loss of some older clients who for some reason did not like dealing with Shareen. One fact about Shareen that worries Jane is that at her previous workplace, she sued the company for discrimination and won. A comment that Jane heard was that Shareen was intense and that nothing would stop her from reaching her goals. Another upper-management individual came into Jane's office and said: 'You know, Jane, Shareen is engaged to my son. I've looked over her personnel files and she looks very good. She looks like a rising star, and I think she should be promoted as soon as possible.'

Finally, the Human Resource Director came to talk to her about Thandi and said: 'Thandi is one of the very few black females in our firm who is qualified for this position. I've been going over the firm's hiring and promotion figures – it would benefit our employment profile tremendously if she could be promoted.'

Source: Adapted from Ferrel, Fraedrich & Ferrel, 2002.

Questions for discussion

1. Discuss the merit of each candidate without taking employment equity (affirmative action) into consideration.
2. How would your evaluation of the merit of the candidates change if you do take employment equity into consideration?
3. What ethical and legal considerations should Jane keep in mind while making her decision?
4. What are the options available to Jane? Discuss the implications of each decision Jane could make.
5. Who would you appoint if you were in Jane's situation? And how would you morally defend your decision to the unsuccessful candidates?

Company expenses

Employees and especially professionals often find themselves in positions where they have to make discretionary expenses in order to fulfil their work obligations. Such expenses often revolve around travel, meal, and accommodation expenses. These discretionary expenses for which the company is ultimately responsible can be abused by employees at the cost of the company. The next case presents a scenario where an employee who recently joined a firm is confronted with the temptation to use the system of company expenses to his personal benefit.

Case study seven: Three nights out of town

'You know, I have no idea how I'm going to manage to reach the end of the month', said Leonard Chasi to his friend and colleague Bill Mather. 'It's great to be a father, but children do not come cheap, and on top of this, I've had to pay the deposit on the house that I am renting. Right now you could turn me upside down and shake me from the ankles and not a cent would fall off me.'

'I'm sure it can't be as bad as that,' answered Bill. 'I've gone through similar situations myself and it is my experience that somehow one always manages to survive until the next pay cheque.'

'Don't worry,' said Leonard laughing. 'I'm not trying to borrow money from you.' He added, 'I agree that somehow or other I will manage to survive this month. What really worries me is that no matter how much I try to economise, there seems no way to bring my expenses into line with my income. This constant worry about financial matters really wears me down.'

Leonard Chasi was a newly hired manager working in the South African subsidiary of a well-known multinational company. Immediately after he completed his studies five years ago, he started to work for an accounting firm. The year before, he had completed his professional exams and had qualified as a professional accountant. It had been only two months prior to the date of this conversation that he had managed to secure his present job. Leonard had been married for two years and as recently as last month his wife had delivered their first child. They were very far from completing the furnishing and equipping of the rented flat in which they lived, but as they optimistically said, the advantage of having so little furniture was that in that way, the flat didn't look so small.

Bill Mather was a manager in the same company. He was also a chartered accountant and was three years older than Leonard. He had been working with the company for five years. Leonard liked Bill. He had found Bill helpful and welcoming during his early days in the new job. The two of them were fast becoming good friends.

'Well, at least you now have your coming trip to Mpumalanga. You're going to spend three nights there, aren't you? You should be able to get at least two or three thousand rand out of it,' Bill said.

'What do you mean?' answered Bill. 'I thought I would be lucky if it didn't cost me any money'.

'Oh! You can always save money if you're ready to rough it,' Bill explained. 'Of course, if you insist on living like a gentleman in a first class hotel, there is no way you will save any money. But I'm sure that you must have some friends in Mpumalanga. If you stay with any of them, you will spend next to nothing and then you can keep your expenses for more urgent needs.'

'But I understood that the company did not pay any overnight allowance. I was told that the policy was to refund reasonable expenses actually incurred, on the presentation of receipts,' Leonard said.

'Yes, that is the official policy,' Bill replied. 'But in practice it's easy to get receipts from a hotel that you can present here on your return. I have never seen the company attempting to verify whether or not you have actually stayed in the hotel.'

Leonard looked doubtful while he considered this suggestion. He said, 'I don't know ... would it not be like stealing the money from the company?'

'What do you mean, stealing the money from the company?!' Bill exclaimed. 'The company counts on you to spend that money in the hotel. You save it only because you are ready to live in more uncomfortable conditions. As a matter of fact, the last time I travelled, I ended up sleeping on a mat in the sitting room of a friend's apartment. Do you think that I should make that type of sacrifice and the company save the money? Come on! In what world do you live? Besides, the company expects to spend on the cost of having you in a certain kind of hotel per day to have you in a given city and, at the end of the day, they spend exactly that. Where is the problem?'

'But ... is this a common practice among the company's managers?' questioned Leonard. 'Do most of them do it?'

'You know, this is not the type of thing that you discuss openly with every Tom, Dick, and Harry in the company's cafeteria', replied Bill. 'But I know for certain that at least two people do it regularly, and among my friends outside the company several do it and do not think anything special about it.'

'I don't know,' said Leonard, 'I certainly need money very badly, and every little bit helps ... and what you say makes a lot of sense ... it's just that I had never thought of things that way. I don't know, I guess I'm just confused.'

Questions for discussion

1. Look critically at the arguments used by Bill to justify his position. Do you think his arguments can be morally justified?
2. What can the company that Leonard and Bill work for do to clarify their position on travel expenses? Do they carry any moral blame for the predicament in which Leonard finds himself?
3. If you were in Leonard's position, would you follow Bill's advice on your upcoming trip to Mpumalanga? How would you explain your decision to Bill and your manager respectively?

Whistle blowing

Whistle blowing occurs when an employee reports illegal or immoral conduct outside official channels to a source that is deemed fit to take appropriate action. Organisations therefore tend to regard whistle blowing as an act of betrayal. It often leads to a breach of trust between the organisation and the whistle blower which results in his or her dismissal. Although legislation such as the Protected Disclosures Act 26 of 2000 exists to protect whistle blowers from retaliation by their employers, it is difficult to enforce in practice. The next case study paints the predicament of a whistle blower.

Case study eight: Suspicious invoices

Renée, an accountant, joined Immaculate Designs, a textile manufacturing company based in the Eastern Cape. Part of her job was to approve suppliers' invoices for payment. Once approved by Renée, one of the directors would sign the cheques. Being new, she studied each invoice carefully to ensure that it was valid and that the goods or services mentioned had actually been received.

Within the first month, some invoices landed on her desk that aroused her suspicion. She noted that the invoices had not been commercially printed and had just been typed out on plain paper. She knew that some small suppliers do operate that way, but, in this case, there were invoices from different suppliers prepared in exactly the same way. Upon further investigation, she could find no evidence that the goods and services specified on the invoices had actually been supplied. There were also no order numbers or the usual signatures indicating that the goods and services had been received. Renée then approached the financial director, who assured her that everything was in order and that the invoices should be paid.

Being quite sure that something untoward was happening and that even senior management were involved, Renée decided to approach the senior partner of the external auditors for advice. They decided that during the forthcoming audit, they would 'discover' the existence of the invoices. This duly happened.

Upon the discovery of the invoices by the external auditors, management became suspicious. They could not understand how the auditors could have discovered the existence of the false invoices so quickly. They suspected that one of the sales managers, Jim, who had recently fallen into disfavour with management, was responsible.

> Although no direct accusations were made, they made life very difficult for Jim and he eventually resigned.
>
> It turned out that the money from the suspicious invoices was being channelled into a secret account held outside the organisation. This money was then used to entertain the buyers of client companies who purchased stock from Immaculate Designs. Sometimes, the money was used to entertain the said buyers in escort clubs, casinos or restaurants when they visited the company's premises. On rare occasions only, the money would be deposited into the personal credit card of a buyer.
>
> The auditors reported this practice to the shareholders, who ordered the practice to cease. The sales staff complained that this made it difficult for them to compete, as competitors did not seem to have any qualms about this kind of practice. 'In any event, what was the big deal? It was not as though we are stealing from the company,' one salesperson remarked.

Questions for discussion

1. Do you agree with the assessment of the sales staff that their behaviour was not unethical, but was normal business practice? Give reasons for your answer.
2. The sales management claimed that the survival of the company depended on its being able to compete using the same methods as competitors. How would you respond to this kind of argument?
3. Was Renée justified in 'blowing the whistle' on the company in the way that she did? Or should she have used other channels to voice her disapproval? Suggest other ways in which she could have approached the problem.
4. Could Renée be held morally responsible for Jim's dismissal? Should she have owned up to having informed the auditors?
5. How do you assess the external auditors' behaviour? Should they have approached the situation differently?

Bibliography

Ferrel, OC, Fraedrich, J & Ferrel, L. 2002. *Business ethics: ethical decision making and cases*, 5th ed. Boston, MA: Houghton Mifflin.

Moloi, M. 2005. 'Facing up to the crippling effects of fronting in SA'. *Business Day*, 22 March. [Online]. Available: <www.businessday.com> [Accessed 20 February 2006].

Moneyweb. *Corporate governance*. [Online]. Available: <www. moneyweb.co.za/specials/corp_gov> [Accessed 5 June 2006].

Part 3
Professional ethics

In Part 3, we focus specifically on professional ethics in the field of accountancy. In *Chapter 12* we first explain what it means to be a professional, clearly demonstrating that ethical strength is central to the true professional, before evaluating whether accountants and auditors can be regarded as professionals. The nature of the accounting and auditing professions is then analysed and the key professional bodies in South Africa identified. The last part of the chapter deals with criticism of the profession in recent years, and highlights questions about the commitment of some accountants and auditors to professional ethics.

We then proceed to a discussion of codes of professional ethics in *Chapter 13*. The approach taken is initially wide-ranging and general. We show why professional codes are essential, what their typical features and structures are, and how they tend to be implemented. Attention is then turned to the codes of professional ethics of accountancy bodies. First the *IFAC Code of Ethics for Professional Accountants* is considered, and the key principles contained therein are identified. As virtually all reputable professional accountancy bodies, including the SA Institute of Chartered Accountants (SAICA), are members of IFAC, these principles have been incorporated into most of the ethical codes for professional accountants. A review of the SAICA *Code of Professional Conduct* confirms this. The chapter concludes with an analysis of the ethical principles vital for the external audit to have value, but which have not been consistently adhered to by auditors, thereby contributing to the auditing scandals of recent years.

Applied ethics is all about putting moral values into practice. Therefore Part 3 and the whole book conclude in *Chapter 14* with a set of case studies covering a number of important ethical challenges facing professional accountants.

12

Accountants and auditors as professionals[*][**]

Frans Prinsloo

Outcomes

After working through this chapter, you should be able to do the following:
- Discuss the difference between personal ethics, business ethics, and professional ethics
- Understand the concepts of 'profession' and 'professionalism'
- Demonstrate an awareness of the background and development of professions
- Discuss the characteristics which are useful in distinguishing professional from non-professional occupations
- Discuss whether accountants and auditors are members of a profession
- Illustrate the dimensions of professionalism with specific reference to the accounting and auditing professions
- Discuss the desirability of 'licensing' of individuals to perform professional services
- Explain the key roles of the professional accountancy bodies operating in South Africa
- Demonstrate an awareness of the major scandals that have affected the accounting and auditing professions in recent years.

Overview

In this chapter the relevance of professional ethics to accountants and auditors is evaluated by first establishing what characteristics need to be satisfied in order for an occupational grouping to be considered a profession. Thereafter, the occupations of accountants and auditors are evaluated with

---

[*] This chapter acknowledges the extracts from the original Chapter 11 of the revised edition by Miné van Zyl.
[**] The contribution of Charl du Plessis in compiling the original Chapter 12 co-authored with Marinda Burger for the revised edition is acknowledged.

reference to these characteristics. Having concluded that accountants and auditors are members of professions, consideration is given to the 'type' of professions to which they belong. The professional bodies in the field of accounting and auditing operating in South Africa are identified and their roles noted. The chapter concludes with the identification of a number of corporate scandals that in recent years have brought the commitment of accountants and auditors to professional ethics into question.

Introduction

Earlier in this text, we noted that the words 'ethics' and 'morality' are often used interchangeably and referred to as behaviour which is acceptable and responsible. Ethics concerns itself with what is good or right in human interaction, and behaviour can therefore be classified as ethical when it is good not only for the 'self', but also for others. When ethical behaviour revolves around personal moral dilemmas, it is referred to as '**personal ethics**'. Personal ethics can therefore be defined as the set of one's own ethical commitments, which is usually acquired in early home or religious training, often modified by later reflection, and sometimes adjusted through later experiences in life (Harris, Pritchard & Rabins, 2005). Personal ethics is also closely linked with common morality, which is a set of moral ideals shared by most members of a society.

> Personal ethics can be defined as the set of one's own ethical commitments.

While personal ethics and common morality deal with human interaction, either on personal or societal levels, business ethics focuses on behaviour during economic activity. Business ethics is concerned with the moral behaviour of participants and activities of businesses on the macro-economic level, the organisational level, and the intra-organisational level, and therefore strives to enhance the interests of all stakeholders. Since the majority of accountants are not engaged in public practice, but employed in commerce and industry and in the public sector, an understanding of business ethics at these three levels is essential.

> Professional ethics is the set of standards adopted by professionals insofar as they see themselves acting as professionals.

Professional ethics is the set of standards adopted by professionals insofar as they see themselves acting as professionals (Harris *et al*, 2005). The purpose of these ethical standards is to ensure adherence to moral behaviour by the members of the profession to the benefit of the clients and the society which they serve.

> Ideally, the three sets of ethical standards – personal ethics, business ethics, and professional ethics – will coincide, but at times situations may occur where moral dilemmas exist and the professional standard may differ from the code of ethics of a business, and even

> from personal morality. In these situations, professionals need to make a choice from among the three sets of ethical standards.

Before proceeding with discussions about professional ethics for accountants and auditors, it is necessary to consider whether accountants and auditors are indeed members of a profession. In order to do this, it is necessary first to consider what criteria have to be satisfied in order for an occupational grouping to be regarded as a profession, and secondly, to evaluate whether accountants and auditors satisfy these criteria.

What is a profession?

An early meaning of 'profession' stems from the word 'professed', referred to in *The Oxford English Dictionary* (1961) as early as the thirteenth century as 'the declaration, promise, or vow made by one entering a religious order'. The meaning later developed to signify:

> '[t]he occupation which one professes to be skilled in and to follow ... a vocation in which a professed knowledge of some department of learning or science is used in its application to the affairs of others or in the practice of an art founded upon it'.

Source: The Oxford English Dictionary, 1961

The Oxford English Dictionary (1961) further defines 'professionalism' as the '... professional quality, character, method or conduct, and the stamp of a particular profession'. In other words, professionalism comprises the conduct and qualities which characterise a profession or professional person.

At the beginning of the nineteenth century the concept of a 'profession' was intended to include only the learned occupations of divinity, law, and medicine. Before the industrial revolution, social class and status determined entry into these professions. After the industrial revolution in England, around 1832, the pursuit of professional careers by the middle classes emerged, which gave them the opportunity to gain status through work as opposed to social class (Larson, 1977:5).

Because of the ambiguous nature of the concept of 'a profession', and because of the market power that may come from professional licensure (Friedman, 1962), many different occupational groups have tried to lay claim to professional status. However few occupations have attained the attributes and recognition ascribed to 'true' professions such as medicine and law (Wilensky, 1964). A profession is born out of a social need for services which require specialised knowledge and skills (Carter, 1998). The professionals, who provide the special services for economic reward, aim to control a market for their expertise by devising a system of education and training, and accepting into the profession only those who are considered competent with reference to their performance in the prescribed education and training. If professions enjoy certain social status by providing services which require specialised knowledge and skill in a market which they control, one should be able to distinguish professional occupations from non-professional occupations.

A number of authors have attempted to identify the criteria that should be satisfied for an occupational grouping to be considered a profession.

> A profession is born out of a social need for services which require specialised knowledge and skills.

Larson (1977) identifies characteristics of professions which include:
- A body of knowledge and techniques which professionals apply in their work
- Training to master knowledge
- Service orientation
- Distinctive ethics which justifies the self-regulation granted by society, and
- Autonomy and prestige.

Based on these characteristics, it is possible that many occupational groups may lay claim to being a 'profession', not only familiar professions such as medicine and engineering, but also service firms such as advertising agencies, accounting and consulting firms, and law firms. The tougher test cases arise when asking how to deal with occupations such as beauticians or hairdressers, both of which could satisfy many of these characteristics and have expressed the ambition to be considered professions. Abbott (1988) introduced a helpful further distinction, emphasising that the key distinguishing characteristic of professions is that they are 'based in *abstract* bodies of knowledge'.

The South African Institute of Chartered Accountants (SAICA) (2008: ET-3) indicates that a profession can be distinguished when members of an occupational grouping:
- Have mastered specific intellectual skills through an education and training process
- Accept duties to society as a whole in addition to duties to the client or employer
- Have an outlook that is essentially objective, and
- Render services to a high standard of conduct and performance.

Sharma (1997:758) indicates that the core characteristics of professionals (members of a profession) are '... having prolonged specialized training in a body of abstract knowledge and output service that is intangible – one that is perishable and, unlike tangible products of a manufacturing entity, impossible to hold in inventory'.

> Huebner (1915) identifies four characteristics of a professional:
> - The professional is involved in a vocation that is useful to society and so noble in its purpose as to inspire the professional to make the vocation his life's work.
> - The professional's vocation involves a science and in its practice requires an expert knowledge of the science.
> - In applying the expert knowledge, the professional should abandon the strictly selfish commercial view and always keep in mind the advantage of the client.
> - The professional should have a spirit of loyalty to fellow professionals and a spirit of helpfulness to achieve the common cause they all profess, and should not allow any unprofessional acts to bring shame upon the entire profession.

Even though these attributes are not considered to be universal standards (as certain professions may not possess a given characteristic, and other occupations may possess some of the characteristics and yet not be regarded as a profession), they are nonetheless useful in classifying occupational groups as professional or non-professional. A good example of an attribute that would not preclude external auditors from being members of a profession is '... always to keep in mind the advantage of the client'. In fact, if the external auditor acts in his client's advantage, rather than in the public interest, it could be argued that the auditor is acting unprofessionally.

The characteristics described by Greenwood (1957:44–55) (cited in Harris *et al*, 2005:4) are also useful in distinguishing professions from non-professional occupations, and will be used to evaluate whether accountants and auditors are members of a profession.

One: Entrance into the profession requires an extensive period of education and training

Many occupations require a period of education and practical training, but the training required of a professional has a more intellectual character. The knowledge and skills attained by professionals are grounded in a body of theory acquired through formal education, usually at an academic institution. A formal education usually requires attaining a bachelor's degree from a university along with a more advanced degree, and often involves completing a professional examination. A close relationship necessarily exists between the profession and universities offering the formal education.

In South Africa, before a person can become a registered auditor (a requirement before one can render external audit services), the Independent Regulatory Board for Auditors (IRBA) will consider whether the applicant '... has complied with the prescribed education, training and competency requirements for a registered auditor ...' in terms of section 37(2)(a) of the Auditing Profession Act 26 of 2005.

A person also cannot become a Chartered Accountant (SA) unless the applicant has satisfied the South African Institute of Chartered Accountants (SAICA) that he or she '... has passed the examinations, and has the practical experience, prescribed' by the Institute (By-Law 29.1 of SAICA).

Currently the prescribed education and training requirements for registered auditors and Chartered Accountants (SA) are very similar:
- Successful completion of the four-year degree/equivalent programme (CTA/equivalent) as accredited by the SAICA.
- The passing of Part I and Part II of the Qualifying Examination set by SAICA/IRBA. The Part I examination is an assessment of the 'core competence' of the candidate in the fields of Financial Accounting, Auditing, Taxation, Management Accounting, and Finance. The Part II examination is a test of 'professional competence' either in Auditing or Financial Management, depending on which training route the candidate has chosen.
- Completion of a training contract (with a minimum duration of three years) in the office of a registered auditor (Registered Training Organisation) or with an Approved Training Organisation in commerce and industry / public sector.
- Successful completion of a 'specialism' programme which is done concurrently with the training contract.

It is submitted that these fairly onerous education and training requirements ensure the development of intellectual knowledge and skills which are thoroughly assessed before a person can become a Chartered Accountant (SA) or registered auditor.

Two: Professional knowledge and skill are essential to the wellbeing of the larger society

> In a sophisticated society, professionals enjoy a certain social status attained through delivery of specialised services. Society, on the other hand, is dependent on the services provided by professionals. Members of society, for example, depend for their wellbeing on the specialised knowledge of physicians in treating illnesses and

> restoring health. Lawyers protect and defend those who have been accused of a crime.
>
> In addition to society depending on professionals, a proliferation of skilled professionals in society enhances the intellectual development, sophistication, and economic wellbeing of the society, and therefore contributes to a higher standard of living.

The core knowledge base of accountants and auditors is ordinarily in the fields of Financial Accounting, Auditing, Taxation, Management Accounting, and Finance. With this specialist knowledge, they perform several functions essential for the economy and society. Some examples include:

Roles in public practice

- *Auditing and assurance:* The auditor is responsible for issuing an opinion on whether or not a company's annual financial statements fairly present its financial performance, financial position and cash flows. Without such opinions expressed by independent, competent auditors, investors and other providers of finance will be reluctant to make funds available to businesses, resulting in an increased cost of capital or, in the extreme, the inability of businesses to operate.
- *Taxation:* Accountants in public practice advise their clients on how to minimise their tax liabilities lawfully through efficient tax planning. They also submit tax returns, resolve tax problems, advise on tax implications, and advise on litigation matters.
- *Management consultancy:* This service involves advising clients on the management of their businesses (and is often accompanied by the preparation of budgets and cash flow forecasts, business plans and valuations). This service is particularly important to the effective management of smaller businesses, which do not have qualified accountants in their employ, yet play a vital role in the economy.
- *Secretarial services:* This service involves maintaining statutory records and filing returns with CIPRO, thereby assisting particularly smaller companies in complying with the requirements of the Companies Act 61 of 1973.
- *Accounting services:* This involves designing, evaluating and/or maintaining of computerised accounting information systems to enhance the integrity of financial information that is available to management for decision-making purposes, and may further include the compilation of the client's annual financial statements.

Roles in commerce and industry

The financial director/financial manager or equivalent will use his or her specialist knowledge to perform duties that will assist in ensuring the financial wellbeing of his or her employer, such as:
- *Preparing financial statements* (both monthly and annually) in order to assist management, shareholders and other stakeholders to monitor the financial performance, financial position and cash flows of the business
- *Interpreting financial information* to assist management to identify areas in the business requiring remedial action timeously
- *Devising and installing financial reporting and cost accounting systems* in order to keep track of transactions and the costs thereof
- *Designing and evaluating internal controls* to ensure the orderly and efficient conduct of the business and the safeguarding of its assets
- *Developing budgets and forecasts* (for example, statements of cash flow) to assist management with its planning for the future.

The importance of the professional knowledge and skills of accountants and auditors to society is evident from the following comment made by Lynn Turner (2001), previously Chief Accountant of the Securities and Exchange Commission (SEC) in the USA:

'The enduring confidence of the investing public in the integrity of our capital markets is vital. In America today, approximately one out of every two adults has invested their savings in the securities markets ... These investments have provided trillions of dollars in capital ... That capital is providing the fuel for our economic engine, funding for the growth of new businesses, and providing ... job opportunities for ... millions of workers. But ... the willingness of investors to continue to invest their money in the markets cannot be taken for granted ... Public trust begins, and ends, with the integrity of the numbers the public uses to form the basis for making their investment decisions ... Accordingly, investors in the US capital markets have depended for over a hundred years on an independent third party, an external auditor, to examine the books and financial reports prepared by management ...'

While this comment was made in relation to the stock (share) market in the USA, it pertains equally to countries across the world, including South Africa. The 'public trust' referred to is dependent on external auditors who express an opinion on the fair presentation of the financial statements. However, it should be noted that the role of accountants and the

> The role of accountants and the management of the business entities responsible for preparing the financial statements should not be ignored – if they cannot be trusted, it will be very difficult (if not impossible) for the external auditor to express an opinion on the fair presentation of the financial statements.

management of the business entities responsible for preparing the financial statements should not be ignored – if they cannot be trusted, it will be very difficult (if not impossible) for the external auditor to express an opinion on the fair presentation of the financial statements.

Three: Professions usually have a monopoly on the provision of professional services

The monopoly on the provision of professional services is achieved in two ways. Firstly, only candidates who have graduated with the appropriate qualification from an accredited academic institution and who have successfully completed a professional exam or who have graduated from a professional school are allowed to hold the professional title. The profession 'controls' the academic institutions and professional schools by regulating their number and quality. The profession also determines the curriculum requirements. Secondly, the profession implements a licensing system or registration with a professional body for candidates who want to practise in that profession. Contravention of this requirement is usually subject to a legal penalty.

In South Africa, SAICA accredits universities to provide education to aspiring Chartered Accountants (SA) and registered auditors. SAICA also prescribes a syllabus that has to be covered during the four year degree/equivalent programme, and adherence to this is verified during monitoring visits that occur at least once in a five year cycle. The results of graduates of the accredited universities in SAICA's Qualifying Examination Part 1 also send a clear message as to the quality of the programme on offer. Consistently poor performance normally results in SAICA initiating remedial action.

Legislation (specifically, section 41(2) of the Auditing Profession Act) prohibits any person who is not registered with the Independent Regulatory Board for Auditors from performing any external audit or using the name of 'registered auditor' or otherwise practising as an external auditor. Also, no person may refer to him- or herself as a Chartered Accountant (SA) unless he or she is a member of SAICA. Should someone falsely purport to be a Chartered Accountant (SA), he or she is guilty of an offence in terms of the Chartered Accountants Designation (Private) Act 67 of 1993.

Four: Professionals often have an unusual degree of autonomy when rendering their services

Law and medical professionals in private practice have considerable freedom in choosing their clients and patients. Even in an organisational setting, professionals may exercise a large degree of personal judgement and creativity when performing their responsibilities. Lawyers can determine the most appropriate defence arguments for their clients and physicians can decide on the best medical treatment for their patients. The justification for this unusual degree of autonomy is that only the professional has the required knowledge and skills to determine the most appropriate professional service. The specialised knowledge and skills give the professional the power to claim a large degree of autonomy in his or her field. This makes for one of the most satisfying aspects of being a professional.

The auditor performing the external audit of financial statements is required '... to obtain reasonable assurance about whether the financial statements as a whole are free from material misstatement ... thereby enabling the auditor to express an opinion on whether the financial statements are prepared, in all material respects, in accordance with an applicable financial reporting framework; and to report on the financial statements ... in accordance with the ... findings' (IFAC, 2010, paragraph 11). In undertaking this work, the auditor has to use his or her expert knowledge about auditing and financial accounting as well as professional judgement to gather audit evidence sufficient to be able to support his or her opinion expressed on the financial statements. In terms of auditing standards, and reinforced by legislation, the client may not in any way attempt to restrict or direct the work of the auditor in order to achieve the objectives of the external audit.

> The accountant has to make judgements about the appropriate accounting policies to be followed by the entity, and prepare estimates about matters such as depreciation rates, doubtful debts, provisions, and fair values when preparing financial statements.

The accountant, in turn, has to make judgements about the appropriate accounting policies to be followed by the entity, and prepare estimates about matters such as depreciation rates, doubtful debts, provisions, and fair values when preparing financial statements. However, it is important to note that while the accountant plays a key role in preparing the financial statements, the management or board of directors of the company still has to assume responsibility for the fair presentation of the financial statements. In this regard, trust of the entity's management in the abilities of the accountant is vital.

Five: Professionals claim to be regulated by ethical standards

To achieve and maintain the professional status enjoyed by professionals in society, most professions attempt to limit abuse of this status by regulating themselves for the benefit of the public. Most professional societies or bodies have a code of ethics or conduct. If professionals want to remain registered as professionals within their particular professional body, they have to adhere to their profession's respective code of ethics. Professional bodies discipline members for contravening the code of ethics thereby promoting adherence and protecting the reputation of the profession. Observing a code of ethics enhances a professional's sense of responsibility towards the wellbeing of society.

> Observing a code of ethics enhances a professional's sense of responsibility towards the wellbeing of society.

Accountants and auditors who are members of accountancy bodies are generally subject to a code of ethics, which is enforced by the professional body of which they are members. This will be explored in more detail in the next chapter.

Types of professionals in society

Figure 12.1 maps the elements of professionalism along two dimensions. On the horizontal axis, the work executed by professionals is assessed to determine if it is performed for the benefit of society (Parsons, 1968), or whether it comes from a biased position as advocate for a specific client's benefit (Donaldson, 2000). The former position is labelled as the 'Altruistic' model of professionalism, and the latter as the 'Advocacy' model. It should be noted, however, that Larson (1977) condemned this romanticised view that professionals are altruistic servers of mankind, claiming that the professions are really economic interests attempting to dominate intellectually the market for necessary expert services.

Figure 12.1 Two dimensions of professionalism

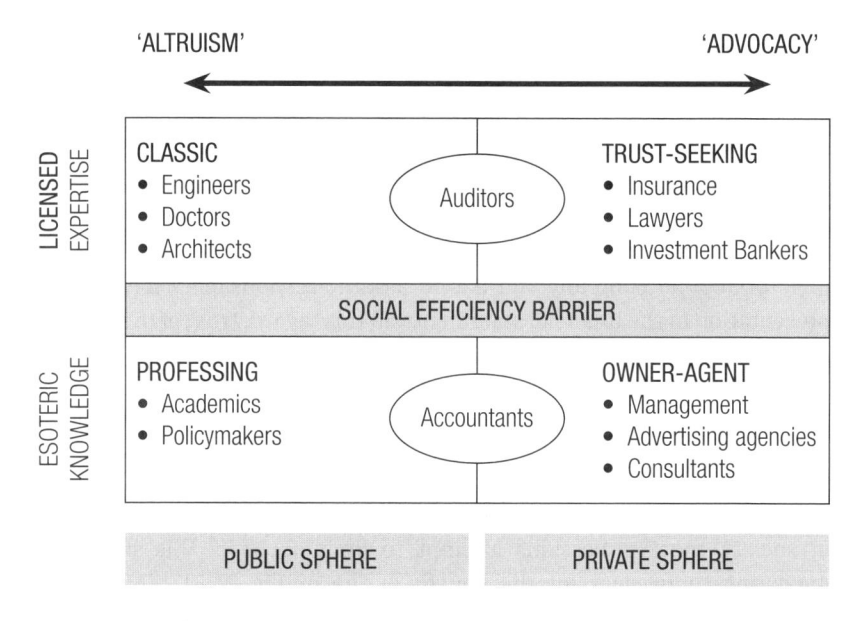

	'ALTRUISM' ←——————————→ 'ADVOCACY'	
LICENSED EXPERTISE	**CLASSIC** • Engineers • Doctors • Architects *(Auditors)*	**TRUST-SEEKING** • Insurance • Lawyers • Investment Bankers
	SOCIAL EFFICIENCY BARRIER	
ESOTERIC KNOWLEDGE	**PROFESSING** • Academics • Policymakers *(Accountants)*	**OWNER-AGENT** • Management • Advertising agencies • Consultants
	PUBLIC SPHERE	PRIVATE SPHERE

The vertical dimension is drawn from discussion on the centrality of knowledge to the professional, and distinguishes between the formally 'licensed' uses of specialised knowledge versus general market entry. In other words, do you need a licence to work as an auditor, lawyer, hairdresser or accountant? Milton Friedman (1962), and later Larson (1977), expressed doubts about the motives behind licensing. Friedman's concern with 'specifying which individuals should be permitted to follow particular pursuits' (1962:138) stems from the restriction of the economic freedoms of individuals.

So what is the justification for not simply allowing everyone to practise in an occupational field requiring a licence, and then allowing the market to weed out poor service? On what basis does society allow certain occupational groups to close their ranks to membership?

In terms of the Social Efficiency Barrier (Sharma, 1997), social welfare is enhanced when professional groups pre-certify through licensing their members' capabilities, as the public and market need not continually establish the competency of service providers. The prior certification represents a reduction in both search costs and in risk. There appears to be broad consensus that medical practitioners and engineers fit this description of licensing comfortably because of public interest. Perhaps it has something to do with the irreversibility of an error of judgement in these spheres? Life-threatening advice from an ill-qualified medical doctor or injury resulting from the collapse of a public structure is hardly made whole through monetary compensation. The public interest in these areas suggests that market imperfections for these services, and the premium pricing that results, may be tolerated in exchange for public peace of mind and a reduction in search costs. However, below the Social Efficiency Barrier, you are on your own. The risk of appointing, for example, an advertising agency falls squarely on your company's shoulders, as no professional body certifies their competency of the service provider by means of a licence.

The two-by-two matrix depicted in Figure 12.1 yields four separate classes of potential professionals. The first quadrant is the most familiar and probably represents what is most generally understood under professionalism. Hence the label 'Classic Professionals', which includes doctors, engineers, and arguably architects, whose specialised design and construction skills have become essential for safety in our urban landscape.

Moving across to the top right quadrant, still above the Social Efficiency Barrier, we encounter a group labelled 'Trust-seeking Professionals'. Common to these occupational groups is that their members require licensing to practise, and furthermore, that the relationship between the aspiring professional and his or her client is a decidedly private affair and serves the specific interest of the client. The label assigned to this group is derived from their attempts to escape the adverse public perceptions and reputation of their occupations. Their agenda is to use the formal tools of professionalisation, for example, licensing, codes of ethics, and membership sanction, to develop better trust among the public.

The bottom left quadrant is labelled 'Professing Professionals'. This group is actively involved in the creation of knowledge and in the professing of knowledge, predominantly in the public interest. However, entry into this public forum for ideas requires no licensing. Academic tenure may be seen as some form of entry control, yet tenure by its very nature intends to create conditions for new and even dissident knowledge, rather than a willingness to subscribe to a uniform body of agreed-upon ideas within the profession.

The final quadrant is called 'Owner-Agents'. Entry into these occupations requires no formal licensing, and the objective of this group, quite like the 'trust-seeking' group above, is to serve the private interests of whoever pays for the service.

Figure 12.1 also maps several 'professions' in terms of this matrix. Next, consideration is given to where the professions of accountants and auditors should be located if placed within this matrix.

Accountants need neither certification nor licensing in order to perform their duties, and therefore fall below the Social Efficiency Barrier. Even though all professional accountancy bodies (for example, SAICA) set requirements for admission, it is important to realise that a person does not have to be a member of a professional body in order to perform duties as an accountant. Furthermore, the varying functional demands currently placed on the typical accountant correspond with two very different positions, and hence, accountants tend to straddle the public and private spheres.

Auditors are placed above the Social Efficiency Barrier, as formal licensing is required to practise as an auditing professional (in terms of the Auditing Profession Act). Auditing is '... the linchpin of our enterprise system. It is supposed to keep companies honest in how they do their accounting and reporting, safeguarding the public's interest in terms of both investing and taxation' (Sayles & Smith 2006:79). This account of the profession would prompt us to shift auditors over to the Classic Professionals quadrant, given that their licensed work would ideally conform to the 'Altruistic', public interest label.

> Even though all professional accountancy bodies set requirements for admission, it is important to realise that a person does not have to be a member of a professional body in order to perform duties as an accountant.

However, Sayles, an emeritus professor of accounting at Columbia University, and his co-author Smith (*ibid*) offer a useful account of the unfortunately all-too-common commercial entrapments that create problems for the profession owing to conflicts of interest. The rendering of consulting services concurrently with the external audit, the pressures to complete the audit work within budget, the sidelining of audit partners who do not reach revenue targets, and fee-based compensation are all examples of how the auditing firm, as competitive player in the private market for professional services, repeatedly places its partners and staff in untenable choice-dilemmas between private and public interests. As long as this tension remains unresolved, the claim to Classic Professionalism is arguably disingenuous.

It is submitted that in the late 1990s the auditing profession was located between the first and second quadrants in Figure 12.1. However, much has been done by the professional bodies, regulators and legislators to reinforce the need for auditors to act in the 'public interest'. Some examples of remedial action taken include the promulgation of the Auditing Profession Act and the replacement of the Companies Act 61 of 1973 by the Companies Act 71 of 2008 by legislators in South Africa (and the Sarbanes-Oxley Act by their counterparts in the USA); the introduction of stronger codes of professional conduct enforced more rigorously by professional bodies; and the issue of more onerous auditing standards, accompanied by stricter monitoring by regulators of audit firms' compliance therewith.

Professional bodies guarding the profession and its ethics

Professional bodies have the responsibility to protect the standing of their respective professions. To this end, a professional body typically performs the following functions:

1. *Regulates entrance to the profession through education and training:* The professional body determines the curriculum requirements for undergraduate and postgraduate programmes as well as the training requirements. It also sets qualifying examinations. In essence, the professional body prescribes the minimum requirements for admission to the profession.
2. *Administers a registration system for candidates who want to practise as professionals:* When the professional body is satisfied that the aspirant professional has conducted him- or herself throughout the period of practical experience or training in a way that satisfies the professional, ethical, and academic requirements expected of a future registered professional, the applicant is admitted to the professional body.
3. *Sets or controls the technical standards with which its members must comply:* The professional body further promotes adherence to the professional standards to ensure a high quality of service.
4. *Issues ethical standards to the members of the profession so that good conduct is the norm:* Compliance with the professional body's code of ethics and ethical standards is enforced upon its members by having a disciplinary committee (or equivalent). If the disciplinary committee

is of the opinion that a member is guilty of contravening the code of ethics or of other improper conduct, an appropriate punishment can be imposed upon the member.

A number of professional bodies in the field of accountancy operate in South Africa, including the South African Institute of Chartered Accountants, the South African Institute of Professional Accountants, the Chartered Institute of Management Accountants, the Association of Chartered Certified Accountants, and the Institute of Internal Auditors. The Independent Regulatory Board for Auditors differs from these bodies in that it is established as a 'public entity' in terms of the Public Finance Management Act 1 of 1999, is partially funded by the government, and has as its core function the regulation of the external auditing profession.

South African Institute of Chartered Accountants (SAICA)

SAICA is arguably the best-known professional accountancy body in South Africa, being formally established in 1980, but with a history dating back to 1894. A member of SAICA is referred to as a 'Chartered Accountant', or in its abbreviated form as a CA (SA). At the end of 2010 SAICA had just over 31 000 members, of whom just under 7 000 were resident outside South Africa.

The mission of SAICA is to serve the interests of the chartered accountancy profession and society, by upholding professional standards and integrity, and the pre-eminence of South African CAs nationally and internationally, by:

- 'Delivering competent entry-level members
- Providing services to the members to maintain and enhance their professional competence thereby enabling them to create value for their clients and employers
- Enhancing the quality of information used in the private and public sectors for measuring and enhancing organisational performance
- Running and facilitating programmes to transform the profession and to facilitate community upliftment
- Fulfilling a leadership role regarding relevant business-related issues and providing reliable and respected public commentary'.

SAICA prides itself that its members are leaders in the business world. For example, nearly a quarter of the directors of the Top 100 companies listed on the JSE are Chartered Accountants (SA).

Source: <www.saica.co.za> [accessed 16 August 2011]

South African Institute of Professional Accountants (SAIPA)

SAIPA aims to ensure that its members '... are able to optimise their accountancy practices or add value to their employers in the corporate world, and, by so doing, create additional wealth for the country and its people'. SAIPA has more than 6 000 professional accountants who work in public practice, commerce and industry, government and academia. The majority of its members are in public practice, offering accounting and related services (but excluding external auditing) to the general public and the business community, especially to small, medium and micro-enterprises.

Source: <www.saipa.co.za> [accessed 16 February 2009]

Chartered Institute of Management Accountants (CIMA)

CIMA is the only international professional body that focuses solely on the education and training of management accountants in business. CIMA represents over 164 000 members and students in 161 countries who work in industry, commerce, not-for-profit and public sector organisations.

Source: <www.cimaglobal.com> [accessed 16 February 2009]

Association of Chartered Certified Accountants (ACCA)

The Association of Chartered Certified Accountants (ACCA) is an international accounting professional body with 147 000 members from 170 countries and offers qualifications for those seeking a career in accountancy, finance and management. Accounting professionals who comply with the registration requirements become members of ACCA and are known as 'Chartered Certified Accountants'. ACCA has statutory recognition in the United Kingdom and Ireland, and is recognised under the European Union's Mutual Recognition Directive and in many other countries around the world.

Source: <www.accaglobal.com> [accessed 16 August 2011]

Institute of Internal Auditors (IIA)

Established in 1941, the Institute of Internal Auditors (IIA) is an international professional association with global headquarters in the United States of America. The IIA is '... the internal audit profession's global voice, recognised authority, acknowledged leader, chief advocate, and principal educator. Members work in internal auditing, risk management, governance, internal control, information technology audit, education, and security'. At the end of 2010 the IIA had just over 170 000 members globally, operating in 165 countries and jurisdictions, including South Africa.

Source: <www.theiia.org> [accessed 31 August 2011]

All of the above professional bodies have their own codes of ethics, together with disciplinary processes to act against improper conduct by members. The technical standards to which members have to adhere in the performance of their duties are developed either by these professional bodies or by international standard setters (such as the International Accounting Standards Board and the International Auditing and Assurance Standards Board).

Independent Regulatory Board for Auditors (IRBA)

The IRBA is the statutory body responsible for regulating the auditing profession in South Africa and functions in terms of the Auditing Profession Act 26 of 2005. The IRBA is funded mainly by fees and levies from Registered Auditors and firms, and monies appropriated by Parliament. The IRBA's mission is to '... protect the financial interest of the South African public and international investors in South Africa through the effective and appropriate regulation of audits conducted by registered auditors, in accordance with internationally recognised standards and processes'.

The key goal of the IRBA is '... to help create an ethical, value-driven financial sector that encourages investment, creates confidence in the financial markets and promotes sound practices'. This can be achieved by:
- Developing and maintaining internationally comparable auditing standards
- Developing and maintaining internationally comparable ethical standards
- auditors who meet the IRBA's registration requirements
- Monitoring compliance with reportable irregularities and anti-money laundering legislation
- Monitoring registered auditors' compliance with professional standards (e.g. auditing and ethical standards)
- Investigating and taking appropriate action against registered auditors in respect of improper conduct
- Developing and maintaining stakeholder relationships to enhance performance, accountability and public confidence
- Strengthening IRBA's organisational capability, capacity and performance to deliver on its mandate in an economically efficient and effective manner, in accordance with the relevant regulatory frameworks

Source: <www.irba.co.za> [accessed 16 August 2011]

The collapse of Enron and Andersen

Despite the existence of these professional bodies, and other similar bodies around the world, the accounting and auditing professions have received significant criticism in recent years following a number of high-profile corporate collapses, which involved questionable conduct on the part of, among others, the accountants and auditors. However, no event in recent memory has had such a significant impact on the profession as the collapse of Enron, followed by the collapse of Enron's auditor, Andersen (previously known as Arthur Andersen). The 'fallout' from Enron can be attributed to factors including the size and perceived good reputation of both entities and the distinct lack of ethical conduct on the part of the company's management and its auditor.

Andersen was a 'big 5' audit firm operating globally with an annual revenue of US$8.4 billion in 2001. As at 31 December 2001 Enron's market capitalisation (market value) exceeded US$60 billion, and the company was rated as 'the most innovative large company in America in *Fortune* magazine's survey of Most Admired Companies' (Healy & Palepu, 2003). However, within a year, Enron's shares were virtually worthless.

Some of the fraudulent or questionable accounting practices adopted by Enron's management, and accepted by the company's auditor, included:

- The values of long-term contracts were recorded at their present values (as required by US Generally Accepted Accounting Practice (GAAP), which involved the determination of the estimated future earnings from these contracts. The problem was that significant estimation was required in valuing these contracts, involving the forecasting of many variables well into the future. In a number of instances, significant profits were recorded despite 'serious questions about the viability of the contracts and their associated costs' (Healy & Palepu, 2003). Losses reported in the third quarter of 2001 in the amount of US$1 billion related mainly to write-downs of Enron's energy contracts and point to '... a lack of proper accounting in earlier periods ...' (Ketz, 2002:6).
- The use of special purpose entities (SPEs) resulting in debts and losses being reflected in separate entities, and not in the financial statements of Enron. Despite the fact that US GAAP required these SPEs to be consolidated into Enron's financial statements, Enron violated these requirements. The result was that on 16 October 2001, Enron announced restatements to its financial statements for years 1997 to 2000 to correct these violations. These restatements resulted in reductions in earnings for this period of US$613 million (or 23 per cent of the reported earnings during this period), an increase in liabilities by US$628 million, and a reduction in shareholders' equity of US$1,2 billion (or 10 per cent of the reported equity) (Healy & Palepu, 2003).

- Enron provided only minimal disclosure on its relationship with the special purpose entities, thereby deceiving investors and other financiers as to the financial risks to which the company was exposed (Ketz, 2002:6).

Following the collapse of Enron, Schuetze (2002) (the then Chief Accountant of the Securities and Exchange Commission (SEC)) made the following statement:

> 'The public's confidence in financial reports and in the audit of those financial reports by the public accounting [auditing] profession, has been shaken badly ... The public's confidence needs to be regained and restored ... [or else] ... investors will bid down the price of stocks and bonds ... This will reduce the market capitalisation of corporations, which in turn will negatively affect capital formation, job creation and job maintenance, and ultimately our standard of living.'

Of concern was that Enron was not an isolated instance of accounting/auditing failure. Even before Enron, McNamee, Dwyer, Schmitt & Lavelle (2000:69) reported that companies were restating their audited annual financial statements at an increasing frequency: 104 companies restated their financial statements in 1997, 118 in 1998, and 142 in 1999. While these restatements were the result of a variety of reasons (from revised accounting policies to the discovery of outright fraud), the validity of Schuetze's views is confirmed by the consequential loss in market capitalisation. Nine of the largest restatements resulted in investors losing US$41 billion following the drop in share prices after the restatement announcements were made (McNamee *et al*, 2000).

In the case of Cendant, the restatement resulted from the company's income being inflated by US$500 million through fraud and accounting errors, and the loss of market capitalisation following the restatement announcement amounted to US$11,3 billion (Byrnes, McNamee, Brady, Lavelle & Palmeri, 2002). Other large losses of market capitalisation resulted from the restatements recorded by Waste Management to account for the overstatement of the company's income from 1992 to 1996 by more than US$1 billion; and from restatements to Rite Aid's revenue figures to correct the more than US$1 billion overstatement in 1998 and 1999. The magnitude of these restatements invariably results in the question being asked: 'Where were the auditors?'

Unreported material misstatements in financial statements have not been confined to the United States of America. In recent years the auditing profession in Europe experienced criticism following discovery of a fictitious bank balance of US$4.9 billion in the consolidated financial statements of Parmalat (representing 38 per cent of the company's assets), and overstated revenues amounting to approximately $500 million at

Royal Ahold, to mention just two examples. In South Africa, the conduct of accountants and auditors at Masterbond, MacMed, Leisurenet and Regal Treasury Bank (to mention just a few) have further tarnished the reputation of the profession.

It is apt to conclude this chapter with the following extract from the editorial which appeared in the *Business Week* of 17 December 2001:

> 'Enron's tale is a clarifying event. It reveals key weaknesses in the financial system that must be corrected as the US moves forward in the 21st century. If America is to have an equity culture in which individuals invest in stocks and provide the capital for fast economic growth, the market must be able to correctly value companies. This requires making [reliable] financial data readily available and easily comprehensible.'

While it would be unreasonable to expect that external auditors must detect all material misstatements in annual financial statements, many of the misstatements in the instances referred to above relate to matters that the auditors were aware of at the time of issuing the audit report, but overlooked or rationalised, possibly because of conflicts of interest and other ethical lapses. Examples of these will be explored further in the next chapter. However, if the perception exists among investors and other providers of finance that auditors' reports on annual financial statements cannot be trusted, it is not too radical to submit that it places the entire capitalistic financial system in jeopardy. Auditors should never forget this unique responsibility.

Conclusion

With reference to the attributes for an occupational grouping to be regarded as a profession identified in the literature, it was concluded that Chartered Accountants (SA) and registered auditors can justifiably be referred to as 'professionals'. As professionals, they should aim to ensure that professional services are rendered in the public interest (rather than in their own self-interest). However, given a number of high-profile scandals in the 1990s and early 2000s (including Enron), the commitment of accountants and auditors to professional ethics has been questioned. In this regard, codes of professional ethics (to be discussed in the next chapter) can play an important role.

Questions for discussion

1. Discuss whether an accountant who is not a member of the SA Institute of Chartered Accountants can claim to be a 'professional'.
2. Explain the differences between the roles of the South African Institute of Chartered Accountants and the Independent Regulatory Board for Auditors, and explain the similarities and differences in the study paths to become members of these bodies.
3. Discuss the validity of the following statement: 'Because audit fees are paid by the client company, rather than by the shareholders or other providers of finance, the external auditor has a professional duty to act at all times in the best interest of the client company.'
4. Respond to the following comment made by an economics student: 'There is no need to restrict entry to the auditing profession – in a free market system, the market should be free to decide who should render the external audit service.'

Bibliography

Abbott, A. 1988. *The system of professions: an essay on the division of expert labor*. Chicago: Chicago University Press.

Byrnes, N, McNamee, M, Brady, D, Lavelle, L & Palmeri, C. 2002. 'Accounting in crisis'. *Business Week*, 28 January, 50–54.

Carter, M. 1998. Increased professionalism: An experience from the United States. *Journal of Leisurability*, 25(21):20–25.

Donaldson, T. 2000. 'Are business managers "professionals"?' *Business Ethics Quarterly*, 10(1):83–94.

Friedman, M. 1962. *Capitalism and freedom*. Chicago: Chicago University Press.

Greenwood, E. 1957. 'Attributes of a profession'. *Social work*, 44–55. In Harris, CE, Pritchard, MS & Rabins, MJ (eds). 2005. *Engineering ethics: concepts and cases*, 3rd edition. Belmont, CA: Thomson Wadsworth.

Harris, CE, Pritchard, MS & Rabins, MJ (eds). 2005. *Engineering ethics: concepts and cases* (3rd edition). Belmont, CA: Thomson Wadsworth.

Healy, PM & Palepu, KG. 2003. 'The fall of Enron'. *Journal of Economic Perspectives*, 17(2):1–26.

Huebner, SS. 1915. 'How the life insurance salesman should view his profession'. [On-line]. Available: <theamericancollege.edu/docs/344.pdf> [Accessed 13 June 2009].

International Federation of Accountants (IFAC). 2010. 'ISA 200: 'Overall objectives of the independent auditor and the conduct of an audit in accordance with International Standards on Auditing' in *Handbook of international quality control, auditing, review, other assurance and related services pronouncements, 2010 edition Part 1*. New York: International Federation of Accountants.

Ketz, JE. 2002. 'Can we prevent future Enrons?' *The Journal of Corporate Accounting and Finance*, 13(4):3–11.

Larson, MS. 1977. *The rise of professionalism: a sociological analysis*. Berkeley, California: University of California Press.

McNamee, M, Dwyer, P, Schmitt, CH & Lavelle, L. 2000. 'Accounting wars'. *Business Week*, 25 September, 68–72.

The Oxford English Dictionary. 1961. Volume VIII (Poy – Ry). London: Oxford University Press.

Parsons, T. 1968. *Professions*. In Sills, D (ed). 1968. *International encyclopedia of the social sciences*, XII, 536–547. New York: Macmillan, Free Press.

Sayles, LR & Smith, CJ. 2006. *The rise of the rogue executive*. Upper Saddle River, NJ: Pearson Education (publishing as Prentice Hall).

Schuetze, W. 2002. Hearing on 'Accounting and investor protection issues raised by Enron and other public companies: Oversight of the accounting profession, audit quality and independence, and formulation of accounting principles'. Prepared Statement to the US Senate Committee on Banking, Housing and Urban Affairs. [On-line]. Available: <banking.senate.gov/02_02hrg/ 022602/ schuetze.htm> [Accessed 15 February 2009].

Sharma, A. 1997. 'Professional as agent: knowledge asymmetry in agency exchange'. *Academy of Management Review*, 22(3):758–798.

South African Institute of Chartered Accountants (SAICA). 2008. *SAICA Handbook 2008/2009 Ethics and Circulars*. Vol. 3. Durban: LexisNexis.

Turner, LE. 2001. 'Independence: A covenant for the ages'. Speech given at the International Organisation of Securities Commissions. Stockholm, Sweden. [On-line]. Available: <www.sec.gov/news/speech/spch504.htm> [Accessed 15 February 2009].

Wilensky, HL. 1964. 'The professionalization of everyone?' *American Journal of Sociology*, 70:137–158.

13

Codes of professional ethics

Frans Prinsloo

Outcomes

After working through this chapter, you should be able to do the following:
- Identify, in general terms, the content of a code of professional ethics
- Discuss the purpose of a code of professional ethics
- Explain the 'conceptual framework approach' adopted by the IFAC *Code of Ethics for Professional Accountants* (including the fundamental principles, types of threats, and safeguards)
- Understand the construction of SAICA's *Code of Professional Conduct* and its applicability
- Illustrate the importance of the fundamental principles of 'integrity', 'professional competence and due care' and 'objectivity/independence' for the value of the external audit
- Contrast self-regulation of a profession with the government oversight thereof; and critically evaluate which is the more desirable for the auditing profession.

Overview

In this chapter consideration is given to understanding what a code of professional ethics is and how it can be of benefit to a profession. Thereafter, the importance of the IFAC *Code of Ethics for Professional Accountants* is explained, together with the conceptual approach, which forms the foundation of this Code. An overview of the *Code of Professional Conduct* of the South African Institute of Chartered Accountants is then provided, to illustrate how a professional body in South Africa has adapted the IFAC *Code of Ethics for Professional Accountants* to suit its particular circumstances. The chapter concludes with a more in-depth analysis of a number of fundamental ethical principles which are of vital importance to registered auditors.

Introduction

In the previous chapter it was concluded that accountants and auditors can be regarded as professionals. Yet it was observed that especially in the 1990s and early 2000s a number of accountants and auditors acted in a manner that served their own interests without sufficient consideration of the public interest (supposedly one of the cornerstones of the accounting and auditing professions). While society has in the past allowed the accounting and auditing professions to self-regulate their activities, this has been increasingly questioned given the manner in which members of the profession have conducted themselves. In attempting to address society's concerns about the conduct of professionals, codes of professional ethics play a vital role.

What is a 'Code of Professional Ethics'?

One of the distinguishing characteristics of a profession is the adherence to ethical standards embodied in a professional code of ethics. A 'code of professional ethics' establishes ethical requirements for members of the profession, to which these members have to adhere. As a consequence of the professional status and unusual degree of autonomy they enjoy, professionals have a responsibility towards the public interest and the wellbeing of the society whom they serve. A code of professional ethics facilitates accountability, responsibility and trust among professionals to the individuals / society whom the profession serves.

> Professionals have a responsibility towards the public interest and the wellbeing of the society whom they serve. A code of professional ethics facilitates accountability, responsibility and trust among professionals to the individuals / society whom the profession serves.

There are numerous codes of ethics which have been written for almost all reputable professions. This has been done in a number of formats and they vary tremendously in terms of the depth and detail of information, but they all promote accepted behaviours, high standards of performance and skill, adherence to regulations and requirements, and serve as a benchmark for occupational identity.

An analysis of the codes of ethics of various professional bodies reveals specific similarities in that they:

- *Start with a preamble* containing declarations of adherence to ethical virtues and values, authority, and responsibility. Values such as integrity, equity, resolution of ethical conflicts, honesty, dignity, morality, equality, justice, independence, openness, accountability, and authority are common in most codes of ethics, with integrity, accountability, and independence featuring in most of the codes of ethics in one way or another. This section of a code might be seen as inspirational, pointing members of the profession towards certain principles that may serve them well in the absence of specific regulations and requirements.

- *Supply definitions for words* to serve as guidance for the specific meaning attached to them in such a code of ethics.
- *State the legislative and regulatory requirements* applicable to their sector in the economy.
- *Highlight specific requirements* pertaining to, for example, conflicts of interest, insider trading, confidentiality of information, and lack of independence, mostly as a separate heading or section within the code of ethics.
- *Deal with the behaviour towards or relations with others* either under a separate heading or in a separate section of the code, but also in an integrated manner with other sections. For example, the *Code of Professional Conduct* of the SA Institute of Chartered Accountants (SAICA) contains a section on the responsibility towards colleagues, but throughout all the other sections of the *Code of Professional Conduct*, reference is made directly or indirectly to behaviour towards or relations with others. Behaviour towards others is of critical importance in codes of ethics and the behaviour focused on relates principally to the professional's behaviour in relation to his or her partners, staff, colleagues, and clients.

The codes of professional ethics, including those for professional accountants, serve several important functions which are discussed below.

One: Guidance on proper conduct for professionals

The codes of professional ethics state what is expected of professionals when providing a professional service or working in a business environment. When faced with an ethical dilemma, the professional is not left alone to decide what the proper course of action should be, but is guided by the code in reaching a decision. According to Duska & Duska (2003:75) a code of ethics can provide a more stable permanent guide to right or wrong than human personalities or continual ad hoc decisions.

The professional can furthermore assume that all other professionals in the profession adhere to the same code of ethics. This creates an equal (but yet still competitive) environment. For example, the *Code of Professional Conduct* of SAICA provides the requirements for determining fees for professional services and 'lowballing' (charging a significantly lower fee than that charged by another professional in the past). Joe Bloggs CA (SA) can therefore assume that other Chartered Accountants (SA) will not quote a significantly lower fee than his in such a way that adherence to the technical standards applicable to the service will be compromised.

Two: Adherence to the Code assists in protecting the public interest

One of the distinguishing characteristics of a profession is the acceptance of its responsibility to act in the public interest. The public interest has been defined in the 2003 version of the *Code of Professional Conduct* of SAICA as the 'collective wellbeing of the community of people and the institutions' that the professional serves. The accountancy profession's public consists of 'clients, government, employers, employees, investors, the business and financial community, and others who rely on the objectivity and integrity of the members of the profession to maintain the orderly functioning of commerce'.

> Members of the public rely on accounting professionals for sound financial reporting and advice and on auditing professionals to enhance the credibility of financial information. It is in the best interest of the accounting and auditing professions that those to whom they provide services trust that these services are executed at the highest level of performance and according to the ethical requirements described in the code of professional ethics that strive to ensure such performance. According to the 2003 version of the SAICA *Code of Professional Conduct*, professional accountants '... can remain in this advantageous position only by continuing to provide the public with these unique services at a level which demonstrates that the public confidence is firmly founded.'

Particular care must, however, be taken in ensuring that the wording used in the Code is sufficiently specific and clear to prevent members of the profession from avoiding their responsibilities to society (Kultgen, 1982:414). If this is not achieved, it could be argued that codes of ethics are '... merely smokescreens for the protection of sectional interest' (Velayutham, 2003:484).

Three: Rationale for adherence even when pressured to violate code of ethics or moral conduct

The code of professional ethics could be said to constitute an agreement among professionals themselves, and also between the professionals and the public. Professionals agree to abide by these uniform standards which will promote the economic wellbeing of the community and ensure the competence of the professionals, thereby protecting the public interest. The following hypothetical but not unrealistic situation illustrates pressure on professionals by others to act improperly.

> **Case study: Vanilla Investments (Pty) Ltd**
>
> Vanilla Investments (Pty) Ltd is an investment group which specialises in advising clients about investing in companies listed on the JSE. One of the analysts of Vanilla Investments (Pty) Ltd contacted Mr. Crawford, senior partner in Crawford & Crubnick Registered Auditors, to obtain information about a listed audit client of the partnership. Vanilla Investments (Pty) Ltd wanted to use this information to provide a reliable recommendation to its clients. If the information was not provided, Vanilla Investments (Pty) Ltd threatened to advise all its clients not to make use of the accounting or auditing services of Crawford & Crubnick Registered Auditors. Mr Crawford responded that the codes of professional ethics of SAICA and the IRBA require that the confidentiality of client information should be observed unless the professional has a legal duty to disclose such information.

In the above case study, a response or defence based on a standard or code of professional ethics that applies to all accounting and auditing professionals is likely to be more successful than one based merely on personal belief of what constitutes moral and professional conduct. A code could also motivate appropriate conduct through peer pressure, by holding up a generally recognised set of behavioural expectations that must be considered in decision making.

Four: Providing a mechanism by which action can be taken against unethical conduct of professionals

> A member of a professional body, upon entering the profession, undertakes to abide by the requirements of the code of professional ethics of the professional body, and therefore any subsequent conduct contrary to the code can be sanctioned by the profession body.

It is fair to say that within any profession there will always be a few 'bad apples'. It is up to the profession to ensure that these 'bad apples' are removed so as not to taint the entire profession – unfettered unethical conduct will create an environment where the society's trust in a profession is lost. That loss will create a reduced demand for the skills of those professionals, with a major negative impact on the economic wellbeing of the professionals, and on the status of the profession within society. In countering this, the code of professional ethics plays a vital role.

A member of a professional body, upon entering the profession, undertakes to abide by the requirements of the code of professional ethics of the professional body, and therefore any subsequent conduct contrary to the code can be sanctioned by the profession body. In initiating the investigation and disciplinary process against the professional, the alleged improper conduct of the professional can be evaluated against the requirements of the code, and all departures will be noted. The severity of the departures will determine the severity of the sanction, which could include a warning or fine, deregistration of the professional, or referring the matter to a statutory body that has jurisdiction over the matter.

To facilitate the accomplishment of the above, the investigations and disciplinary processes and accompanying sanctions for improper conduct need to be clearly defined by the professional body, and all substantive complaints lodged should be investigated, and if necessary referred for disciplinary action.

Five: Achieving the objectives of the profession

The objectives of the accounting profession are to work to the highest standards of professionalism, to attain the highest level of performance, and, generally, to meet the public interest. The 2003 version of SAICA's *Code of Professional Conduct* identified four basic needs which the accounting and auditing professions should satisfy in order to ensure that it achieves its overall objectives. The four basic needs are:

1. *Credibility:* There is a need for credible information at all levels of society.
2. *Professionalism:* There is a need for individuals who can be clearly identified by clients, employers, and other interested parties as professional persons in the accounting field.
3. *Quality of services:* There is a need for assurance that all services obtained from members are executed to the highest standards of performance.
4. *Confidence:* Users of professional accounting services should be able to have confidence in the services that they receive knowing that these services are governed by a framework of professional ethics.

If the principles of integrity, objectivity, professional competence and due care, confidentiality, professional behaviour, and technical standards contained in the *Code of Professional Conduct* of SAICA are adhered to, the four basic needs can be met, which will go a long way towards ensuring that the services rendered by the profession will remain in demand and that the profession therefore remains relevant in society. The accounting and auditing professions have been granted exclusive rights to perform certain services such as the external audit or independent review of financial statements, and serving as accounting officers of close corporations. Should society's needs, as specified above, not be satisfied, there is a distinct risk that the profession will lose the benefits resulting from this 'monopoly'.

Six: The Code provides a basis for debate about future changes and improvements to ethical standards

The ethical codes of the accounting profession internationally and in South Africa have undergone considerable changes in the last few years. Even though the underlying principles have remained the same, the application of the principles has changed and is likely to change further in future. A good example of this is the extent to which advertising of professional services has been permitted. Up until about twenty years ago, the ability of professional accountants to advertise their services was severely restricted. Today, advertising of such services is permitted provided it does 'not bring the profession into disrepute' and the advertising is 'honest and truthful' and is undertaken 'with a due sense of responsibility to the profession and the public as a whole' (e.g. 'aimed at informing the public in an objective manner' and is in 'good taste as to content and presentation').

> Changes within the profession and within the financial and business community as well as global changes affect the ethical requirements by which professional accountants operate. The code of ethics of the profession therefore needs to be evaluated on a regular basis with reference to the experiences of professionals in practice and in business and societal expectations, and then used as a debate about future changes that may be required.

Dissemination and enforcement of professional codes of ethics

Codes of ethics, as well as any further amendments, are enforced on all members registered in the profession from their implementation dates, and are also applicable to any new member entering the profession.

Professional codes of ethics are made available to members in a variety of ways, not least by being on the web sites of professional bodies – thereby also being available for scrutiny by non-members. Compliance with these codes of ethics should be formally monitored. This is best achieved by the professional body having an appropriate system in place to investigate complaints that are lodged by members of the profession, regulatory bodies and the general public, followed by a disciplinary process for any substantive allegations. Possible breaches of the codes of ethics should be handled by the professional body as soon as possible in a fair and transparent manner – so as to ensure continued public trust in the profession.

Professional bodies should also establish thorough and transparent processes by which changes are made to professional codes of ethics. Formally-appointed working committees should formulate exposure drafts to enable the views of members of the profession and other interested stakeholders to be elicited. These exposure drafts can usually be viewed on the web site of the professional body and may also be distributed in a printed version for comment. All comments are then reviewed and amendments made to the code of ethics where necessary. Amended professional codes of ethics very often have a specific implementation date which members must honour. These codes of ethics, as well as any further amendments, are enforced on all members registered in the profession from their implementation dates, and are also applicable to any new member entering the profession.

Codes of professional ethics in the accounting profession

As indicated in the previous chapter, each professional body in the field of accounting and auditing has its own code of professional ethics. However, most of these professional bodies are members of the International Federation of Accountants (IFAC), and as such they may not apply less stringent standards than those contained in the IFAC *Code of Ethics for Professional Accountants* (hereafter referred to as the 'IFAC *Code of Ethics*'). The professional bodies therefore typically use IFAC's *Code of Ethics* as the point of departure in determining their own codes of professional ethics, and then add additional sections to deal with local matters affecting the particular members of the professional bodies and, if considered necessary, to amplify certain sections of the IFAC *Code of Ethics*.

International Federation of Accountants (IFAC)

IFAC was founded in 1977 and at the time of writing had 164 members and associates (primarily national professional accountancy bodies) in 125 countries and jurisdictions. These members and associates represent 2.5 million professional accountants across the world who are employed in public practice, industry and commerce, government, and academia.

> IFAC's mission is to serve the public interest by:
> - contributing to the development, adoption and implementation of high-quality international standards and guidance (in areas such as ethics, education and auditing and assurance, and public sector accounting),
> - contributing to the development of strong professional accountancy organizations and accounting firms, and to high-quality practices by professional accountants,

- promoting the value of professional accountants worldwide, and
- speaking out on public interest issues where the accountancy profession's expertise is most relevant.

Source: <www.ifac.org/About/> (accessed 5 August 2011)

Given that IFAC is the international body to which virtually all reputable professional accountancy bodies belong, and that member bodies may not apply less stringent standards than those contained in the IFAC *Code of Ethics*, the importance of understanding the key aspects of this Code should be self-evident.

Fundamental principles

The following fundamental principles are identified in paragraph 100.5 of the IFAC *Code of Ethics*:

- *Integrity:* A professional accountant should be straightforward and honest in all professional and business relationships.
- *Objectivity:* A professional accountant should not allow bias, conflict of interest or undue influence of others to override professional or business judgments.
- *Professional competence and due care:* A professional accountant has a continuing duty to maintain professional knowledge and skill at the level required to ensure that a client or employer receives competent professional service based on current developments in practice, legislation and techniques. A professional accountant should act diligently and in accordance with applicable technical and professional standards when providing professional services.
- *Confidentiality:* A professional accountant should respect the confidentiality of information acquired as a result of professional and business relationships and should not disclose any such information to third parties without proper and specific authority unless there is a legal or professional right or duty to disclose. Confidential information acquired as a result of professional and business relationships should not be used for the personal advantage of the professional accountant or third parties.
- *Professional behaviour:* A professional accountant should comply with relevant laws and regulations and should avoid any action that discredits the profession.

> A professional accountant should comply with relevant laws and regulations and should avoid any action that discredits the profession.

Conceptual framework approach

With the June 2005 revision of the IFAC *Code of Ethics*, a 'conceptual framework approach' was adopted where professional accountants are required '... to identify, evaluate and address threats to compliance with the fundamental principles, rather than merely comply with a set of specific rules'.

In terms of this conceptual framework approach (IFAC *Code of Ethics* para 100.2), the professional accountant must specifically:
- Identify threats to compliance with the fundamental principles;
- Evaluate the significance of the threats identified; and
- Apply safeguards, when necessary, to eliminate the threats or reduce them to an acceptable level.

> The threats to the fundamental principles ordinarily fall into one of the following categories (IFAC *Code of Ethics* para 100.12):
> - *Self-interest threats*: Threats that financial or other interests will inappropriately influence the professional accountant's judgement or behaviour.
> - *Self-review threats*: Threats that the professional accountant will not appropriately evaluate the results of a previous judgement made (or service rendered) by the accountant, on which s/he will rely when forming a judgement as part of providing the current service.
> - *Advocacy threats:* Threats that the professional accountant will promote a client's position to the point that his/her objectivity is compromised.
> - *Familiarity threats:* Threats that due to a long or close relationship with the client the professional accountant is too sympathetic to the client's interests (or accepting of the client's work).
> - *Intimidation threats*: Threats that a professional accountant will be deterred from acting objectively because of actual or perceived pressures.

Case study: Kool Trading (Pty) Ltd

You are a partner in Tick & Bash, a firm of registered auditors. One of the firm's trainee accountants, Gary Kool, attempted to recruit a new audit client, Kool Trading (Pty) Ltd, by approaching his cousin, Rodney Kool, the sole shareholder and managing director of Kool (Pty) Ltd.

> Rodney Kool indicated that he would appoint Tick & Bash as Kool Trading (Pty) Ltd's registered auditor at the company's next Annual General Meeting on two conditions:
> 1. Gary Kool must receive a bonus equal to 10 per cent of the first year's audit fee, and
> 2. Gary Kool must be in charge of the audit.
>
> On the agenda for the next partners' meeting, you note that it is proposed that Kool Trading (Pty) Ltd be accepted as an audit client of the firm.
> Having considered this set of facts, you commence preparing a list of threats to compliance with the fundamental principles for presentation to the partner's meeting. The three threats that immediately come to mind are:
> - *Familiarity threat to objectivity* (owing to Gary's close family links to the potential client)
> - *Self-interest threat to integrity* (as Gary is entitled to a bonus based on the audit fee charged – he may therefore spend more time on the audit than is required by the auditing standards), and
> - *Intimidation threat to professional competence and due care* (as Rodney Kool is already dictating the manner in which the audit should be done – for example, Gary Kool should be in charge).
>
> Can you think of any other threats that should be added to this list?

Once the threats to compliance with the fundamental principles have been identified and evaluated, the conceptual framework requires a determination of safeguards for those threats that are not at an acceptable level. According to the IFAC *Code of Ethics*, safeguards that may eliminate or reduce threats to an acceptable level fall into two categories:
- Safeguards created by the profession, legislation or regulation, and
- Safeguards in the work environment.

The first category of safeguards (which includes the profession setting of requirements for entry into the profession and for continuing professional development and the profession undertaking monitoring and disciplinary action) essentially creates 'an environment' conducive to the mitigation of threats in general (by ensuring that only competent persons with integrity work in the profession and that they know what the ethical requirements are) and are relevant to those both in public practice and in commerce and industry. The second category of safeguards aims at dealing with specific threats identified by professionals in the conduct of their work (either in

public practice or in business). Examples of these safeguards include (IFAC *Code of Ethics* para 200.13):
- Involving another professional accountant to review the work undertaken.
- Consulting an independent third party, such as a committee of independent directors (for example, audit committee) of the engagement client, a professional regulatory body or another professional accountant.
- Discussing ethical issues with those charged with governance of the client (for example, the board of directors or audit committee).
- Disclosing to those charged with governance of the client the nature of services provided and extent of fees charged.
- Involving another firm to perform or re-perform part of the engagement.
- Rotating senior team personnel periodically.

So, for example, the objectivity/independence of the audit team may be threatened (in appearance, if not in fact) if a director of the audit client is in a position to exert direct and significant influence over the annual financial statements and he was a partner of the audit firm in the recent past. As the threat is not at an acceptable level, safeguards such as involving another audit partner to review the work undertaken will be required to reduce the threat to an acceptable level.

> The following test should be used to determine whether the threat has been eliminated or reduced to an acceptably low level: Will a reasonable and informed third party, weighing all the specific facts and circumstances available at the time, probably conclude that compliance with the fundamental principle is not compromised?

In the final analysis, the following test should be used to determine whether the threat has been eliminated or reduced to an acceptably low level: Will a reasonable and informed third party, weighing all the specific facts and circumstances available at the time, probably conclude that compliance with the fundamental principle is not compromised?

The advantage of following this conceptual approach to dealing with ethical matters, rather than a rules-based approach, is that many different circumstances may be encountered by professionals and accordingly it is impossible to deal with every situation in the code. A conceptual framework which requires firms and their staff to identify, evaluate and address threats to the fundamental principles, rather than merely requiring them to comply with a set of specific rules which may be arbitrary, is therefore considered to be in the public interest.

Structure of IFAC Code of Ethics

The IFAC Code of Ethics consists of three parts:
- Part A: General Application of the Code
- Part B: Professional Accountants in Public Practice
- Part C: Professional Accountants in Business

Part A explains the conceptual framework approach and the fundamental principles. Part B deals with matters of specific relevance to those who are in 'public practice' – those who work in firms offering professional services, such as audit, tax advice or consulting to the public. Of particular importance in Part B is the section dealing with the independence requirements for audit and review engagements (paragraph 290). Part C illustrates how the conceptual framework contained in Part A is to be applied by professional accountants in business (for example, those who are responsible for the preparation and reporting of financial and other information for use by the companies they own or work for and/or third parties, such as the company's bankers).

SAICA's *Code of Professional Conduct*

Overview

SAICA's current *Code of Professional Conduct* (hereafter referred to as 'the SAICA Code') was revised and issued in November 2010 following changes made to the IFAC *Code of Ethics*. The structure and content of the SAICA Code is consistent with that of the IFAC Code of Ethics, except that some additions have been made to Part A of the Code to assist with the local application of certain requirements applicable to all chartered accountants in South Africa.

Table 13.1 Contents of the SAICA *Code of Professional Conduct*

STATUS OF THE CODE	
DEFINITIONS	
PART A: GENERAL APPLICATION OF THE CODE	
100	Introduction and Fundamental Principles
110	Integrity
120	Objectivity
130	Professional Competence and Due Care
140	Confidentiality
150	Professional Behaviour
PART B: CHARTERED ACCOUNTANTS IN PUBLIC PRACTICE	
200	Introduction
210	Professional Appointment
220	Conflicts of Interest

230	Second Opinions
240	Fees and Other Types of Remuneration
250	Marketing Professional Services
260	Gifts and Hospitality
270	Custody of Clients Assets
280	Objectivity – All Services
290	Independence – Audit and Review Engagements
291	Independence – Other Assurance Engagements
PART C: CHARTERED ACCOUNTANTS IN BUSINESS	
300	Introduction
310	Potential Conflicts
320	Preparation and Reporting of Information
330	Acting with Sufficient Expertise
340	Financial Interests
350	Inducements
EFFECTIVE DATE	

Role of the SAICA Code in the disciplinary process

The SAICA Code is applicable to members of the Institute (Chartered Accountants (SA)), associates of the Institute (Associate General Accountants (SA)) and trainee accountants. As the CA (SA) or AGA (SA) will also be responsible for any failure to comply with the code by his or her employees and fellow partners (in terms of International Standard on Quality Control 1 para 20), he or she should ensure that policies and procedures are implemented to ensure that all staff within the professional services firm abide by the SAICA Code.

Should a complaint be laid (ordinarily in the form of an affidavit), the disciplinary process prescribed in SAICA's by-laws will be followed. The Professional Conduct Committee of SAICA will obtain a response from the accused (either in writing or in person). If it is clear that no 'punishable offence' (as prescribed in the by-laws, and which includes contraventions of the SAICA Code) has been committed, no further action will be taken and the complainant will be informed accordingly. If there is a relatively minor 'punishable offence', the Professional Conduct Committee can impose the punishment. However, all serious matters are referred to the Disciplinary Committee for a hearing. Should the accused be found guilty

at the hearing, a range of punishments can be imposed, including the termination of the membership of SAICA or a fine of up to R100 000. In order to engender public trust, it is vitally important that the disciplinary process should be:
- Transparent, and
- Thorough and/or rigorous, but
- Expeditious.

It is submitted that with mechanisms such as Disciplinary Committee hearings being open to the public, and the Professional Conduct Committee resolving less egregious matters quickly, SAICA's process satisfies these requirements.

Further analysis of selected fundamental principles of relevance to external auditors

As indicated in the previous chapter, no person may perform external audit services unless he or she has registered as an auditor with the Independent Regulatory Board for Auditors (IRBA). All registered auditors are required to adhere to the IRBA's *Code of Professional Conduct*. This Code, the current version which was issued on 1 June 2010, is based on Parts A and B of the IFAC *Code of Ethics*. The text is virtually identical to the IFAC Code except that a few matters considered important to Registered Auditors in South Africa have been added (indicated via underlining and italic text in the IRBA Code).

While the external auditor has to adhere to all of the fundamental principles, it is submitted that for the external audit to remain relevant and to be of value to users of audit reports, the following principles are paramount:
- Integrity
- Independence (objectivity)
- Professional competence and due care.

Failure by external auditors to comply with these principles will result in serious questioning on the part of legislators, regulators and the investing public about the future of auditing in its current form, and is likely to be accompanied by significant changes in the way in which the audit is undertaken. Articles such as 'Accounting in Crisis' (Byrnes, McNamee, Brady, Lavelle & Palmeri, 2002) and 'Called to Account' (*The Economist*, 2004) explore this matter further.

Integrity

According to section 110.1 of the IRBA Code of Professional Conduct, the principle of integrity imposes an obligation on all registered auditors to be straightforward and honest in professional and business relationships. Integrity also implies fair dealing and truthfulness.

But why is 'integrity' such an important attribute to the external auditor? Flint (1988) (cited in Porter, Simon & Hatherly, 2008:72) observes:

> 'Public trust and confidence in auditors are dependent on a continuing belief in their unqualified *integrity*, objectivity, and, in appropriate circumstances, acceptance of a duty to the public interest, with a consequential subordination of self-interest ...' (italics added)

If Flint is correct, the lack of 'unqualified integrity' will translate into the loss of trust in auditors, which will render the external audit service irrelevant. This is because the purpose of the audit is to enhance the credibility of the information contained in the financial statements being reported on. The need for an external audit arose following the separation of ownership of a business from its day-to-day management, when the owners of the business (who were not involved in the day-to-day management) required credible information about the financial performance of the business.

Of course, the professional managers had conflicts of interest when reporting on the financial performance of the business, because poor results were likely to adversely affect their remuneration or lead to the termination of their employment. Therefore, business owners (shareholders) sought the services of an independent, trustworthy third party, knowledgeable in Financial Accounting, to report on the 'fair presentation' of the financial information. It follows that the business owners would not appoint a third party with questionable honesty as they would still not know if the information was credible (in other words, the 'dishonest' third party might collude with management for his or her own benefit).

> The need for an external audit arose following the separation of ownership of a business from its day-to-day management, when the owners of the business (who were not involved in the day-to-day management) required credible information about the financial performance of the business.

Independence

In order to enhance the credibility of the financial statements of the entity subject to audit, it is essential that the registered auditor expressing the opinion on the fair presentation of the financial statements is independent from the entity's management, who is responsible for the preparation thereof. Bluntly stated, if the auditor expressing the opinion is not independent from the management preparing the financial statements, why have an auditor? Bogle (2000), founder of The Vanguard Group, put the requirement for independence more eloquently, as follows:

> 'It is unarguable ... that the independent oversight of finance figures is central to that disclosure system. Indeed, independence is at integrity's very core. And, for more than a century, the responsibility for the independent oversight of corporate financial statements has fallen to America's public accounting [auditing] profession. It is the auditor's stamp on a financial statement that gives it its validity, its respect, and its acceptability by investors. And only if the auditor's work is comprehensive, skeptical, inquisitive, and rigorous, can we have confidence that financial statements speak the truth.'

In terms of paragraph 290.6 of the IRBA's *Code of Professional Conduct*, independence comprises:
- *Independence of mind:* The state of mind that permits the expression of a conclusion without being affected by influences that compromise professional judgement, thereby allowing the auditor to act with integrity, and exercise objectivity and professional skepticism.
- *Independence in appearance:* The avoidance of facts and circumstances that are so significant that a reasonable and informed third party would be likely to conclude, weighing all the specific facts and circumstances, that a firm's or member's integrity, objectivity or professional skepticism has been compromised.

Lee (1993:98) noted that '... it is exceedingly difficult to give operational meaning to what is essentially a state of mind', but added that 'at least there is general agreement that independence is an attitude of mind which does not allow the viewpoints or conclusions of the corporate auditor to become reliant on or subordinate to the influences and pressure of conflicting interests'.

'Independence' should not be seen as requiring the external auditor necessarily to be free of all economic, financial and other relationships. As a member of society, every auditor will have relationships with others. Rather, the significance of economic, financial and other relationships should be evaluated in the light of what a reasonable and informed third party, weighing all the specific facts and circumstances available at the time, will conclude as an unacceptable threat to independence. To achieve this, paragraph 290 of the IRBA Code of Professional Conduct introduces a 'conceptual approach to independence' along similar lines to the conceptual framework approach to the fundamental principles, discussed earlier in this chapter. This approach also requires the identification of threats (but this time to independence), the evaluation of the significance of the threats and the implementation of safeguards to mitigate the threats to acceptable levels.

Examples of situations where threats to independence arise are provided in the IRBA Code of Professional Conduct, and include:
- Financial interests in clients (for example, a direct or indirect investment in the shares of an audit client).
- Loans and guarantees provided to or obtained from the audit client.
- Close business relationships with an audit client (for example, the audit firm and the client are joint owners of another business).
- Family and personal relationships with senior management of an audit client.
- Where a member of audit team is due to take up employment with the client shortly after completion of the audit.
- Where a member of audit team was recently an employee of the audit client (especially if he or she was involved in the preparation of the client's financial statements).
- A partner in the audit firm serves as a director on the board of the audit client.
- The same registered auditor has served in this capacity for a client for more than, say, ten years.
- The audit firm provides non-audit services (such as accounting, taxation or company secretarial services) to the audit client.
- A large portion of the audit firm's revenue is dependent on one audit client or the fees from an audit client are long overdue.
- A member of the audit team is remunerated for selling non-audit services (e.g. tax and management consulting services) to the audit client.
- A member of the audit team receives a new sports utility vehicle from the audit client on his birthday.
- The audit client is threatening to initiate a major lawsuit against the auditor owing to a statement made in the audit report on the prior year financial statements that the client is not happy with.

Consider the above examples, and identify the specific type of threat to independence that arises (for example, self-interest, or familiarity). The safeguards available are similar to those identified previously. However, sometimes the threats are so significant that safeguards cannot reduce the threat to independence to an acceptable level (for example, the registered auditor of a client holds a large shareholding in the audit client). In such instances, either the threat must be eliminated (for example, by disposing of the shares) or the engagement should not be accepted or continued.

Questions have increasingly been asked about the level of independence of external auditors, especially after a number of high-profile financial reporting scandals, including Enron and Waste Management. Audit firms operate in the private sector, which means that they strive to earn profits and compete in a free market for clients and work. The major dilemma is that the same professional whom society expects to perform certain duties in the public interest, also needs to curry favour with that same client for repeat and further business, and to ensure payment for services. These conflicts came to the fore particularly in the 1990s, when audit firms began to diversify the range of services in an effort to grow their revenues.

Specific examples of problems with the independence of external auditors cited in the literature include:

- '...Andersen had been Enron's outside auditor since the 1980s, but in the mid-1990s, the firm was given another assignment: to conduct Enron's internal audits as well. In effect, the firm was working on the accounting systems and controls with one hand and attesting to the numbers they produced with the other. And the ties went even deeper ... Enron's own in-house financial team was dominated by former Andersen partners ...' (Byrnes *et al*, 2002:50).
- Three significant threats to independence should be evident from this quotation. Yet despite this, Andersen continued to accept the audit engagement of Enron year after year (until Enron's and its own demise).
- 'A 1999 investigation at PwC's Tampa, USA office revealed that employees were buying shares in companies they audited – violating the most basic independence requirement. More than 8 000 violations were found following a more extensive investigation by the firm. Half of the firm's partners were found to have conflicts – averaging five apiece.' (McNamee, Dwyer, Schmitt, & Lavelle, 2000:71)
- Where the Big Six audit firms in 1993 earned just 31 per cent of revenue from management consulting, the Big Five audit firms generated 51 per cent of their revenue from such services in 1999. The share earned in auditing and assurance services in turn declined from 45 per cent to 30 per cent (McNamee *et al*, 2000: 71). This change in the revenue mix can be ascribed to audit firms increasingly using the audit engagement as a 'stepping-stone' to obtaining consulting services. 'They began to emphasize too much, being a business partner' to their audit clients (Byrnes *et al*, 2002:51).

According to Siegal and McGrath (2003), when a team of people, such as auditors, directors or managers, all come from a rather homogeneous cultural set and power-group, and rely on each other for their promotion and compensation, they face certain threats to their independence. Such threats would develop in due time among any group of people who spend enough time in each other's spheres of influence and information. Despite policy-makers striving for independence of judgement, they have not been able to find a way of avoiding these threats to independent-mindedness. This failure may explain in a large part why some of the major accounting scandals have gone undetected for so long, and reached such large proportions.

Professional competence and due care

According to paragraph 130.1 of the IRBA Code of Professional Conduct, the principle of professional competence and due care imposes the following obligations on all registered auditors:
a) To maintain professional knowledge and skill required to ensure that clients/employers receive competent professional service, and
b) To act diligently in accordance with applicable technical and professional standards when providing the professional services.

In the context of external auditing, before a person can become a registered auditor, he or she has to satisfy the prescribed education and training requirements of the IRBA. These requirements, specified in the previous chapter, are the minimum requirements that must be attained by a person in order to be considered by the IRBA as being able to act as a registered auditor and perform satisfactory audit work. However, as the technical body of knowledge (for example, auditing standards) continues to evolve, the registered auditor must devote time in remaining abreast of new developments in order to render a professional service. Therefore, in addition to meeting the prescribed requirements at the point of being admitted as a registered auditor, he or she is required to undertake continuing professional development (CPD), which involves completing a prescribed number of hours of verifiable learning over a three-year period (the IRBA at the time of writing prescribed a minimum of 90 hours of verifiable audit-relevant learning over a three-year period). This will contribute towards ensuring that registered auditors maintain the required knowledge and skills to perform audit engagements in accordance with the technical standards and applicable laws and regulations.

In addition to the registered auditor possessing the requisite competence, it is necessary to ensure that the audit work is performed diligently in accordance with the prescribed technical standards (the International Standards on Auditing) to achieve a competent professional service. In order to ensure that the registered auditor and his or her staff do this, all audit firms implement a system of quality control policies and procedures aimed at ensuring that sufficiently competent staff with integrity are employed, that particular care is taken in accepting

> All audit firms implement a system of quality control policies and procedures aimed at ensuring that sufficiently competent staff with integrity are employed, that particular care is taken in accepting appropriate clients, that guidance is available to staff when performing engagements, and, importantly, that the firm's leadership demonstrate a sufficient commitment to quality work.

appropriate clients, that guidance is available to staff when performing engagements, and, importantly, that the firm's leadership demonstrate a sufficient commitment to quality work. When performing engagements, it is permitted that registered auditors can draw on the expertise of others in areas where the auditor does not have the requisite knowledge (for example, in interpreting a legal agreement). However, auditors should not take on engagements should they lack the requisite competence to ensure that the engagement is completed fully in terms of the requirements of the auditing standards.

Adherence to the fundamental principle of professional competence and due care is particularly important in the context of the external audit because of the difficulty for external parties to gauge the quality of the work undertaken. The only part of the external audit that is made public is the 'independent auditors report'. The structure of this report is prescribed in the International Auditing Standards and contains the following paragraphs:

- An introductory paragraph identifying the financial statements that were audited.
- A paragraph explaining management's responsibility for the financial statements.
- A number of paragraphs describing the auditor's responsibility in performing the engagement.
- An opinion paragraph.

The first three bullet points involve the use of standardised, prescribed wording, and the user would tend to focus on the content of the 'opinion paragraph'. If the registered auditor is satisfied with the fair presentation of the client's financial statements, the following text would be used in this paragraph:

> 'In our opinion, the financial statements present fairly, in all material respects, the financial position of ABC Company at 31 December 20X1, and its financial performance and cash flows for the year then ended, in accordance with International Financial Reporting Standards and the requirements of the Companies Act of South Africa.'

Before issuing this report, however, a significant amount of work must be undertaken, in the following stages:
- *Planning the audit:* This stage involves identifying the risks of material misstatement (owing to error or fraud) in the client's financial statements. Once these risks have been identified and assessed, the auditor plans procedures to gather evidence to address the assessed risks.

- *Gathering of audit evidence:* In responding to the assessed risks, the planned procedures will be performed to gather sufficient appropriate audit evidence to ascertain (with reasonable assurance) whether in fact material misstatements are present in the financial statements. Based on the evidence gathered, further procedures may have to be performed to gather sufficient appropriate evidence about the fair presentation of the financial statements.
- *Evaluating, concluding and reporting:* Once the evidence has been gathered, it must be evaluated to determine whether any misstatements identified in the financial statements are in fact material (either individually or in aggregate with other misstatements). If no material misstatements are found, the opinion presented above will be expressed. If material misstatements are present, the opinion will have to be suitably modified (either qualified, adverse or disclaimer).

Undertaking this work will involve many hours of work, and the fees charged for the audits of listed companies often run into millions of rands. Given that users cannot assess the quality of the work performed, and that users of the audit report will make financial decisions (often involving large amounts of money) based on the now 'credible' financial information in the accompanying audited financial statements, the external auditor has an important responsibility to render the service in a competent manner. After all, if the opinion is incorrect, the user of the audit report risks losing large amounts of money.

Unfortunately, all external auditors have not entirely satisfied this responsibility as is evidenced by the following:

> 'Few school pupils would rush home to show a test score of 50 per cent to their parents. America's auditors therefore have some explaining to do. Of the 174 auditors inspected by their industry's newish regulator, almost half have been deemed to have some trouble doing their job satisfactorily ...' (*The Economist*, 2006:74).

The future of self-regulation

Given the failure to comply with the fundamental principles described above, it appears as if enhanced policing of the auditing profession may be required. The question arises whether government, as society's elected agent, should attempt to enforce behavioural norms through legislation, or whether professional bodies should continue to be allowed to regulate themselves.

The legislation approach (also called a 'compliance mode') tends to refocus the professional's attention simply to meeting

> When following the self-regulatory approach, professional bodies become the watchdog of their professions and create trust by carrying out their standard-setting and monitoring duties.

the lowest possible necessary standards prescribed by the law. However, beyond the law, there is always the possibility of far more exemplary ethical and professional conduct guided by strong principles, but the compliance mode shifts things the other way – and arguably the wrong way.

When following the self-regulatory approach, professional bodies become the watchdog of their professions and create trust by carrying out their standard-setting and monitoring duties. With this more principled approach, a higher average standard of behaviour should result, despite the possibility of some egregious misconduct escaping the professional body. In the self-regulatory approach, codes of professional ethics (as explained earlier) are the tool used by professional bodies to regulate their members.

> In South Africa, concerns about the ability of auditors to regulate themselves have resulted in the Auditing Profession Act 26 of 2005 establishing the Independent Regulatory Board for Auditors, with the majority of members on the governance structure of the Board being non-auditors.

However, as a consequence of the violations of the fundamental ethical principles (referred to previously), the auditing profession in the USA is increasingly losing its self-regulatory status. One example (following the enactment of the Sarbanes-Oxley legislation in the USA) is the fact that the majority of the members on the governing board of the Public Company Oversight Board, responsible for regulating the auditing profession in the USA, are non-auditors. The legislation also outlaws the rendering of many professional services concurrently with the external audit. In South Africa, concerns about the ability of auditors to regulate themselves have resulted in the Auditing Profession Act 26 of 2005 establishing the Independent Regulatory Board for Auditors, with the majority of members on the governance structure of the Board being non-auditors. The practice of the IRBA undertaking reviews on the quality of work of registered auditors (via the Board's practice review department) has now also become well-established (in the past the quality of work was solely undertaken via peer-reviews – where one partner or firm reviewed the work of another). The bottom-line is that if auditors cannot themselves ensure adherence to fundamental principles, increased government oversight and regulation is inevitable, and the status of the auditing profession is likely to diminish.

Conclusion

Professionals are allowed by society to practise in a quasi-monopolistic fashion. Because society has deemed it more effective to allow professions to regulate themselves within the absolute minimum of legislative framework, the onus shifts towards the leadership of professional bodies to provide their members with clear entry requirements and acceptable standards of conduct. To this end, codes of professional ethics provide a variety of particular and general guidelines for professionals, with the risk of exclusion from the profession, or of other punitive measures, should they fail to comply.

Codes of ethics will certainly not guarantee completely that all members of each profession always meet the minimum required standards of behaviour. This has been particularly evident from a number of high-profile accounting scandals in the 1990s and early 2000s. The onus is on all professional accountants to work together to ensure adherence to the codes of professional ethics (both in terms of the letter and in spirit), thereby ensuring that public interest is put ahead of self-interests. Should this not be successful, the future of the accounting and auditing professions in their current form is questionable, and increased government intervention is a likely consequence.

> The onus is on all professional accountants to work together to ensure adherence to the codes of professional ethics (both in terms of the letter and in spirit), thereby ensuring that public interest is put ahead of self-interests.

Questions for discussion

1. Comment on the following statement: 'As a professional body will carefully review all applications for membership for any evidence of a lack of ethical conduct on the part of the applicants, a code of professional ethics is not necessary.'
2. Assume you are in your third year of your training contract at a major auditing firm in South Africa. The firm is planning to hold a workshop on the *Code of Professional Conduct* in light of recent ethical problems within the firm. You have been asked to prepare a presentation on the benefits and functions of the Code. You are required to prepare the notes for your presentation (in the form of an essay) in which you explain:
   a) Who the auditing profession's public is, and
   b) How adherence to the Code assists in protecting the public interest (you are not required to prepare the presentation).
3. Identify from the following scenario the threats to compliance with the fundamental principles that need to be reduced to an acceptable level by the audit firm:

Chemklear (Pty) Ltd ('Chemklear') is a company that operates a hazardous waste dump (also known as a 'landfill site') on the outskirts of Port Elizabeth. The dump has been designed to accept hazardous chemicals, and partially processes these chemicals through a series of filtration ponds before final disposal in the dump.

Shortly after the members of the audit team were introduced to the Chemklear financial director, she contacted the engagement partner and in an aggressive manner demanded that Bunny Hager, a senior member of the audit team, be removed immediately. Her demand was expressed as follows:

> 'Our operations director has informed me that Bunny Hager is very active in community environmental issues. As he will have access to confidential information while on this audit, we demand that he should be removed from the audit team. He is reputed to have a negative attitude towards our industry and we believe that this will cloud his judgement in his work.'

4. Critically evaluate the disciplinary process followed by the SA Institute of Chartered Accountants.
5. Discuss the following statement: 'Given the problems that have arisen as a result of external auditors operating in the private sector, it would be preferable for all audits to be undertaken by a public sector body, similar to the Office of the Auditor General.'

Bibliography

Bogle, J. 2000. 'Public accounting: profession or business?' [On-line]. Available: <johncbogle.com/speeches/JCB_NYU_Lecture_10-00.pdf> [Accessed 18 February 2009].

Byrnes, N, McNamee, M, Brady, D, Lavelle, L & Palmeri, C. 2002. 'Accounting in crisis'. *Business Week*, 28 January, 50–54.

Duska, RF & Duska BS. 2003. *Accounting ethics*. Malden, MA: Blackwell Publishing.

The Economist. 2004. 'Called to account'. 20 November, 71–73.

The Economist. 2006. 'Ticks and crosses'. 28 January, 74–75.

International Federation of Accountants (IFAC). 2010. '*Code of ethics for professional accountants*'. In *Handbook of international quality control, auditing, review, other assurance and related services pronouncements, 2010 edition Part 1*. New York: IFAC.

Kultgen, J. 1982. 'The ideological use of professional codes'. In Callahan, JC. 1988. *Ethical issues in professional life*. New York: Oxford University Press.

Lee, T. 1993. *Corporate audit theory*. London: Chapman & Hall.

McNamee M, Dwyer, P, Schmitt, CH & Lavelle, L. 2000. 'Accounting wars'. *Business Week*, 25 September, 68–72.

Porter, B, Simon, J & Hatherly, D. 2008. *Principles of external auditing*, 3rd ed. Chichester, England: John Wiley & Sons.

Siegal, A & McGrath, S. 2003. 'Recognizing and addressing conflicts of interest'. *The Critical Perspectives on Accounting (CPA) Journal*, 73(4):6–11.

South African Institute of Chartered Accountants (SAICA). 2010. '*Code of professional conduct*'. In *SAICA Handbook 2010/2011 Volume 3: Accounting, Ethics and Circulars*. Durban: LexisNexis.

Velayutham, S. 2003. 'The accounting profession's code of ethics: Is it a code of ethics or a code of quality assurance?' *Critical Perspectives on Accounting*, 14:483–503.

14

Case studies in accounting ethics

Korien Sander

Outcomes

After working through this chapter, you should be able to do the following:
- Integrate your knowledge of ethics in general with the specifics of accounting ethics obtained in this textbook
- Apply your knowledge to real-life situations
- Supply solutions when confronted with ethical dilemmas in order to recognize the interconnectedness with others.

Overview

The case method has as its objective, with the ethical decision-making principles covered in this course, the integration of real-life situations which you may anticipate in practice. The case study method is held in high regard and is widely used in business schools across the world. At this stage you have already covered both ethical theories and the requirements of the codes of professional conduct that is necessary to have a meaningful discussion of the cases. The case studies should engage your ethical imagination which is necessary to ensure that you "see" the issues at stake and "picture" possible solutions.

Introduction

In this chapter, you will encounter several short case studies for discussion, either in class or in smaller study groups. This is not a test where you hope to get to the right answer. Decision-making in the business world is often far more complicated than clear right-wrong answers, and is mostly dependent on the context (situation) within which you need to make the decision and act. For that reason, there may be several ways of approaching each case. Your challenge is to work with your classmates, both in finding as many options and solutions as possible, as well as refining your understanding and use of certain ethical principles. This will equip you to, in a different situation and at a different time and place, make the right choices.

Approach each case study using the following set of questions as your framework for discussion:
- What is the problematic choice that presents itself to the main actor(s) in the case?
- What are all the possible decisions or actions that this actor may make/take?
- What are the ethical issues relevant to each possible decision or actions, and how do we draw on either ethical theories or the requirements of the professional codes of conduct, to determine the right course of action?
- What are the possible consequences of the preferred decision or action? Is it ethical, legal, practical?

Case study one: Recruiting and employing trainees

Tamar Arch, senior audit manager at Crane Chartered Accountants and Auditors Inc. (Cranes), was exhausted. It had already felt like a particularly long week, and to end it with a phone call like the one she just concluded was not what she was hoping for on any Friday afternoon. She had just finished speaking with George Prince, the managing partner of Prince Auditors Inc. To say that he was upset would be a gross understatement.

Melissa Smith had applied for a position as trainee at Cranes in response to an advertisement in Accountancy SA. During the interview she told John Crane, founder and senior partner, that she was currently employed at Prince Auditors, but wanted to resign. When prompted she told John that although she had been employed at Prince's for a year and a half, her training contract had still not been registered with SAICA. She further indicated that George Prince was never available at the office and when she went out to clients, she mostly did that on her own. John considered Melissa to be a strong candidate and Cranes was in desperate need of more trainees.

After the interview John called George Prince a number of times to discuss the situation, but George was never available. When George called Cranes on Friday afternoon, John was already out so Tamar took the call. "How dare you poach my staff? You know that trainees are useless until the last year of their training contract! You are stealing the time and money I have invested! You are a bunch of common thieves!" And that is the family version of his comments!

Questions

1. Were Cranes' actions in recruiting trainees through advertisements appropriate?
2. What obligations do Cranes have if an employee of another audit firm applies for a position with them?
3. How should Melissa have gone about applying for the position at Cranes?
4. What should be done about George Prince's actions?

Comments

Audit firms require staff in the same manner that other organisations do. Details of training offices registered with SAICA (i.e. audit firms who are allowed to offer SAICA training contracts or "articles") are available on SAICA's website, but audit firms will also look for trainees or other staff through other means, like placing advertisements or using recruitment agencies. Outside the profession a call to an applicant's current employer may just be to obtain a reference, but maintaining collegial relationships with fellow members of the profession, by informing them of such an application, is considered to be good practice.

There typically exists a power imbalance between employer and employee which may result in abuse of power by the employer. In the absence of reporting unethical and unprofessional conduct, the behaviour will most likely continue.

Case study two: Reporting time spent on timesheets

On another Friday afternoon Melissa was finalising her timesheet. She was sitting in one of the small meeting rooms at Cranes along with JP Shaw and Lerato Khumalo. On the last Friday of the month, affectionately known as "timesheet Friday", it was not only impossible to find a parking space close to the office, but also a desk in the open plan office. Although Melissa worked as a senior on most jobs, the other trainees considered her a junior because she had only been at Cranes for four months. JP and Lerato were both first-years and so the three of them most often wound up stuffed into a meeting room on "timesheet Friday". The desk and floor was covered with laptops, audit files, Lerato's designer handbag and JP's camera bag.

Melissa was looking forward to the weekend, even though she knew that she would have to fit in at least four hours of study time. Working and studying at the same time was tougher than she had thought, but if she got her degree at the end of the year it would mean both a promotion and (more importantly!) a very good increase. As she clicked the "Submit" button to send the timesheet to Tamar for electronic approval, she sat back and looked at the mess around her. How did Lerato afford her designer handbag? And JP his camera equipment? She had seen some of JP's photos and they were absolutely stunning.

"I need a break from putting this timesheet together." JP said, as he got up for a smoke break. Melissa tried to sound as casual as possible when she asked Lerato about her designer bag. "Don't you just love it? It was a gift from my dad for my 21st. I had been nagging him for months, so he finally gave in. But he said I shouldn't expect another such expensive gift at least until my 30th. But I don't mind – it goes with everything and it is such good quality that it should last me until I retire. Which is hopefully sooner rather than later." Melissa felt she was blushing and tried, unsuccessfully, to change the topic. Lerato noticed the blushing and asked, "Did you think it was a fake?" "No, no, no" Melissa protested, "I was just wondering how you could afford it on a trainee salary? I mean..." "If you want to talk about affording expensive things... Did you know that JP has a photography business? I know, I know. There is nothing wrong with having a hobby, but I have heard him take calls from his clients, and seen him edit photos, while we were working on an audit. And then there is a rumour that he used the four days' study leave we got for last month's exams to attend a photography course."

Melissa wished she had never asked Lerato about her handbag. In the induction course which Tamar presented when Melissa started at Cranes, Tamar explained that Cranes took the profession's code of conduct very seriously and that the code also applied to trainees. Melissa remembered signing a declaration committing not only to act in accordance with the code, but also to report instances of violations.

Questions:

1. How detailed should timesheet entries be? If you receive a personal call while working, is it acceptable to count that as time spent on the client's work?
2. Is running your own business, while you are employed, acceptable?
3. Should Melissa report what she heard from Lerato? If so, to whom?

Comments:

Almost all professional services firms require that staff keep detailed timesheets, and then compare those to the budget set for an assignment. While the firm will typically indicate the expected amount they will charge a client for an assignment and use this to give the audit team a budget, the information from the timesheets is used as the basis for charging clients. If an assignment has taken longer than planned, detailed timesheets make it possible for the firm to explain to the client the reasons for charging them higher fees. Staff often feel pressure (explicit or implicit) not to charge time once the budget has been reached. This however results in the firm not being given the opportunity to try and recover the fees from the client. Despite detailed timesheets a firm may nevertheless have to write off fees. Write offs are often a key performance area for managers. There are a number of reasons why staff spend more time than was budgeted for, including inadequate guidance and supervision to junior staff. If this is the case, and the juniors do not charge all the time spent, it will make the manager's performance appear to be something that it is not.

An employer's time and assets should be used in order to do the job that you were employed to do. Most employers however would not object to incidental personal use e.g. using your internet access to check your exam results, or taking a call from your mom to let her know that you will join the family for Sunday lunch. Reporting incidences of unethical and unprofessional conduct is often required by organisations' codes of conduct. Doing so should however be based on fact rather than rumour, because otherwise such a system could be used to "get at" a colleague.

Case study 3: Networking and new clients

John Crane sat back and looked across the room as the applause died down and people started to get up. Tamar was being congratulated by the staff who had just heard that she had formally been made partner in Cranes as at the beginning of next month. She had worked very hard since first joining the firm as a trainee many, many years ago and exhibited both the technical skills and people management skills that John belied to be necessary to be successful as partner. He had hoped to offer her the partnership some years ago, but the difficult economic conditions had given his other partner a good reason to motivate waiting with the offer. Recently Tamar had brought in a very prominent client with the potential to become one of Cranes biggest.

Tamar met Gugu Tutani at a Women's Day breakfast where they sat at the same table. In the course of their conversation they discovered that they had both studied at the same university, and lived in the same on-campus residence, but a couple of years apart. Gugu had considered completing her training contract at Cranes, but when she was offered a training contract from a large financial services organisation she decided to complete her training contract there. Shortly after qualifying as a chartered accountant, Gugu was headhunted to become the financial director of a listed company. She had started her own company a year ago, and after being unhappy with the services of the current auditors wanted to appoint a new audit firm. Tamar had offered to prepare a presentation on Cranes. Although Cranes is a smaller audit firm, Gugu was impressed with Tamar and started the process of replacing her company's auditors with Cranes. Gugu's company had already invested in a number of businesses, and if its growth continued at the current pace it would soon become a force to be reckoned with in the South African market.

Almost all of the staff had left the room when John saw Melissa talking to Tamar. He assumed Melissa was congratulating her, but the expression on Tamar's face was not a happy one. He walked over to them and Tamar told him that Melissa had just given her some unexpected news that could affect their appointment as auditors of Gugu's company. Gugu was about to marry one of Melissa's cousins.

Questions:

1. Was it appropriate of Tamar to offer to prepare a presentation for Gugu?
2. Was it appropriate of Gugu to consider Cranes as the auditors of her company?
3. Is it relevant to the appointment that Cranes is a "smaller" audit firm? If so, why?
4. How does Melissa's news affect the appointment of Cranes as the auditors of Gugu's company?

Comments:

Networking takes place in a variety of environments, and learning of the products and services provided by other companies in such an environment is not necessarily problematic. No deal was made at the breakfast and Tamar's offer could well have been declined by Gugu. The appointment of auditors is also regulated by law (Companies' Act 2008) and cannot be done by Gugu only. "Professional competence and due care" is one of the fundamental principles of the IFAC code of conduct. This means that a firm should not accept work that it does not have the necessary technical skills to do, or that it would be able to execute due to the size of the firm. While the so-called big four audit firms are the firms that are well-known, there are hundreds of registered audit firms who are guided by the same standards, and subject to the same monitoring by the Independent Regulatory Board for Auditors.

In order to ensure the reliability of the opinion of the external auditor, it is critical that the auditor is objective. Objectivity means that the auditor should not be biased and avoids any conflicts of interest. Independence, which is a means of ensuring objectivity, should be both "in fact" and "in appearance". The family relationship between Gugu's fiancé and Melissa would at a minimum be considered to influence the appearance of independence, although it may well be that Melissa and her cousin have no contact and Melissa just happened to hear about the engagement. There are specific guidelines in the IFAC code of conduct which guide the behaviour of the chartered accountant in these situations, and it should be possible to address the perceived conflict of interest, e.g. by not having Melissa work on the audit at any point in time.

Case study 4: Parental leave and a BBBEE offer

Lerato had now been the senior manager on Cranes' largest audit client (BAC Limited) for the past four years, except last year when she had been on maternity leave. She had considered resigning from Cranes, but she found her work very rewarding, and also the family needed both her and her husband's income. Her husband was wonderfully supportive and hands-on (although he still complained every time he changed the baby's nappy!), but it was still tough to get to everything she wanted to do. With John Crane retiring last year, it meant that there may be a partnership offered to her although she wasn't sure whether it would happen any time soon. She remembered how Tamar had waited for years to become a partner. On the other hand, she was both black and a woman, which made hers a very desirable name to have on the firm's website and stationery.

Lerato had options in commerce and industry as well, but she was concerned that she would not find the same kind of support she had at Cranes. If her child was ill, Tamar was happy for Lerato to work from home for a couple of days. And then there was that other option…

Cecil John Williams, the operations manager of BAC Limited, had approached her after she was the only audit team member left working in the BAC boardroom one evening. He explained that BAC was under increasing pressure to improve its BEE score. He proposed registering a company with Lerato as sole shareholder. This would then allow this new company to qualify for one of the many B-BBEE deals that BAC was considering. He would do all the work: arrange for the financing, run the operations and take care of everything else, and then buy out Lerato after a year at an agreed price. His closing comment was that "after all, this has become standard practice".

Questions:

1. What maternity benefits should employers offer their professional staff? What about paternity benefits?
2. How can the workplace be changed so that the change is positive and lasting (not just superficial change)?
3. Should Lerato consider Cecil John Williams' offer, and why (or why not)?

Comments:

While South Africa has made large strides towards racial equality since the end of apartheid, gender inequality remains prevalent. Some professional women, who also choose to have families, have reported receiving the unspoken message that they will be side-lined when it comes to promotions and career progression. The labour legislation is clear about what the legal obligations of employers are, and it is worth noting that legislation differs vastly from country to country. An employer's ethical obligation may well be to offer more than what is required by law (the law is the ethical minimum).

Various pieces of legislation were promulgated in order to achieve economic transformation in South Africa, and include employment equity, black economic empowerment and broad-based black economic empowerment. The objective is to attempt restoring justice. As "the law is enforced through external pressures such as state authority" (see page 23) the reason for workplace transformation may only be to comply with the law. Employees are quick to realise when efforts speak of a genuine commitment, and in the absence thereof employees typically do not change their behaviour.

Recently various efforts have been made to ensure that B-BBEE deals are in fact legitimate. The Independent Regulatory Board for Auditors was appointed an "approved regulatory body" to approve auditors who meet the requirements to provide B-BBEE verification services (the South African National Accreditation System also accredits B-BBEE verification agents).

Case study 5: Environmental and social impacts

While Melissa had enjoyed her time at Cranes, she had always had the objective of entering the financial services industry. Now employed as financial analyst at a large investment bank, she was enjoying her new position. She was a member of a team that investigated companies that had applied to the bank for financing. This was a critical part for the bank to determine the risks involved in lending. As Melissa sat down with fellow analysts Ben Fisher and Mohamed Saloojee for lunch, Ben said "Let's hope you can break the deadlock". Ben and Mohamed explained that they were disagreeing about the level of risk of a project.

Mr Mara Diego was a South African who now lived in Colombia, South America. His company had obtained the necessary licences from the Colombian government to conduct exploration in the Angostura region. Based on the findings, the company was seeking finance in order to start operations. "So far so good" said Ben, and Melissa wondered what "deadlock" Ben and Mohamed could have. Ben went on to explain that the mine was located next to the La Paya National Park which is one of many national parks that lay in the ecologically sensitive Amazon jungle. "Surely the Colombian government would have considered the results of an environmental impact study before issuing the licence?" Melissa asked. "My point exactly!" exclaimed Mohamed, and he continued to explain that Colombian legislation required that 80% of mining royalties were required to return to the region for investment in development projects. Ben shook his head and said "Even if we had absolute certainty that these development projects were receiving the money, this remains an environmentally sensitive area. And the best practices in mining still have a significant impact on the environment. This is the Amazon after all!" "We are a bank and our business is providing finance", countered Mohamed. "If our clients have met all the legal requirements, we have done what we can."

Ben was still not satisfied. "You seem to have forgotten the Diamonds Affair, Mohamed." Ben was referring to a scandal which had been in the headlines for a full year before the investment bank in question finally closed their doors. Even two years later the scandal still reared its head on occasion. The scandal had resulted in the retrenchment of most of the staff of that investment bank which had provided the financing for a diamond mine in the Central African Republic. It had come to light that the licences for the mine had been obtained through the payment of bribes. The company in question had argued that they had disclosed the payments of "facilitation fees" in their financial statements, which were both audited and publicly available. They had also argued that the payment of "facilitation fees" was general practice, and that they were being unfairly targeted by the media for a practice that all companies were involved in. "In the most recent Corruption Perceptions Index, Colombia was perceived as being more corrupt than South Africa. The Diego mine is definitely a high risk project for us to be financing."

Questions:

1. Should the investment bank be considering the environmental impact of its client's operations?
2. Should other organisations be held accountable for the activities of their clients? And the activities of their suppliers?
3. Is "general practice" a valid reason for paying bribes?
4. What other examples of "general practice" may be considered unethical?
5. Should the disclosure of "facilitation fees" be accepted as sufficient disclosure (or sufficient transparency)?

Comments:

The globalised world that we live in has resulted in benefits, but also challenges in the business environment. It is now possible to outsource various functions to countries in order to make use of better cost structures. It is not possible however to outsource responsibilities, as has been evident by the response to evidence of sweatshops, using child labour and other unethical practices such as not paying minimum wage, harassment and verbal, physical and sexual assault of employees in the supply chain of companies such as Nike and, very recently, Apple. A bank would be considered complicit if it was financing illegal operations, and this again raises questions about what is legal, the reactive nature of the law and what is ethical.

Trying to justify bribing as an acceptable practice is short-termism (i.e. focussing on short-term results as opposed to long-term, sustainable results). The results of corruption are devastating to economies. What has been general practice in the past has subsequently been found to be unacceptable and this is evidence in practices ranging from slavery to denying women the right to vote to apartheid to many more.

The intention of financial statements is to provide users thereof with the information required in order to make informed decisions about whether to invest (potential shareholders), the return on their investment (current shareholders), and whether to lend (providers of financing). Disclosing all expenses incurred in doing business is a valid principle, but the choice of a euphemism "facilitation fees" to describe the expense still results in obscuring some of the facts.

Case study 6: Fraud red flags

Tamar looked at the report on her desk and sighed. The client was going to be very upset when the report was issued. When Melissa had reported her suspicions to her manager, he authorised her to engage an audit firm to conduct a forensic investigation, grumbling that the external auditors (not Cranes) should have picked this up during the audit. Melissa's claims appeared to have substance, but he wanted to make absolutely sure before taking this further. So Melissa approached Tamar, who was now senior partner at Cranes, and Cranes was appointed to conduct the investigation. Tamar's team had completed the investigation and the report, and it was about to be issued.

Melissa had been moved to another team at the bank and over a short period of time had become suspicious of the team leader, Laurie Johnson. At first Melissa had thought that Laurie may well be the hardest worker she had ever come across, but after a while she realised that there was no reason for the extraordinarily long hours Laurie worked. Laurie had also refused to delegate certain tasks that a team leader was not really supposed to be responsible for. The final "red flag" was when she had heard that it had literally been more than a year since Laurie had taken any leave. All of these were still only suspicions, until Melissa had accidentally picked up some of Laurie's printing at the shared printer. This had included an email sent from theman@hotmail.com with details of a bank account. The email had instructed Laurie to "make sure that the Glen Jiang deposit was made without delay". Glen Jiang was a project Laurie's team had been working on and Melissa had known that the bank account referred to in the email had nothing to do with Glen Jiang. At this point Melissa had met with her manager and explained her concerns.

Tamar's investigation found that Laurie had been falsifying bank account details to have payments made to an account set up in the name of Simpson (Pty) Ltd. This had started two years ago. All the payments had involved transactions with companies located in foreign, non-English speaking countries, and mostly China. Tamar's theory was that this was because a delay in delivering of the goods ordered by the clients (in one case two 70-seater luxury coaches) could be easily explained due to the distance and challenges of delivery and importation, and also not easily followed up due to the language barriers. An interesting "twist" in this case was that it had not been Laurie who had initiated the fraud. The investigation found that Laurie was drowning in debt and was targeted by a syndicate who "got to know" Laurie through Facebook posts and Twitter tweets.

Questions:

1. Whose responsibility is it to detect fraud?
2. What mechanisms should organisations implement to prevent fraud?
3. Should employers monitor employees' emails? What about social media activity (e.g. Facebook, Twitter, LinkedIn)?

Comments:

When fraud is discovered by someone other than the external auditor, the auditors are criticised for failing to identify fraud. The responsibility for the prevention and detection of fraud lies with "those charged with the governance of the entity and management" (ISA240), and organisations will implement internal controls to limit opportunities for fraud or to detect fraud. Because fraud typically involves hiding the evidence (concealment), there is an unavoidable risk that the auditor's procedures may not detect fraud. In addition to internal controls, the organisation should also create an ethical organisational culture with zero-tolerance for fraud. Management's response to the report on Laurie's fraud will send a message to other employees: if the fraud is covered up and Laurie not dealt with, it will undermine other activities (e.g. the establishment of a code of conduct, making available an anonymous reporting line) an organisation may have implemented to prevent fraud.

Information technology has become an integral part of conducting business. Initially technology was used to automate manual functions, but increasingly technology (including the Internet and the World Wide Web) is used to conduct business. Organisations and individuals should ensure that their electronic data and transactions are as secured as they would secure their physical data, transactions and assets. The information shared by individuals on social networks could be used by cybercriminals e.g. if your bank uses your mother's maiden name as a security question, and you have disclosed this on a social network, a criminal could access your account by calling your bank and asking to change the password. The practice of phishing is another way of getting access to usernames, passwords or credit card information by pretending to be from a valid entity e.g. your bank.

The South African constitution contains the right to privacy including the right not to have private communications be violated. Organisations will formulate internet and email use policies detailing what is acceptable use of these mediums.

Bibliography

Carroll & Buchholtz. 2000. *Business and society, 4th edition*. Cincinatti: South-Western Thompson Learning.

Cushman, JH. 1998. *Nike pledges to end child labor and apply US rules abroad*. [On-line]. <www.nytimes.com/1998/05/13/business/international-business-nike-pledges-to-end-child-labor-and-apply-us-rules-abroad.html?pagewanted=all&src=pm> [Accessed 1 August 2012].

Daily Mail. 2011. *Nike workers 'kicked, slapped and verbally abused' at factories making Converse.* [On-line]. <www.dailymail.co.uk/news/article-2014325/Nike-workers-kicked-slapped-verbally-abused-factories-making-Converse-line-Indonesia.html> [Accessed 1 August 2012].

Duhigg, C & Barboza, D. 2012. *In China, human costs are built into an iPad*. [On-line]. <www.nytimes.com/2012/01/26/business/ieconomy-apples-ipad-and-the-human-costs-for-workers-in-china.html?pagewanted=all> [Accessed 1 August 2012].

Griseri & Seppala. 2010. *Business ethics and corporate social responsibility.* Hampshire: South-Western Cengage Learning.

Wingfield, N. 2012. *Apple chief puts stamp on labor issues.* [On-line]. <www.nytimes.com/2012/04/02/technology/apple-presses-its-suppliers-to-improve-conditions.html?_r=1&pagewanted=all> [Accessed 1 August 2012].

Addendum: Learning journal assignment

A suggested form of assignment for Accounting Ethics students

An innovative way of demonstrating the quality of your learning in a subject is to write a learning journal in which you record, explore, interpret, comment on and evaluate your learning experiences in connection with the contact sessions (lectures, workshops), and also beyond these contact sessions. Here are the guidelines for such an assignment:

1. The first step is for you to understand the purpose of this exercise, namely to link what you learn in the contact sessions with your readings and with relevant, practical experiences after the contact sessions, in other relevant studies, and in society at large.

2. For some reading recommendations, see below. Your readings must include at least Duska and Duska (2003) and one other substantial text. However, the depth and quality of your reading counts more than the quantity of your reading.

3. In order to read meaningfully, it is best to make regular and detailed notes after contact sessions and regularly thereafter about readings and relevant experiences.

4. Next, be especially alert to anything in your wider experience (such as work or society) which strikes you as being relevant to, or which links up with, what you learn in the contact sessions. Make clear notes of these, with dates and source details where appropriate.

5. See yourself as your own creative educator – by doing more than just noting the issues covered in the classes and in your wider experience. Try to probe issues, interrogate them, seek insight, make imaginative connections with them, be alert to problems, and above all, ponder possible solutions – and keep notes of these episodes of creative thinking.

6. Start shaping your growing body of notes into a well-written and well-presented learning journal. Feel free to find creative ways of presenting your material, so long as these do not give the reader headaches. Add full bibliographical details and other appropriate source references for material written by somebody else, or derived from such material.

7. Please do not exceed 3 000 words or drop below 2 500 words.

8. Feel free to contact your lecturers about anything in this process.

Recommended core readings

Bowie, NE (ed). 2002. *The Blackwell guide to business ethics*. Oxford and Malden, MA: Blackwell Publishers.

Duksa, RF & Duska, BS. 2003. *Accounting ethics*. Oxford and Malden, MA: Blackwell Publishing.

Rossouw, D. 2005. *Business ethics*, 3rd ed. Cape Town: Oxford University Press.

Singer, P. 1995. *Practical ethics*, 2nd ed. Cape Town: Cambridge University Press

Glossary

Advocacy threat – with reference to an auditor's independence, this threat occurs when an auditor compromises his or her independence in promoting an auditee's position or opinion by acting on behalf of the auditee

African ethics – used to describe the collective set of values that derive from traditional black African people. It can be done alone as a distinct field of study or as part of comparative ethics

Agent – one who acts for another (the principal) in a representative capacity and who may or may not be endowed with rights to act on behalf of the principal depending on the contract of agency between principal and agent

Altruistic standard – a principle of behaviour where one acts for the benefit of others

Aspirational codes – codes of ethics that articulate the core ethical values that should guide members of organisations in their behaviour and ethical decision-making. Aspirational codes are normally value-based codes and much shorter than directional codes

Audit – an audit is an evaluation of an organisation, system, process, project, or product. It is performed by a competent, independent, objective, and unbiased person or persons, known as auditors. The purpose is to make an independent assessment based on management's representation of their financial condition (through their financial statements). Another purpose of the audit is to ensure that the internal accounting system is effective and in accordance with approved and accepted accounting standards, statutes, regulations, or practices. It also evaluates the internal controls to determine if conformance to good accounting procedures will continue, and recommends necessary changes in policies, procedures, or controls

Auditing Profession Act 26 of 2005 – this act regulates the auditing profession in South Africa. Among other things, the Act provides for the establishment of a committee for auditor ethics as well as a disciplinary committee to deal with improper conduct by auditors in practice

Broad (corporate) governance – broad governance is the regulation and control of companies by the state and judiciary with various forms of legislation, such as the Companies Act and labour laws. The state can also delegate some of its control functions to regulatory bodies. Regulatory bodies are entities formed by the state with representatives from the state, the industry, and stakeholders

Business ethics – the concept of 'ethics' (see 'ethics') as it applies to economic activity, i.e. what constitutes good and morally acceptable economic behaviour. As a field of study it focuses on determining what is morally acceptable in economics and business

Business sustainability – Business sustainability is the ability of corporations to continue as going concerns and sustain business for future generations. Business sustainability is important to avoid the cost of corporate failures and the effect thereof on employees, suppliers, customers, and the surrounding community

Capitalism – an economic system in which the means of production are mostly privately owned, and capital is invested in the production, distribution, and other trade of goods and services, for profit. These include factors of production such as land and other natural resources, labour, and capital goods. Capitalism is also usually considered to involve the right of individuals and groups of individuals acting as 'legal persons' (or corporations) to trade in a free market

Caste – one of the several hereditary classes into which society in India has been divided as far back as history can document; the members of each caste are socially equal, have the same religious rites, and generally follow the same occupation or profession; members of one caste have no social interactions with those of another. In modern, democratic India the caste system has been significantly modified

Categorical imperative – the philosophical concept central to the philosophy of Immanuel

Kant. Kant defined an imperative as any proposition that declares a certain kind of action (or inaction) to be necessary. A hypothetical imperative would compel action under a particular circumstance, e.g. if I wish to satisfy my thirst, then I must drink this lemonade. A categorical imperative would denote an absolute, unconditional requirement that overrides all other options for action in all circumstances, and is both required and justified as an end in itself. It is best known in its first formulation: 'Act only according to that maxim by which you can at the same time will that it would become a universal law'

Code of ethics – in the context of an organisation, a code of ethics is often a formal statement of the organisation's values and standards of behaviour on certain ethical and social issues. The effectiveness of such codes of ethics depends on the extent to which management supports and enforces these codes

Communist ethics – the approach to ethics and values based largely on the work of Karl Marx, but developed since his time by other leading Marxists, including a few members of the South African Communist Party. It treats the overthrow of exploitative economic structures, which it identifies with capitalism, as a central value

Comparative ethics – a study of different value systems, such as African ethical traditions, Christian ethics, Buddhist ethics and others from around the world, done with respect and empathy for them in order to understand each one better and detect points of agreement and difference

Compliance strategy – a mode of managing the ethical performance of an organisation where the emphasis is on ensuring that members of the organisation abide by the ethical norms and standards of the organisation. Those who transgress the ethical standards of the organisation are disciplined, while those who abide may be rewarded. A compliance strategy is often premised on a directional code of ethics

Corporate governance – corporate governance is the set of processes, customs, policies, laws, and institutions affecting the way a corporation is directed, administered, or controlled. An important aspect of corporate governance deals with accountability and fiduciary duties, basically advocating the implementation of guidelines and mechanisms to ensure good behaviour and to protect the interest of stakeholders. In recent years, the stakeholder view of corporate governance has called for more accountability to stakeholders other than the shareholder, e.g. for more accountability to employees

Corporate internal decision structure – the system of policies, procedures, and lines of authority that an organisation follows in making decisions. Decisions that are made according to the corporate internal decision structure are regarded as corporate decisions and not merely as personal decisions

Creative middle way solutions – a solution to a social dilemma that all parties to a dilemma can live with because compromises have been made in finding a solution that pleases everyone

Demographics – the study, in terms of size, density and distribution, of the structure of populations

Deontological ethics – a theory stating that decisions should be based primarily on one's duty to do the right thing and the rights of others. Deontology goes further than having or acting in accordance with mere moral obligations, and suggests that people should live according to a framework of defined principles that do not change merely because the circumstances or situations have changed. One of the most important implications of deontology is that great goals can never justify immoral actions; in other words, the ends cannot justify the means, because the means or manner of doing something is crucial in itself

Directional codes – codes of ethics that provide detailed guidelines on how members of organisations should behave in specific situations or with regard to specific issues. Directional codes are normally rule-based codes and tend to be rather detailed and lengthy

Economic system level (macro-economic level) – one of the levels on which a moral evaluation of economic activity can occur; the level at which economic systems or macro-economic policies and trade agreements are scrutinised to see that they are equitable and fair

Economics – a social science that seeks to analyse and describe the production, distribution, and consumption of goods and services. Economics therefore studies how individuals, coalitions, and societies seek to satisfy needs and wants. Economics has two broad branches: micro-economics, where the unit of analysis is the individual agent, such as a household or firm, and macro-economics, where the unit of analysis is an economy as a whole

Ethical risk – the risks inherent in ethical decisions that have to be made by boards of directors in managing and directing companies

Ethical risk analysis – the systematic investigation and forecasting of risks in business and commerce, especially as this would pertain to making choices in support of ethical conduct

Ethical standards – these are standards or guidelines that guide ethical behaviour in people, organisations, societies, and professions

Ethics – the moral principles by which a person or group is guided; ethics as a field of study is concerned with the principles of human duty and morality in general

Exclusive approach (to corporate governance) – in the exclusive approach to corporate governance, the directors of a company are regarded as agents of the shareholders only. The corporate governance processes within the company therefore exist to protect only the interests of the shareholders of the company, and the interests of other stakeholders are ignored

Familiarity threat – although legally auditors are answerable to shareholders, doubt has been cast on how independent they are from the directors of the company which is audited. A factor which has been shown in many studies as possibly having eroded auditor independence is the close nature of the relationship between the auditor and the directors of the company. This has been termed the 'familiarity threat'

Feminist ethics – a branch of ethics that revises, reformulates, or rethinks those aspects of women's moral experience that are seemingly inaccurately or not sufficiently dealt with in traditional western ethics. Proponents of feminist ethics feel that in general western ethics and the policies derived from these are deficient to the degree that they lack, ignore, trivialise, or demean those personality traits and virtues which are culturally associated with women

Global sustainability – global sustainability is the ability of our planet to sustain an environmental resource base sufficient to meet the needs of future generations. National governments around the world have the responsibility of controlling their companies in a way that ensures environmental sustainability of our planet

Greatest Happiness principle – this is the foundation of utilitarian moral theory (see 'utilitarian moral theory'), and states that the correct action in any situation is that action which brings the most happiness to the most people

Inclusive approach (to corporate governance) – in the inclusive approach to corporate governance, directors are responsible to all the stakeholders of the company and not only to the shareholders. The corporate governance processes within the company are established to protect the interest of all stakeholders (e.g. shareholders, employees, customers, government, society). All relevant stakeholders of the company should be identified. A relationship should be established and maintained with the all the stakeholders to identify the interests of the relevant stakeholders

Integrity strategy – a mode of managing the ethical performance of an organisation where the emphasis is on the internal commitment of each member of the organisation to the values and norms of the organisation. Members of the organisation are encouraged to internalise the values of the organisation and to use their discretion in applying it to their behaviour and decisions. An integrity strategy is often premised upon an aspirational code of ethics

Intimidation threat – this threat to an auditor's independence occurs when an auditor's professional skepticism and opinion are deterred by threats from an auditee's personnel and/or management, for instance, a threat to not appoint the auditor again

Intra-organisational level (micro-economic level) – the level at which economic activity and decisions taken within organisations are evaluated so that these decisions apply fairly to all employees

Invisible hand doctrine – the invisible hand is a metaphor created by Adam Smith to illustrate how those who seek wealth inadvertently stimulate the economy and assist the poor, by following their individual self-interest

Laissez-faire capitalism – a system based on personal interest and competition, and the acquisition and persuit of private property and freedom – the latter two being institutional prerequisites that guarantee the existence of the first two concepts. This system seeks to limit the role of government to the protection and reinforcement of private property and freedom

Law – the body of rules which a particular state or community recognises as binding on its members or subjects. These rules could be either formally enacted, such as Acts of Parliament, or be derived from customs and traditions that have become formalised as 'rules'

Lowballing – occurs when an auditor charges a lower fee than previously for the same standard of work and calculated according to the required rules, but with the intention to retain an auditee. Auditors should be aware that their independence is not compromised by lowballing

Macro-economic level – see 'economic system level'

Macro-ethics – Macro-ethics is the study of what constitutes right or wrong or good or bad economic principles as it pertains to society as a whole, for instance in deciding which economic system is best for a society and on what basis one makes such a claim

Management consultants – experts in some area of corporate management, who offer their advice or services to organisations in exchange for a consultancy fee

Mean – the midpoint between morally going too far (e.g. being too generous) and not going far enough (e.g. being stingy). So, for example, the virtue of generosity is a mean between stinginess and a tendency to give far too much or to the wrong kinds of people

Meso-economic level – see 'organisational level'

Moral dilemmas – a dilemma of a moral nature which occurs when one has evaluated one's choices or options going forward, and what results is two (or more) conflicting judgements or choices. In each case, the person having to resolve the moral dilemma regards him- or herself as having moral reasons to do each of two actions, but doing both actions is not possible

Narrow (corporate) governance – Narrow corporate governance is the set of processes, customs, policies, rules, and culture which were implemented by the company and which exist within the company. Narrow governance comprises the corporate governance processes which exist within the company to ensure good behaviour by its employees and the protection of its stakeholders' interests

Natural disposition – one's natural instinct or tendency to act in particular way in a given situation

Natural law – the law as based on the principles of natural morality, and subject to rational thought and action. The appeal to natural law has been an important part of the approach to Christian ethics that developed in the Catholic tradition in the Middle Ages

Organisational ethics – the 'ethos' of an organisation or the prevailing climate of acceptable behaviour in the organisation which sets the standard for what is 'right' and 'wrong'. Sometimes these standards are explicitly stated, such as in a code of behaviour that is applicable to all employees in an organisation

Organisational level (meso-economic level) – the level at which the impact of business on broader society is evaluated, for example, it looks at the social responsibility of business towards society and also at the impact of business on the natural environment

Personal ethical dilemma – see 'personal moral dilemma'

Personal ethics – Personal ethics is the set of one's own ethical commitments (i.e. moral values, beliefs, attitudes) which is usually acquired in early home or religious training and often modified through later experiences in life

Personal moral dilemma – a moral dilemma (see 'moral dilemma') which is of a personal nature and results in someone having to make a personal decision between two conflicting moral choices

Principle of reversibility – this follows on from the principle of universalisability (see 'Principle of universalisability') and states that we should be willing to put ourselves in the position of those who will be at the receiving end of our intended action and ask ourselves whether the intended action would be acceptable from that perspective

Principle of universalisability – a consequence of the categorical imperative (see 'categorical imperative') which states that we should have enough conviction in the principles informing our actions that we would be willing for these principles to be followed by all

Professional codes of conduct – see 'code of ethics'

Professional ethics – the norms and guidelines for moral and ethical behaviour for professionals. Guidelines for professional ethics are usually codified in codes of conduct (see 'codes of ethics')

Professionalism – the qualities, conduct, and kinds of behaviour expected from a professional or a profession

Rational Interaction for Moral Sensitivity (RIMS) – an approach to resolving moral dilemmas in which rational discussion is used to mould conflicting points of view into a morally sensitive compromise that respects the moral views of all parties in a dispute

Risk – kinds of behaviour that can lead to the chance or hazard of commercial loss or liability. Risk can also be positively seen as opportunities that companies can exploit for their own financial gain

Secular humanist ethics – the understanding of morality that has developed independently of religion, and sometimes in opposition to it, mostly in western societies over the past two or three centuries

Self-interest threat – this threat to an auditor's independence occurs when an auditor could benefit from a financial or other interest in an auditee, for example, undue dependence on the fees from one auditee, or having a material share in an auditee's business

Self-review threat – this threat to an auditor's independence occurs when there were previous connections between the auditor and the auditee, for example, acting as an auditor for an auditee of whom the books were previously written up or where the auditor was previously employed by the auditee

Social dilemma – a moral dilemma (see 'moral dilemma') occurs when different persons or groups take conflicting moral positions on a decision that needs to be made in a situation that affects them all

Social ethical dilemma – see 'social dilemma'

Social responsibility – or corporate social responsibility is an expression used to describe a company's moral obligations to its stakeholders, i.e. employees, customers, suppliers, community organisations, subsidiaries and affiliates, joint venture partners, local neighborhoods, investors, shareholders, and others. Social responsibility is seen as the contribution of a company towards the sustainability and wellbeing of society

Stakeholder – a person or party who is affected by a business or who has the potential to affect the performance of a business

Stakeholder engagement – involving all those stakeholders who are to be affected by a business action or decision or who can influence the actions or decisions of a business. Determining the perceptions of stakeholders

Stakeholder theory – this theory attempts to ascertain which groups are stakeholders in a corporation and therefore deserve management's attention. Stakeholder theory recognises that there are other parties that have a decisive impact on business such as governmental bodies, political groups, trade associations, trade unions, communities, associated corporations, and so on. Thus the specific stakeholders of a corporation are defined (the normative theory of stakeholder identification) and the conditions under which these parties should be treated as stakeholders are examined (the descriptive theory of stakeholder salience). These two questions make up the modern treatment of stakeholder theory

Talmud – in a wide sense, this refers to the body of Jewish civil and ceremonial traditional law independently of religion, and sometimes in opposition to it, mostly in western societies over the past two or three centuries

Triple bottom-line reporting – a method of corporate reporting that captures an expanded spectrum of values and criteria for measuring organisational (and societal) success – economic, environmental, and social. This translates into expanding the traditional company reporting framework to take into account environmental and social performance in addition to financial outcomes

Utilitarian moral theory – a moral theory which states that right actions are those that produce the greatest total amount of human well-being

Values – convictions, principles or standards of behaviour which inform one's sense of what is good or appropriate behaviour in any given situation

Virtue – a certain character trait that predisposes one to doing the right thing. It affects one's emotions and emotional reactions, choices, values, desires, perceptions, attitudes, interests, expectations, and sensibilities. To possess a virtue is therefore also to possess a certain complex mindset and set of emotional and psychological factors which guides one to do the right thing and, indeed, almost compels one to do so

Virtue theory – an approach to ethics that shifts the emphasis from rules, consequences, and particular acts and places the focus on the kind of person who is acting. The overriding issues are not whether an intention is right, or whether one is following the correct rule, or whether the consequences of actions are good, although all these factors are relevant. The overriding concern is whether the person acting is doing so in accordance with moral virtues or not

Index

Page numbers in **bold** refer to figures and tables.

A

AA1000 standard 194
abortion 60
ACCA (Association of Chartered Certified Accountants) 232, 233
accountability 28, 33, 56, 67, 68, 164, 170, 173, 234, 241
accountancy 1, 2, 66, 112, 217, 232, 233, 243, 247, 248
    management 64
    professional bodies 217, 218, 228, 230, 232, 247, 248
accountant(s) 1, 24, 25, 28, 29, 61, 86, 89, 127, 151, 152, 165, 178, 179, 181, 185, 197, 217, 218–239, 241, 242, 243, 246, 247, 248, 249, 251, 252, 253, 263, 271
    ethical issues 33
accounting services 224, 245
accounting profession 24, 25, 28, 63, 66, 76, 127, 165, 185, 197, 233, 245, 246
    codes of professional ethics 247–254
action, ethic of 49
advertising 221, **228**, 229, 246
advocacy **228**
    threats 249
Advocacy Model (of professionalism) 228, **228**
affirmative action (AA) 19, 20, 197, 211
African ethics, traditional 34–37
    ancestors 35, 36
    context 36
    ubuntu 35
African Christians 36
African societies, traditional 36
Agency Argument 154
agency problems 163, 166, 169, 170
altruism **228**
Altruistic Model (of professionalism) 228, **228**
ancestors 35, 36
    guardians of morality 36
apartheid 24, 46, 62, 90, 130, 138, 211, 272, 274
Approved Training Organisation 223
arguments, moral 102, 103, 105
Aristotle 1, 74, 75
    concept of the 'mean' position 74, **75**
    ethics 65
    happiness (*eudaimonia*) 73, 74
    goals (*telos*) 73, 74, 75

    justice 138
    natural dispositions 74
    virtue theory 71, 73
Arthur Andersen 33, 170, 235–237, 258
aspirational codes of ethics 189
assets 110, 130, 133, 225, 236, 269, 276
    intangible 136
    tangible 135, 136, 178
Association of Chartered Certified Accountants (ACCA) 232, 233
assurance 165, 175, 180, 181, 224, 245, 247, 258, 261
audit 152, 181, 230, 233, 236, 251, 252, **253**, 254, 255, 257, 258, 259, 261, 268
    external 165, 179, 180, 217, 223, 226, 227, 230, 240, 245, 254, 255, 260, 262
    firm(s) 65, 170, 180, 181, 231, 235, 251, 257, 258, 259, 260, 261, 267, 270
    gathering evidence 227, 261
    internal 164, 165, 175, 179, 180, 181, 187
    planning 260
    qualified statement 76, 82
    reporting 170, 237, 254
    risk assessment 165
    unqualified statement 76, 79, 82, 83
audit committee 165, 175, 179, 181, 251
    duties of 180
    role of 179–180
audit process 175, 180
audit report 170, 237, 254, 257, 261
auditing profession, governance role 179–181
Auditing Profession Act 26 of 2005 223, 226, 230, 231, 234, 262
auditing 16, 25, 27, 28, 22, 61, 64, 66, 68, 71, 79, 83, 127, 152, 163, 179, 180, 182, 184, 185, 195, 196, 217, 218, 219, 223, 224, 227, 230, 231, 232, 233, 234, 235, 236, 240, 241, 243, 244, 245, 246, 254, 256, 258, 259, 261, 262, 263
    standards 234, 250, 260
auditors 25, 28, 29, 61, 79, 83, 86, 112, 127, 151, 152, 165, 169, 178, 179, 180, 181, 197, 217, 218–239, 254, 255, 256, 257, 258, 259, 260, 261, 262, 270, 272, 276
    ethical issues 33
    external 165, 180–181, 222, 225, 226, 237, 254–261, 270, 276
    internal 165, 181
autonomy 34, 63, 221, 227, 241

285

B

Basic Conditions of Employment Act 75 of 1997 203
basic needs 245
benevolence 56, 67
Berlin Wall, fall of 57, 132
best practice (corporate governance) 172, 174, 177, 186, 187, 188
Bhagavad Gita 51, 52, 53
Bill of Rights 58, 59
Black Economic Empowerment (BEE) 133, 197, 207–208, 272
board of directors 157, 163, 164, 165, 166, 170, 171, 172, 174, 175, 181, 187, 227, 251
Broad-based Black Economic Empowerment Act 53 of 2003 133, 207
Buddhism 30, 50
business
    and morality 64–65
    key concepts 16–26
    sustainability 152, 169, 172, 174, 175, 178, 180, 182, 186, 194
business ethics 20–22, 127–216
    economic system level (macro-economic level) 21
    intra-organisational level (micro-economic level) 21, 22
    moral evaluation 20
    organisational level (meso-economic level) 21–22

C

capital 44, 133, 134, 136, 137, 146, 167, 169, 170, 171, 224, 225, 236, 237
capitalism 21, 30, 40, 57, 58, 128, 129, 130, 131–132, 133, 134, 135, 136, 137, 138, 148, 158, 187
    Anglo-American model 133
    dynamic nature 133–134
    European model 133
    globalised 129
    key features 127, 129, 134–137
    laissez faire 131, 132
    rise of 131–134
care, ethic of 60
cartels 137
case studies
    Aids anxiety 202–206
    Black front, white back 207–208
    Cheating and eating 198–199
    Chris 72
    Credible credentials? 200–201
    Dilemma in professional and business ethics 2–15
    Email dilemma 103–105
    Environmental and social impacts 272–273
    Fraud red flags 274–275
    Jane Peterson's downsizing assignment (and applications) 87, 90, 92, 93, 96–97
    Kool Trading (Pty) Ltd 249–250
    Miriam's brainwave 113–125
    Networking and new clients 269–270
    Parental leave and a BBBEE offer 271
    Promotion problems 211–212
    Recruiting an employing trainees 266
    Reporting time spent on timesheets 267–268
    Suspicious invoices 215–216
    Tempting tickets 209–210
    Thandi and government tenders 31–32
    Three nights out of town 213–214
    Using ethical skills and insights 113–125
    Vanilla Investments (Pty) Ltd 244
caste discrimination 54
categorical imperative 77–78
Catholics 40, 43, 44, 62
character 42
Chartered Accountant (CA) (SA) 223, 226, 232, 237, 242, 253
Chartered Institute of Management Accountants (CIMA) 232, 233
cheating 36, 48, 197, 198–199
child marriage 54, 55
Christian(s) 29, 30, 63, 66
    ethics 39–46, 67
    tradition 39, 60
Christianity 33, 36
    ethics in 39–46
    Jesus of Nazareth 39–40, 41, 42
    modern morality 39
    world view 40–42
CID structure (corporate internal decision structure) 156–157
CIMA (Chartered Institute of Management Accountants) 232, 233
clarity 63, 152, 186, 192, 195
classic professionals **229**, 230, 231
client information, confidentiality 105, 106, **107**, 108, 110, 242, 245, 248, **252**
code of conduct 107, 270, 271, 276
code of ethics 28, 90, 91, 170, 184, 185, 188, 189, 190, 192, 193, 217, 219, 228, 231, 232, 241, 242, 246
    aspirational 189
    directional 188–189
Code of Ethics for Professional Accountants (IFAC) 217, 240, 247
Code of Professional Conduct (IRBA) 254, 255, 256, 257, 259

INDEX

Code of Professional Conduct (SAICA) 217, 240, 242, 243, 245, 252–254
    contents **252–253**
    role in disciplinary process 253–254
codes of professional ethics 217, 237, 240–264
    [*see also* professional ethics]
    accounting profession 247–254
    adherence 263
    dissemination and enforcement 246–247
colleagues, responsibility to 242
collective bargaining 158
combined assurance concept 165, 180
commerce and industry 112, 127, 219, 223, 233, 250
    roles in 225–226
common moral decencies (Kurtz) 56
common morality 219
communalistic ethic 60
communication 133, 193, 276
    corporate 180
    email 107
    external 105, 106, 109
    ineffective **107**, 109–110
    internal 105, 106, 109
    system 192, 194
    technology 200
Communism 29, 30, 33, 57, 58
communist(s) 63, 64,
    ethics 57–58
    revolution 132
    value system 55
Companies Act 61 of 1973 224, 231
Companies Act 71 of 2008 172, 173, 177, 231
company expenses 212–214
company standards 90–92
comparability 195
compassion 31, 35, 39, 40, 42, 46, 47, 49, 55, 60
competence 25, 164, 180, 223, 232, 240, 243, 245, 248, **252**, 254, 259–261, 270
competition 65, 89, 127, 131, 133, 134, 136–137
    perfect 137
competitive free markets 258
compliance strategy 190–191
conduct (ethical/professional) 38, 46, 48, 49, 61, 67, 76, 181, 190, 192, 220, 225, 228, 234, 235, 237, 241, 243, 244, 250, 262
    code(s) of 31, 33, 43, 107, 231, 265, 266, 270, 271, 276
    [*see also* the main entries for various Codes of Conduct]
    proper 242
    rules 189, 190

standards of 221
    unethical/illegal/improper 23, 24, 188, 191, 244, 245, 262, 267, 269
confidence **75**, 225, 234, 236, 243, 245, 255, 256
confidentiality 105, 106, **107**, 108, 110, 242, 245, 248, **252**
conflict(s) of interest 33, 174, 180, 230, 237, 242, 248, **252**, 255, 270, 271
consensus 30, 101, 134, 229
consequences 21, 82, 83, 127, 129, 138, 139, 145, 162, 167, 211
    actions/decisions 1, 28, 52, 53, 71, 79, 82, 85, 159, 266
    ethical 86
Constitution of the Republic of South Africa, 1996 59, 276
controversial practices in Hinduism 54
core concepts in ethics 16, **18**
core values 59, 91
corporate citizenship 174
corporate governance 33, 127, 163–183
    [*see also* the main entry for *King Report*]
    agency problem/relationships 163, 166, 169, 170
    definition of 164–166
    double agency construct 127
    history 167–169
    importance 166–167
    increased focus since 1980 169–170
    King Reports 127, 151, 172, 173, 186
    substantive 170
    superficial 170
    triple bottom-line reporting 151, 185, 186, 194
corporate internal decision (CID) structure 156–157
corporate moral agency 155–156
corporate social responsibility 150, 152–155
corporation(s) 21, 66, 127, 134–135, 136, **160**
    corporate moral agency 155–156
    corporate social responsibility 150, 152–155
    law 155
    legal identity 135
    limited liability 135
    moral obligations 150–162
    multi-national 135, 151
    perpetual lifetime 134
    stakeholder theory 158, 159
    triple bottom-line reporting 151, 185, 186, 194
creative middle way solutions 20
creativity 41, 93, 100, 101, 160, 227
credibility 33, 63, 159, 175, 177, 182, 243, 245, 255
culture 19, 21, 22, 27, 30, 36, 59, 61, 63, 101, 151

D

decision-making (ethical) 85–98, 123–125
    process 85, 88, 95, 103
    rules 157
decisions, ethical 30, 85, 96, 88–89, 92, 102, 112, 113, 190
deontological ethics 71, 73, 76–79, 83
    categorical imperative 77–78
    respect for persons 78–79
deontological theory 71, 73, 79
dharma 52, 53
difference principle 142
dignity 18, 20, 34, 38, 59, 130, 241
dilemma(s) 20, 60, 99, 100, 105, 231, 258
    ethical 2, 60, 197, 242, 265
    moral 1, 16, 17, 19–20, 24, 25, 82, 86, 97, 99, 100, 101, 105, 110, 112, 113, 219
    personal ethical 16, 100
    social 19, 99, 100, 103, 106
    social ethical 16, 100
directional codes of ethics 188–189
disciplinary system (ethics) 193
discipline 41, 76, 185, 194
disclosure test 85, 89, 93, 95–97
dissensus 99, 101
distributive justice 128, 130, 138, 139, 145, 146, 147
division of labour 131
Diwali (Hindu festival of lights) 34, 55
due care 240, 245, 248, 250, **252**, 254, 259–261, 270

E

economic
    argument 158–159
    challenges 29, 32–33
    distribution [*see* wealth distribution]
    equilibrium 137
    inequality 142
economic justice 59, 127, 145
economic systems 21, 22, 33, 127, 133
education 30, 43, 45, 143, 153, 221, 222–223, 226, 231, 233, 247, 259
egalitarian theory of justice 140–143
empathy 60
employees 17, 22, 38, 45, 88, 91, 99, 105, 107, 108, 109, 153, 158, 159, 160, **160**, 165, 169, 171, 176, 181, 188, 189, 190, 191, 192, 193, 194, 212, 215, 243, 257, 258, 267, 272, 274, 276
employment equity 211–212, 272
Employment Equity Act 55 of 1998 133, 211
Enron (USA) 33, 63, 166, 170, 173, 235–237, 258
entitlement theory 145, 146, 147
entrepreneurship 187

equality 18, 19, 54, 58, 59, 130, 138, 139, 141, 142, 143, 161, 241, 272
ethic
    of action 49
    of care 60
ethical consequences 86
ethical decision-making 85–98, 123–125
ethical decisions 30, 88–89, 102, 113, 190
    business or professional 88–89, 92, 112
    criteria 85, 86
ethical dilemmas 2, 60, 197, 242, 265
    personal 100
    resolving 1, 20, 99–111, 112, 198
    social 100
ethical performance 184, 185, 186, 190, 191, 192, 193, 194–195, 196
    reporting and disclosing 186, 194–195
ethical reporting 184, 186, 194, 195
    principles of 184
ethical risk 190, 192, 194, 195
    analysis 184
    assessment 187–188
    determination of 185, 186–188
ethical standards 16, 24, 76, 85, 90–92, 164, 190, 191, 219, 220, 234, 241
    changes and improvement 246
    codifying of 184, 185, 188–189
    institutionalising 185
    regulation of professionals 221–222, 231
ethical traditions 1, 36, 39, 50, 66
ethical values 19, 27, 39, 102, 164, 188, 189, 191, 192, 234
ethics
    and family 33–34
    Aristotle 65
    business 42–45, 127–216, 219
    communist 57–58
    definition 17–18, **18**
    disciplinary system 193
    economy 42–45
    evaluation system 194
    feminist 60–61
    induction system 193
    institutionalisation of 189–195
    and law 23–24, **24**
    management systems 192
    managing 184–196
    monitoring system 108
    performance appraisal system 193, 194
    personal 219
    personal and organisational 16, 22–23, **23**
    philosophical foundations 71–84
    principles 1–125

professional 219
    staffing system 193
    training system 193
ethics management systems 192
    communication 192
    disciplinary 193
    induction 193
    monitoring and evaluation 194
    staffing 193
    training 193
eudaimonia 73, 74
European Enlightenment 37
evaluation system 194
expediency 82
external audit 165, 179, 180, 217, 223, 226, 227, 230, 240, 245, 254, 255, 260, 262
external auditors 165, 180, 222, 225, 226, 237, 270, 276
    fundamental principles of relevance 254–261
    role 180–181

F
fairness 43, 56, 59, 66, 67, 97, 164, 170
    justice as, theory 141
    test 89, 92, 93
familiarity threat 249, 250
feminist ethics 60–61
forbidden acts 48
Four Vedas 51
fraud 17, 24, 33, 41, 144, 145, 177, 180, 181, 194, 197, 236, 260, 276
    qualification 200–201
freedom 18, 19, 21, 28, 51, 52, 58, 59, 63, 102, 130, 142, 144, 161, 227, 229
Freeman, Edward 150, 157, 158–161, **160**
free market 127
    capitalism 158
    competitive 258
French, Peter 150, 156, 157
Friedman, Milton 150, 152–154, 155, 156, 157, 161, 229
fundamental principles 42, 240, 248, 249, 250, 251, 252, **252**, 254–261, 262
    independence 240
    integrity 240
    professional competence and due care 240, 270

G
Gandhi, Mahatma 51, 54, 55
gifts and gratuities 208–210
Gilligan, Carol 60
Gini-coefficient 32, 130

global ethic 56
globalisation 55
Global Reporting Initiative 178, 194
'good' (core concept in ethics) 16, **18**
good life, definition 64–65
Goodpaster, Kenneth 150, 161
governance role of auditing profession 179–181
Great Epic 53
greatest happiness principle 79–80, 83, 139

H
harassment 66, 194
Hillel, Rabbi 38, 40
Hindu
    caste system 54
    dharma 52, 53
    karma 52–53
    morality 52
    scriptures 51, 53
Hindu ethics 50–55
    sources 53–54
Hinduism 30, 33, 50–52, 53, 54
    controversial practices 54
    goals of life 52, 53
    revitalising of 54–55
    way of life 51–52
HIV in workplace 201–207
HIV/Aids 197, 201–207
Holy *Qur'an* 47, 48
homo economicus 129, 136
honesty 18, 30, 38, 42, 44, 48, 54, 56, 66, 91, 170, 241, 255
human dignity 18, 34, 59
humanism, secular 29, 33, 55, 56–57
human (natural) dispositions (Aristotle) 75, **75**
human responsibilities 58–59
human rights 29, 33, 54, 55, 58–59, 63, 66, 130

I
IFAC (International Federation of Accountants) 247–252
    [*see also* the main entry for International Federation of Accountants (IFAC)]
IIA (Institute of Internal Auditors) 232, 233–234
implications
    ethical 22, 35, 50, 86, 88, 97, 100
    financial 86
    identification of 103, 106
    moral 35, 50, 52, 80
    RIMS 103
    tax 224
independence 255–259
    in appearance 256

of mind 256
    threats to 257, 258
independent director 165, 174, 251
Independent Regulatory Board for Auditors
    (IRBA) 223, 226, 232, 234, 254, 262, 270, 272
    Code of Professional Conduct 254, 255, 256,
        257, 259
indifference 41
individualistic ethics 60
induction system 193
inequality 130, 143, 168
    economic 129, 130
    gender 272
    socio-economic 129, 142, 143
insider trading 242
Institute for Social and Ethical Accountability 194
Institute of Internal Auditors (IIA) 232, 233–234
institutional investor(s) 175–177
institutionalisation of ethics 184, 189–194
    strategic level 189–192
    systems level 192–194
integrated reporting 177–179
integrity 25, 28, 31, 33, 36, 42, 46, 56, 59, 61, 66, 67,
    68, 71, 76, 109, 127, 164, 170, 179, 180, 181, 193,
    224, 225, 232, 240, 241, 243, 245, 248, 250, **252**,
    254, 255, 256, 259
    organisational 186, 189
    strategy 190, 191–192
internal audit 164, 165, 175, 179, 180, 181, 187
    process 175
internal auditors 165, 181
    role 181
International Accounting Standards Board 234
International Auditing and Assurance Standards
    Board 234
International Federation of Accountants
    (IFAC) 247–252
    Code of Ethics for Professional Accountants
        217, 240, 247
    conceptual framework approach 249–251
    fundamental principles 248
    structure of *Code of Ethics* 251–252
International Financial Reporting Standards
    (IFRS) 177, 260
International Standards on Auditing 259
intimidation threat 249, 250
invasion of privacy 105, **107**, 108, 109
invisible hand doctrine 131, 136, 137, 159
IRBA (Independent Regulatory Board for
    Auditors) 223, 226, 232, 234, 254, 262, 270, 272
    [*see also* the main entry for Independent
        Regulatory Board for Auditors (IRBA)]

Islam
    beliefs and principles 30
    ethic of action 49
    modern debate 49–50
Islamic culture
Islamic ethics 33, 47–50
    character 47
    nature of
    sources of 47–49
Islamic law (*shari'a*) 48–49
Islamic tradition 47, 49

J
Jainism 50
Jesus of Nazareth 39–40, 41, 42
Jewish
    ethics 37–38, 39, 42, 65
    prophets 38
    traditions 39
Judaism 37–38
    ethics in 37–38, 39, 42, 65
    golden rule of 38, 40
    mitzvoth (ethical commandments) 37
    prophets 38
    Talmud 38
    Torah 37, 38
justice 31, 35, 37, 38, 39, 40, 41, 42, 46, 56, 58, 59,
    60, 67, 127, 241, 272
    as fairness theory 141
    definition 138–139
    egalitarian theory 140–143
    in original acquisition 145
    libertarian theory 143–146
    theories 138–146
    utilitarian theory 139–140
'just war' teaching 51

K
Kant, Immanuel 1, 63, 71, 73, 76, 77, 78, 79,
    140, 159
    categorical imperative 77–78
    deontological ethics 71, 73, 76–79, 83
    deontological theory 71, 73, 79
karma 52–53
King Committee on Corporate Governance
    163, 172–175, 179
*King Report on Corporate Governance for South
    Africa, Third* (King III) 127, 151–152, 163, 164,
    168, 172, 174, 175, 181, 186
    [*see also* corporate governance]
    principles-based approach 173
    rules-based approach 173, 251

knowledge
    abstract bodies of 221
    and skill 185, 221, 222, 223, 225, 227, 248, 259
Kohlberg, Lawrence 60
Kurtz, Paul 56, 67

L

Labour Relations Act 66 of 1995 203
laissez-faire capitalism 132
leadership 61, 67, 174, 181, 192, 232, 260, 262
legal argument (Freeman) 158-159
legal positivism 139
legality 85, 89-90
    and morality 16, 24, **24**
    state 138, 139
legislation 158, 168, 173, 215, 226, 227, 234, 248, 250, 261, 272
libertarian theory of justice 128, 139, 143-146
licensing 218, 226, 229, 230
limited liability corporations 135, 167
local communities 21, 46, 153, 158, 159, 160, **160**, 195
Locke, John 135, 136, 144, 145

M

macro-ethics 128-149
management consultants 151, 224
managers 22, 67, 142, 154, 158, 159, 160, **160**, 161, 165, 166, 168, 169, 170, 176, 255, 258, 269
    obligation to stakeholders 154-155
managing ethics 184-196
market socialism 132
Marx, Karl 21, 57, 132
Marxism 57, 58
Marxist philosophy 57
maximum principle 142
mean (midpoint) disposition (Aristotle) 74, **75**
Mill, John Stuart 1, 71, 73, 79, 80, 81, 82, 139
money laundering 234
monitoring system 108, 110
monopolies 137
moral
    agents 127, 150, 151, 152, 153, 155, 156, 157, 162
    arguments 102, 103, 105
    communities 28, 61, 67-68
    conduct 67, 243-244
    consensus 30, 101
    decision-making 101, 103
    [*see also* Rational Interaction for Moral Sensitivity (RIMS)]
    dilemmas 1, 16, 17, 19-20, 24, 25, 82, 86, 97, 99, 100, 101, 105, 110, 112, 113, 219
    dissensus 99, 101

equality 54, 138, 142
imagination 93
judgements 60, 100, 102
obligations (of corporations) 34, 58, 64, 127, 150-162
points of view 103, 105, 106
traditions 102
value systems 27-70
virtue(s) 36, 42, 66, 74
morality 1, 29, 30-32, 35, 36, 37, 39, 43, 49, 50, 52, 55, 57, 60, 62, 63, 64-67, 76, 90, 112, 139, 198, 219, 220, 241
    ethics 17-18
    legality 16, **24**
Moses 37
motives, focusing on 101-102
Muhammad, Prophet 47, 48, 49
multi-fiduciary stakeholder concept 161
multi-national corporations 151
Muslims 29, 30, 33, 47, 48, 49, 50, 62, 66

N

natural dispositions (Aristotle) 74
natural environment 21, 30, 46
needs (basic) 245
New Testament 39, 41, 66
Noddings, Nel 60
Nozick, Robert 143, 144, 145, 146

O

objectivity 25, 76, 188, 240, 243, 248, 251, **252**, 254, 255, 256, 270, 271
obligatory acts 48
Occupational Health and Safety Act 85 of 1993 203
oligopolies 137
organisational ethics 22-23, **23**
organogram (CID) 156
original acquisition, justice in 145
original position 141
'other' (core concept in ethics) 16, **18**
outcastes 54, 55
Owner-Agents **228**, 230

P

pain **75**, 75, 80, 82, 133
performance appraisal system 193, 194
personal ethical dilemma 100
personal ethics 22-23, **23**
    and organisational ethics 23
personal moral dilemma 19, 219
personal values 19, 22, 23
plagiarism 198

pleasure 30,52, **75**, 75, 76, 80, 81, 82
policy directive 107, 108, 110
positive and negative concerns 99, 103, 106, **107**, 107
price manipulation 137
Principle of Corporate Legitimacy 159
principle of reversibility 78, 229
principle of universalisability 78
privacy, invasion of 105, 106, **107**, 108, 109
private property 134, 135–136
Professing Professionals **228**, 230
profession
    achieving objectives 245
    definition 220–228
    entrance into 222–223
professional
    behaviour 245, 248, **252**
    bodies 217, 219, 228, 231–234, 235, 241, 246, 247, 261, 262
    competence 223, 232, 240, 245, 248, **252**, 254, 259–261, 270
    knowledge and skills 185, 221, 222, 223, 225, 227, 248, 259
    services 218, 226, 227, 231, 242, 246, 248, 252, **253**, 253, 259, 262, 268
    virtues 16, 24–25
professional ethics 16, 24, 25, 29, 112, 217–276
    Code of Ethics for Professional Accountants (IFAC) 217, 240, 247
    Code of Professional Conduct (IRBA) 254, 255, 256, 257, 259
    Code of Professional Conduct (SAICA) 217, 240, 242, 243, 245, 252–254, **252–253**
    codes of 217, 237, 240–264
    dissemination and enforcement of codes of ethics 246–247
    key concepts 16–26
professionalism 1, 218, 220, 229, 231
    Advocacy model 228, **228**
    Altruistic model 228, **228**
    dimensions of **228**
    standards of 245
professionals
    degree of autonomy 227
    ethical standards 227–228
    guidance on proper conduct 242
    types 228–231
    unethical conduct 244–245
profit motive 134, 136
Promissory Argument 154
Promotion of Equality and Prevention of Unfair Discrimination Act 4 of 2000 203
Protected Disclosures Act 26 of 2000 215

Public Finance Management Act 1 of 1999 232
public interest 179, 222, 229, 230, 231, 232, 237, 241, 245, 247, 248, 251, 255, 258, 263
    protection of 243
public practice 219, 233, 247, 250, 251, 252, **252**
    roles in 224

Q
qualification fraud 200–201
qualified audit statement 76, 82
quality of services 231, 245
Qur'an 47, 48

R
Ramayana 51, 53, 54
Rational Interaction for Moral Sensitivity (RIMS) 99, 100, 108, 112
    assumptions behind strategy 101–102
    points of view 100, 102, 103
    rational interaction 100, 102
    steps 103
    strategy 87, 99, 100, 101, 102–105
rationality 76
Rawls, John 140, 141, 142, 143, 144
recommended acts 48
recruiting 193, 211
Registered Training Organisation 223
reincarnation 52
relevance 195
reliability 195
reprehensible acts 48
reputation(s) 19, 25, 83, 97, 167, 175, 179, 184, 187, 194, 228, 230, 235, 237
respect for persons 78–79, 159
reversibility 78
RIMS (Rational Interaction for Moral Sensitivity) 99, 100, 108, 112
    [*see also* the main entry for Rational Interaction for Moral Sensitivity (RIMS)]
risk 166
    analysis 184
    assessment 165, 187–188
    identification 187, 188
    management 109, 164, 175, 180, 181, 233
Roman Catholics 40, 43, 44, 62

S
SAICA (South African Institute of Chartered Accountants) 67, 221, 223, 232, 240
    [*see also* the main entry for South African Institute of Chartered Accountants (SAICA)]

INDEX

SAIPA (South African Institute of Professional Accountants) 232, 233
Sarbanes-Oxley Act (2002) (USA) 173, 182, 231
scandals, corporate 33, 63, 173, 217, 218, 219, 258, 259, 263
secretarial services 224
secular
    ethics/morality 27–70
    humanism 29, 33, 55, 56–57, 63, 67
    humanist ethics 56
secularist(s) 56, 63, 66, 67
Securities and Exchange Commission (SEC) 225, 236
'self' (core concept in ethics) 16, **18**
self-interest 18, 64, 93, 129, 137, 141, 166, 179, 237, 255, 263
    threat 249, 250, 257
self-regulation 221, 240, 261–262
self-review threat 249
seriti 34
shareholder activism 175–177
shareholder dominant theory 157
    economic argument 158–159
    legal argument 158
shari'a (Islamic law) 48–49
Sikhism 50
skills 1, 113, 153, 185, 196, 197, 220, 221, 222, 223, 225, 227, 244, 259, 270
slavery 44, 45, 62, 274
Smith, Adam 21, 64, 131–132, 136, 137
social
    dilemma 19, 99, 100, 103, 106
    ethical dilemma 16, 100
    inequality 142
    justice 35, 38, 39
    protest 38
    reporting 186, 194, 195
    responsibility 46, 150, 151, 152, 153
    utility 139, 140
Social Efficiency Barrier **228**, 229, 230
socialism 21, 58, 129, 132, 136, 152
    market 132, 136
socio-economic inequality 129, 142, 143
solutions 20, 61, 88, 99, 100, 101, 102, 103, 107, 108, 197, 265
sources of Islamic ethics 47–49
    Qu'ran 47
    Prophet Muhammad 48
    shari'a 48–49
South African Communist Party 57
South African Institute of Chartered Accountants (SAICA) 67, 221, 223, 232, 240

Code of Professional Conduct 217, 240, 242, 243, 245, 252–254, **252–253**
South African Institute of Professional Accountants (SAIPA) 232, 233
specialisation 64, 131
staffing system (ethics) 193
stakeholder(s) 92–95
    corporation 159–161, **160**
    engagement 93
    managers' obligation 154–155
    multi-fiduciary concept 161
    network of **160**
    theory 157–161
standards, ethical 16, 24, 76, 85, 90–92, 164, 184, 185, 188–189, 190, 191, 219, 220, 221–222, 231, 234, 241, 246
statism 128, 131–132
Stone, Christopher 154–155
strategic level ethics 189–190
Sufi (spiritual dimension of Islam) 49, 50
sustainability 169, 172, 174, 175, 194
    reporting guidelines 178–179
    report(s) 152, 178
    risks 186
systems level ethics 192–194

T

taxation 146, 153, 223, 224, 230, 257
Talmud 38
technical standards 231, 234, 242, 245, 259
telos 73, 74, 75
Ten Commandments 30, 42
Third King Report on Corporate Governance for South Africa 127, 151–152, 163, 164, 168, 172, 173, 174, 175, 181, 186, 251
timeliness 195
Torah (holy law) 37, 38
traditional African ethics 34–37
    ancestors 35, 36
    context 36
    ubuntu 35
traditions 102
training 25, 76, 83, 89, 108, 109, 110, 130, 193, 196, 219, 221, 222–223, 231, 233, 259, 263, 267
training system (ethics) 193
transparency 91, 164, 170, 173, 274
triple bottom-line reporting 181, 185, 186, 194
    dimensions of model 185–186
trust, destruction of **107**, 109
Trust-seeking Professionals 229
trustworthiness 42, 56, 67
Turnbull Report (UK) 186

293

U

ubuntu 35
unemployment 32, 44
Universal Declaration of Human Rights 58
universal standards 222
universalisability 78
unqualified audit statement 76, 79, 82, 83
untouchables 54
utilitarian ethics 71, 79–83
utilitarianism 79, 139, 140, 141, 142
    criticisms 80–83
utilitarian moral theory 79
    Greatest Happiness principle 79–80, 83, 139
utilitarian theory of justice 71, 73, 82, 83, 128, 139–140, 144, 147
utility 129, 136, 140, 142
    social 139, 140

V

value(s)
    ethical 19, 27, 39, 102, 164, 188, 189, 191, 192, 234
    judgements 101

value-based approach 91, 109, 110, 191
value systems
    modern 55–61
    religious and secular 27–70
veil of ignorance 141
verifiability 195
vice 25
virtue(s) 73–74
virtue ethics 65, 71, 76
virtue theory 57, 73–76
    Aristotle's concept of the 'mean' position 74–76, **75**
    mean 74–76

W

wealth 28, 38, 45, 127, 129, 132, 136, 142, 233
    distribution 46, 136, 143
whistle blowing 197, 215–216
WorldCom (US) 166, 170, 173
world views, strengths and weaknesses
    religious 62–63
    secular 63–64